Mediterranean Diet Cookbook

1500 Mouthwatering Days of Easy and Healthy Recipes for Beginners and Advanced Users. Include 30 Days Meal Plan and Shopping list.

Chloe Sabia

TABLE OF CONTENTS

MEDITERRANEAN DIET SHOPPING LIST

STAPLES

Oils
- [ ] Olive Oil
- [ ] Extra-virgin olive oil

Vinegar
- [ ] Balsamic
- [ ] Red wine
- [ ] White wine

A variety of dried herbs & spices
- [ ] Basil
- [ ] Parsley
- [ ] Oregano
- [ ] Cayenne pepper
- [ ] Cinnamon
- [ ] Cloves
- [ ] Cumin
- [ ] Coriander
- [ ] Dill
- [ ] Fennel seed
- [ ] Ginger
- [ ] Rosemary
- [ ] Red and white wine
- [ ] Garlic

MEAT & SEAFOOD

- [ ] Clams
- [ ] Cod
- [ ] Crab meat
- [ ] Halibut
- [ ] Mussels
- [ ] Salmon
- [ ] Scallops
- [ ] Shrimp
- [ ] Tilapia
- [ ] Tuna
- [ ] Chicken breast*
- [ ] Chicken thighs*
- [ ] Lean red meat**

CANNED & PACKAGED

- [ ] Olives
- [ ] Canned Tomatoes

Dried & canned beans
- [ ] Cannellini beans
- [ ] Navy beans
- [ ] Chickpeas
- [ ] Black beans
- [ ] Kidney beans
- [ ] Lentils
- [ ] Canned tuna

Whole Grains
- [ ] Whole grain pasta
- [ ] Bulgur
- [ ] Whole wheat couscous
- [ ] Quinoa
- [ ] Brown rice
- [ ] Barley
- [ ] Faro
- [ ] Polenta
- [ ] Oats
- [ ] Whole wheat bread or pita
- [ ] Whole grain crackers

Nuts & seeds
- [ ] Almonds
- [ ] Hazelnuts
- [ ] Pine nuts
- [ ] Walnuts
- [ ] Cashews
- [ ] Sunflower seeds
- [ ] Sesame seeds

REFRIGERATED

Cheese
- [ ] Cream cheese
- [ ] Feta
- [ ] Goat cheese
- [ ] Mozzarella
- [ ] Parmesan
- [ ] Ricotta
- [ ] Low-fat milk
- [ ] Plain or Greek yogurt
- [ ] Eggs

PRODUCE

- [ ] Apples
- [ ] Artichokes
- [ ] Asparagus
- [ ] Avocado
- [ ] Bananas
- [ ] Beets
- [ ] Bell peppers
- [ ] Berries (all types)
- [ ] Broccoli
- [ ] Brussels sprouts
- [ ] Cabbage
- [ ] Carrots
- [ ] Celery
- [ ] Cherries
- [ ] Cucumbers
- [ ] Dates
- [ ] Eggplant
- [ ] Fennel
- [ ] Figs
- [ ] Grapes
- [ ] Green beans
- [ ] Kiwi
- [ ] Leafy greens
- [ ] Lemons
- [ ] Lettuce
- [ ] Limes
- [ ] Melons
- [ ] Mushrooms
- [ ] Nectarines
- [ ] Onions
- [ ] Oranges
- [ ] Peas
- [ ] Peaches
- [ ] Pears
- [ ] Plums
- [ ] Pomegranate
- [ ] Potatoes
- [ ] Shallots
- [ ] Spinach
- [ ] Squash
- [ ] Tomatoes
- [ ] Zucchini

* In moderation, once to twice per week
** On rare occasions, once to twice monthly

INTRODUCTION

"Mediterranean diet" is a generic term based on the traditional eating habits in the countries bordering the Mediterranean Sea. There's not one standard Mediterranean diet. At least 16 countries border the Mediterranean. Eating styles vary among these countries and even among regions within each country because of differences in culture, ethnic background, religion, economy, geography and agricultural production. However, there are some common factors.

Interest in the Mediterranean diet began in the 1960s with the observation that coronary heart disease caused fewer deaths in Mediterranean countries, such as Greece and Italy, than in the U.S. and northern Europe. Subsequent studies found that the Mediterranean diet is associated with reduced risk factors for cardiovascular disease. The Mediterranean diet is a way of eating based on the traditional cuisine of countries bordering the Mediterranean Sea. The foundation of the Mediterranean diet is vegetables, fruits, herbs, nuts, beans and whole grains. Meals are built around these plant-based foods. Moderate amounts of dairy, poultry and eggs are also central to the Mediterranean Diet, as is seafood. In contrast, red meat is eaten only occasionally. Healthy fats are a mainstay of the Mediterranean diet. They're eaten instead of less healthy fats, such as saturated and trans fats, which contribute to heart disease.

Olive oil is the primary source of added fat in the Mediterranean diet. Olive oil provides monounsaturated fat, which has been found to lower total cholesterol and low-density lipoprotein (LDL or "bad") cholesterol levels. The Mediterranean diet typically allows red wine in moderation. Although alcohol has been associated with a reduced risk of heart disease in some studies, it's by no means risk free. Below you can find the shopping list of the most common in the Mediterranean diet. They are divided by category; they are the most used but you will also find recipes with not present in this list.

30-Days Meal Plan

	Breakfast	Lunch	Dinner	Total Calories
DAY 1	Breakfast Wraps with Spinach and Eggs Calories: 434	Mixture of Baby Squash and Lentils (Greek) Calories: 438	Asparagus and Broccoli Primavera Farfalle Calories: 544	1416
DAY 2	Salsa and eggs (Italian) Calories: 383	Grilled Caesar Salad Sandwiches Calories: 949	Super Cheesy TagliatelleCalories: 511	1643
DAY 3	Breakfast Yogurt Sundae Calories: 415	Falafel Balls with Tahini Calories: 574	Cannellini Beans in Italian Sauté Calories: 435	1424
DAY 4	Bacon & Cream Cheese Mug Muffins (Italian) Calories: 511	Fajitas with Mushrooms and Vegetables in a Glaze Calories: 403	Lentil and Vegetable Curry Stew Calories: 530	1444
DAY 5	Frittata with Feta and Spinach Calories: 529	Green Veggie Sandwiches Calories: 617	Veggie Chili Ritzy Calories: 633	1478
DAY 6	Pumpkin Soup with Crispy Sage Leaves Calories: 380	Tuna and Olive Salad Sandwiches Calories: 952	Pearl Barley Risotto with Parmesan Cheese Calories: 421	1673
DAY 7	Israeli Salad (Greek) Calories: 414	Oatmeal Baked with Pears and Pecans Calories: 479	Caprese Fusilli Calories: 589	1482

DAY 8	Breakfast Wraps with Spinach and Eggs Calories: 434	Mixture of Baby Squash and Lentils (Greek) Calories: 438	Asparagus and Broccoli Primavera Farfalle Calories: 544	1416
DAY 9	Salsa and eggs (Italian) Calories: 383	Grilled Caesar Salad Sandwiches Calories: 949	Super Cheesy TagliatelleCalories: 511	1643
DAY 10	Breakfast Yogurt Sundae Calories: 415	Falafel Balls with Tahini Calories: 574	Cannellini Beans in Italian Sauté Calories: 435	1424
DAY 11	Bacon & Cream Cheese Mug Muffins (Italian) Calories: 511	Fajitas with Mushrooms and Vegetables in a Glaze Calories: 403	Lentil and Vegetable Curry Stew Calories: 530	1444
DAY 12	Frittata with Feta and Spinach Calories: 529	Green Veggie Sandwiches Calories: 617	Veggie Chili Ritzy Calories: 633	1478
DAY 13	Pumpkin Soup with Crispy Sage Leaves Calories: 380	Tuna and Olive Salad Sandwiches Calories: 952	Pearl Barley Risotto with Parmesan Cheese Calories: 421	1673
DAY 14	Israeli Salad (Greek) Calories: 414	Oatmeal Baked with Pears and Pecans Calories: 479	Caprese Fusilli Calories: 589	1482
DAY 15	Breakfast Wraps with Spinach and Eggs Calories: 434	Mixture of Baby Squash and Lentils (Greek) Calories: 438	Asparagus and Broccoli Primavera Farfalle Calories: 544	1416
DAY 16	Salsa and eggs (Italian) Calories: 383	Grilled Caesar Salad Sandwiches Calories: 949	Super Cheesy TagliatelleCalories: 511	1643

DAY 17	Breakfast Yogurt Sundae Calories: 415	Falafel Balls with Tahini Calories: 574	Cannellini Beans in Italian Sauté Calories: 435	1424
DAY 18	Bacon & Cream Cheese Mug Muffins (Italian) Calories: 511	Fajitas with Mushrooms and Vegetables in a Glaze Calories: 403	Lentil and Vegetable Curry Stew Calories: 530	1444
DAY 19	Frittata with Feta and Spinach Calories: 529	Green Veggie Sandwiches Calories: 617	Veggie Chili Ritzy Calories: 633	1478
DAY 20	Pumpkin Soup with Crispy Sage Leaves Calories: 380	Tuna and Olive Salad Sandwiches Calories: 952	Pearl Barley Risotto with Parmesan Cheese Calories: 421	1673
DAY 21	Israeli Salad (Greek) Calories: 414	Oatmeal Baked with Pears and Pecans Calories: 479	Caprese Fusilli Calories: 589	1482
DAY 22	Breakfast Wraps with Spinach and Eggs Calories: 434	Mixture of Baby Squash and Lentils (Greek) Calories: 438	Asparagus and Broccoli Primavera Farfalle Calories: 544	1416
DAY 23	Salsa and eggs (Italian) Calories: 383	Grilled Caesar Salad Sandwiches Calories: 949	Super Cheesy TagliatelleCalories: 511	1643
DAY 24	Breakfast Yogurt Sundae Calories: 415	Falafel Balls with Tahini Calories: 574	Cannellini Beans in Italian Sauté Calories: 435	1424

DAY 25	Bacon & Cream Cheese Mug Muffins (Italian) Calories: 511	Fajitas with Mushrooms and Vegetables in a Glaze Calories: 403	Lentil and Vegetable Curry Stew Calories: 530	1444
DAY 26	Frittata with Feta and Spinach Calories: 529	Green Veggie Sandwiches Calories: 617	Veggie Chili Ritzy Calories: 633	1478
DAY 27	Pumpkin Soup with Crispy Sage Leaves Calories: 380	Tuna and Olive Salad Sandwiches Calories: 952	Pearl Barley Risotto with Parmesan Cheese Calories: 421	1673
DAY 28	Israeli Salad (Greek) Calories: 414	Oatmeal Baked with Pears and Pecans Calories: 479	Caprese Fusilli Calories: 589	1482
DAY 29	Breakfast Wraps with Spinach and Eggs Calories: 434	Mixture of Baby Squash and Lentils (Greek) Calories: 438	Asparagus and Broccoli Primavera Farfalle Calories: 544	1416
DAY 30	Salsa and eggs (Italian) Calories: 383	Grilled Caesar Salad Sandwiches Calories: 949	Super Cheesy TagliatelleCalories: 511	1643

Chapter 2
Breakfast Recipes

Breakfast Wraps with Spinach and Eggs

Prep Time: 10 minutes | **Cooking Time:** 7 minutes | **Servings:** 2

Ingredients

1 tablespoon olive oil
¼ cup minced onion
3 to 4 tablespoons minced sun-dried tomatoes in olive oil and herbs
3 large eggs, whisked
1½ cups packed baby spinach
1 ounce (28 g) crumbled feta cheese
Salt, to taste
2 (8-inch) whole-wheat tortillas

Directions

1. Heat the olive oil in a large skillet over medium-high heat.
2. Sauté the onion and tomatoes for about 3 minutes, stirring occasionally, until softened.
3. Reduce the heat to medium. Add the whisked eggs and stir-fry for 1 to 2 minutes.
4. Stir in the baby spinach and scatter with the crumbled feta cheese. Season as needed with salt.
5. Remove the egg mixture from the heat to a plate. Set aside.
6. Working in batches, place 2 tortillas on a microwave-safe dish and microwave for about 20 seconds to make them warm.
7. Spoon half of the egg mixture into each tortilla. Fold them in half and roll up, then serve.

Per Serving

calories: 434 | fat: 28.1g | protein: 17.2g | carbs: 30.8g | fiber: 6.0g | sodium: 551mg

Ricotta Toast with Strawberries

Prep Time: 10 minutes | **Cooking Time:** 0 minutes | **Servings:** 2

Ingredients

½ cup crumbled ricotta cheese
1 tablespoon honey, plus additional as needed
Pinch of sea salt, plus additional as needed
4 slices of whole-grain bread, toasted
1 cup sliced fresh strawberries
4 large fresh basil leaves, sliced into thin shreds

Directions

1. Mix together the cheese, honey, and salt in a small bowl until well incorporated.
2. Taste and add additional salt and honey as needed.
3. Spoon 2 tablespoons of the cheese mixture onto each slice of bread and spread it all over.
4. Sprinkle the sliced strawberry and basil leaves on top before serving.

Per Serving calories: 274 | fat: 7.9g | protein: 15.1g | carbs: 39.8g | fiber: 5.0g | sodium: 322mg

Eggs from the Mediterranean (Shakshuka)

Prep Time: 5 minutes | **Cooking Time:** 20 minutes | **Servings:** 4

Ingredients

2 tablespoons extra-virgin olive oil
1 cup chopped shallots
1 teaspoon garlic powder
1 cup finely diced potato
1 cup chopped red bell peppers
1 (14.5-ounce/ 411-g) can diced tomatoes, drained
¼ teaspoon ground cardamom
¼ teaspoon paprika
¼ teaspoon turmeric
4 large eggs
¼ cup chopped fresh cilantro

Directions

1. Preheat the oven to 350°F (180°C).
2. Heat the olive oil in an ovenproof skillet over medium-high heat until it shimmers.
3. Add the shallots and sauté for about 3 minutes, stirring occasionally, until fragrant.
4. Fold in the garlic powder, potato, and bell peppers and stir to combine.
5. Cover and cook for 10 minutes, stirring frequently.
6. Add the tomatoes, cardamon, paprika, and turmeric and mix well.
7. When the mixture begins to bubble, remove from the heat and crack the eggs into the skillet.
8. Transfer the skillet to the preheated oven and bake for 5 to 10 minutes, or until the egg whites are set and the yolks are cooked to your liking.
9. Remove from the oven and garnish with the cilantro before serving.

Per Serving

calories: 223 | fat: 11.8g | protein: 9.1g | carbs: 19.5g | fiber: 3.0g | sodium: 277mg

Salad with Spinach, Tomatoes, and Poached Egg (Italian)

Prep Time: 13 minutes | **Cooking Time:** 5 minutes | Servings: 2

Ingredients

3 oz. spinach

2 chicken egg

1 tbsp. vegetable oil

2 tbsps. agave syrup

1 tbsp. dill

Salt and pepper to taste

2 tomatoes

2 oz. Feta cheese

1 ½ tsp. sour cream 15%

2 tsps. lemon juice

1 ½ oz. red onion

Directions

1. Pour the vegetable oil onto the cling film.
2. Gently break the egg so that the yolk remains intact.
3. Collect the film with the egg in a bag, squeeze out the air, tie and cook for 5 minutes.
4. Mix the lemon juice, agave syrup (1 tbsp.), and vegetable oil, let the dressing rest.
5. Cut the tomatoes into a cube and the onion into strips, fill with salt and pepper dressing.
6. Add the spinach leaves, mix.
7. Top with Feta cheese and poached egg.
8. Mix the sour cream with the chopped dill and syrup (1 tbsp.).
9. Pour over the salad dressing with the prepared sauce.

Nutrition:

Calories: 200 Fat: 12 g. Protein: 7.5 g.

Potato Scallops with Truffle Oil (Spanish)

Prep Time: 8 minutes | **Cooking Time:** 24 minutes | Servings: 1

Ingredients

4 oz. scallops

½ oz. Parmesan cheese

½ oz. butter

1 ½ tsp. truffle oil

1 tsp. arugula

½ tsp. thyme Sea salt to taste

3 oz. potato

½ tsp. lime zest

1 tbsp. olive oil

2/3 oz. cherry tomatoes

1 chive

Ground black pepper to taste

Directions

1. Fry the scallops on both sides in olive oil with thyme, salt, and pepper.
2. Separately, boil the potatoes and rub them through a sieve. Add the zest of lime, grated Parmesan cheese, butter, salt, and pepper.
3. Lightly warm the arugula and cherry tomatoes in olive oil.
4. Put the mashed potatoes through the ring on a plate, scallops symmetrically put on it, arugula and cherry on the scallops, garnish with the thyme and onion, and pour with the truffle oil.

Nutrition:

Calories: 279 Fat: 59.8 g. Protein: 24.5 g.

Salsa and eggs (Italian)

Prep Time: 5 minutes | **Cooking Time:** 5 minutes | Servings: 2

Ingredients

1 cups tomatoes.

1 bunch of cilantros, chopped.

2 small habanero chilies, chopped.

A drizzle of olive oil.

1 green onion (bunch).

Juice from 1 lime.

1 cup red onion, chopped.

8 eggs, whisked.

Sea salt.

2 garlic cloves, minced.

Directions

1. Mix tomatoes, green onions, red onion, habaneros, garlic, cilantro, and lime juice and toss well.
2. Add a pinch of salt, toss again and keep this in the fridge until you serve it.
3. Heat up a pan with a drizzle of oil, add eggs, and scramble them for 4–5 minutes.
4. Divide scrambled eggs on plates, add salsa on top and serve.

Nutrition:

Calories: 383 g. Fat: 14 g. Fiber: 4 g. Carbs: 3 g. Protein: 8 g.

Bacon & Cream Cheese Mug Muffins (Italian)

Prep Time: 15 minutes | **Cooking Time:** 15 minutes | Servings: 2

Ingredients

¼ cup flaxseed meal.

1 egg.

¼ cup almond flour.

Salt and black pepper, to taste.

½ medium avocado, sliced.

1 tbsps. heavy cream.

2 tbsps. pesto.

¼ tsp. baking soda.

4 bacon slices.

2 tbsps. cream cheese

Directions

1. Mix the flaxseed meal, almond flour, and baking soda in a bowl. Add the egg, heavy cream, and pesto. Then whisk well. Season with salt and pepper.
2. Divide the mixture between 2 ramekins. Microwave for 60–90 seconds. Let cool slightly before filling.
3. Put the bacon in a nonstick skillet and cook until crispy, then set aside.
4. Transfer the muffins onto a plate and cut them in half crosswise. Assemble the sandwiches by spreading the cream cheese and topping with the bacon and avocado slices.

Nutrition:

Calories: 511 g. Fats: 38 g. Protein: 16 g. 31 mg of cholesterol 387 mg of sodium

Crustless Tiropita (Greek Cheese Pie)

Prep Time: 10 minutes | **Cooking Time:** 35 to 40 mins | **Servings:** 6

Ingredients

4 tablespoons extra-virgin olive oil, divided
½ cup whole-milk ricotta cheese
1¼ cups crumbled feta cheese
2 tablespoons chopped fresh mint

½ teaspoon lemon zest
¼ teaspoon freshly ground black pepper
2 large eggs
½ teaspoon baking powder
1 tablespoon chopped fresh dill

Directions

1. Preheat the oven to 350°F (180°C). Coat the bottom and sides of a baking dish with 2 tablespoons of olive oil. Set aside.
2. Mix together the ricotta and feta cheese in a medium bowl and stir with a fork until well combined. Add the dill, mint, lemon zest, and black pepper and mix well. In a separate bowl, whisk together the eggs and baking powder. Pour the whisked eggs into the bowl of cheese mixture. Blend well.
3. Slowly pour the mixture into the coated baking dish and drizzle with the remaining 2 tablespoons of olive oil.
4. Bake in the preheated oven for about 35 to 40 minutes, or until the pie is browned around the edges and cooked through.
5. Cool for 5 minutes before slicing into wedges.

Per Serving

calories: 181 | fat: 16.6g | protein: 7.0g | carbs: 1.8g | fiber: 0g | sodium: 321mg

Fluffy Almond Flour Pancakes with Strawberries

Prep Time: 5 minutes | **Cooking Time:** 15 minutes | **Servings:** 4

Ingredients

1 cup plus 2 tablespoons unsweetened almond milk
1 cup almond flour
2 large eggs, whisked ⅓ cup honey

1 teaspoon baking soda
¼ teaspoon salt
2 tablespoons extra-virgin olive oil
1 cup sliced strawberries

Directions

1. Combine the almond milk, almond flour, whisked eggs, honey, baking soda, and salt in a large bowl and whisk to incorporate.
2. Heat the olive oil in a large skillet over medium-high heat.
3. Make the pancakes: Pour ⅓ cup of batter into the hot skillet and swirl the pan so the batter covers the bottom evenly. Cook for 2 to 3 minutes until the pancake turns golden brown around the edges. Gently flip the pancake with a spatula and cook for 2 to 3 minutes until cooked through. Repeat with the remaining batter.
4. Serve the pancakes with the sliced strawberries on top.

Per Serving

calories: 298 | fat: 11.7g | protein: 11.8g | carbs: 34.8g | fiber: 3.9g | sodium: 195mg

Sundae with Yogurt for Breakfast

Prep Time: 5 minutes | **Cooking Time:** 0 minutes | **Servings:** 1

Ingredients

¾ cup plain Greek yogurt
¼ cup fresh mixed berries (blueberries, strawberries, blackberries)

2 tablespoons walnut pieces
1 tablespoon ground flaxseed
2 fresh mint leaves, shredded

Directions

1. Pour the yogurt into a tall parfait glass and sprinkle with the mixed berries, walnut pieces, and flaxseed.
2. Garnish with the shredded mint leaves and serve immediately.

Per Serving

calories: 236 | fat: 10.8g | protein: 21.1g | carbs: 15.9g | fiber: 4.1g | sodium: 63mg

Avocado Toast with Goat Cheese

Prep Time: 5 minutes | **Cooking Time:** 2 to 3 minutes | **Servings:** 2

Ingredients

2 slices whole-wheat thin-sliced bread
½ avocado

2 tablespoons crumbled goat cheese
Salt, to taste

Directions

1. Toast the bread slices in a toaster for 2 to 3 minutes on each side until browned.
2. Scoop out the flesh from the avocado into a medium bowl and mash it with a fork to desired consistency. Spread the mash onto each piece of toast.
3. Scatter the crumbled goat cheese on top and season as needed with salt.
4. Serve immediately.

Per Serving

calories: 136 | fat: 5.9g | protein: 5.0g | carbs: 17.5g | fiber: 5.1g | sodium: 194mg

Healthy Chia Pudding

Prep Time: 5 minutes | **Cooking Time:** 0 minutes | **Servings:** 4

Ingredients

4 cups unsweetened almond milk
¾ cup chia seeds

1 teaspoon ground cinnamon
Pinch sea salt

Directions

1. In a medium bowl, whisk together the almond milk, chia seeds, cinnamon, and sea salt until well incorporated.
2. Cover and transfer to the refrigerator to thicken for about 1 hour, or until a pudding-like texture is achieved.
3. Serve chilled.

Per Serving calories: 236 | fat: 9.8g | protein: 13.1g | carbs: 24.8g | fiber: 11.0g | sodium: 133mg

Spring Ramen Bowl (Italian)

Prep Time: 15 minutes | **Cooking Time:** 20 minutes | **Servings:** 4

Ingredients

oz. (100g) soba noodles.	1 medium zucchini, julienned or grated.
4 eggs.	½ cup snap peas.
2 cups watercress.	1 leek (white part only), finely sliced.
1 cup mushrooms, finely sliced	2 cloves garlic, minced.
4 cups chicken stock.	1 tsp. sesame oil.
1 long red chili, seeded and finely chopped. 1.6-inch ginger, minced.	1 lemon, cut into wedges.
2 nori sheets, crumbled.	1 tbsp. olive oil

Directions

1. To boil the eggs, fill a saucepan with enough water to cover the eggs and set them over medium heat. Bring water to a gentle boil. Add the eggs and cook for 7 minutes. Drain and transfer the eggs into cold water. Set aside.
2. Place a medium-sized saucepan over medium-low heat. Heat the olive oil and sauté the garlic, ginger, leek, and chili for 5 minutes. Add the stock, noodles, and sesame oil. Cook for another 8 minutes or until noodles are cooked according to your desired doneness. During the last minute, add the zucchini, mushroom, and watercress.
3. Divide the ramen between four bowls and top with nori. Serve with eggs and lemon wedges.

Nutrition:
Calories: 300 g. Fat: 12 g. Fiber: 1 g. Carbs: 3 g. Protein: 9 g.

Spring Ramen Bowl (Italian)

Prep Time: 15 minutes | **Cooking Time:** 20 minutes | **Servings:** 4

Ingredients

oz. (100g) soba noodles.	1 medium zucchini, julienned or grated.
4 eggs.	½ cup snap peas.
2 cups watercress.	1 leek (white part only), finely sliced.
1 cup mushrooms, finely sliced.	2 cloves garlic, minced.
4 cups chicken stock	1 tsp. sesame oil.
1 long red chili, seeded and finely chopped. 1.6-inch ginger, minced.	1 lemon, cut into wedges.
2 nori sheets, crumbled.	1 tbsp. olive oil.

Directions

1. To boil the eggs, fill a saucepan with enough water to cover the eggs and set them over medium heat. Bring water to a gentle boil. Add the eggs and cook for 7 minutes. Drain and transfer the eggs into cold water. Set aside.
2. Place a medium-sized saucepan over medium-low heat. Heat the olive oil and sauté the garlic, ginger, leek, and chili for 5 minutes. Add the stock, noodles, and sesame oil. Cook for another 8 minutes or until noodles are cooked according to your desired doneness. During the last minute, add the zucchini, mushroom, and watercress. Divide the ramen between four bowls and top with nori. Serve with eggs and lemon wedges.

Nutrition:
Calories: 300 g. Fat: 12 g. Fiber: 1 g. Carbs: 3 g. Protein: 9 g.

Cherry Smoothie Bowl (Greek)

Prep Time: 15 minutes | **Cooking Time:** 0 minutes | **Servings:** 1

Ingredients

½ cup organic rolled oats.	½ cup almond milk, unsweetened.
1 tbsp. chia seeds.	2 tsps. almonds, sliced.
1 tsp. hemp seeds.	1 cup cherries, frozen.
1 tbsp. almond butter.	1 cup plain Greek yogurt
1 tsp. vanilla extract	
½ cup berries, fresh.	

Directions

1. Soak the organic rolled oats in almond milk.
2. Prepare a smooth blend with the soaked oats, frozen cherries, yogurt, chia seeds, almond butter, and vanilla extract. Pour the mixture into 2 bowls.
3. To each bowl, add equal parts of the hemp seeds, sliced almonds, and fresh cherries.

Nutrition:
Calories: 130 g. Fats: 0 g. Protein: 1 g.

Pepperoni Eggs (Italian)

Prep Time: 10 minutes | **Cooking Time:** 20 minutes | **Servings:** 2
Servings:

Ingredients

1 cup of egg substitute	1 egg
3 green onions	minced meat
8 slices of pepperoni	diced
1 teaspoon melted butter	1 pinch of salt and ground black pepper to taste
1/4 cup grated Romano cheese	1/2 teaspoon of garlic powder

Directions

1. Combine the egg substitute, the egg, the green onions, the pepperoni slices, and the garlic powder in a bowl.
2. Heat the butter in a non-stick frying pan over low heat; Add the egg mixture, cover the pan and cook until the eggs are set, 10 to 15 minutes. Sprinkle Romano's eggs and season with salt and pepper.

Nutrition:
266 calories 16.2 g fat 3.7 grams of carbohydrates 25.3 g of protein 124 mg of cholesterol 586 mg of sodium

Breakfast Pancakes with Berry Sauce

Prep Time: 5 minutes | **Cooking Time:** 10 minutes | **Servings:** 4

Ingredients

Pancakes:
1 cup almond flour
1 teaspoon baking powder
¼ teaspoon salt
6 tablespoon extra-virgin olive oil, divided
2 large eggs, beaten

Zest and juice of 1 lemon
½ teaspoon vanilla extract
Berry Sauce:
1 cup frozen mixed berries
1 tablespoon water, plus more as needed
½ teaspoon vanilla extract

Directions

Make the Pancakes
1. In a large bowl, combine the almond flour, baking powder, and salt and stir to break up any clumps.
2. Add 4 tablespoons olive oil, beaten eggs, lemon zest and juice, and vanilla extract and stir until well mixed.
3. Heat 1 tablespoon of olive oil in a large skillet. Spoon about 2 tablespoons of batter for each pancake. Cook until bubbles begin to form, 4 to 5 minutes. Flip and cook for another 2 to 3 minutes. Repeat with the remaining 1 tablespoon of olive oil and batter.

Make the Berry Sauce
4. Combine the frozen berries, water, and vanilla extract in a small saucepan and heat over medium-high heat for 3 to 4 minutes until bubbly, adding more water as needed. Using the back of a spoon or fork, mash the berries and whisk until smooth. Serve the pancakes with the berry sauce.

Per Serving calories: 275 | fat: 26.0g | protein: 4.0g | carbs: 8.0g | fiber: 2.0g | sodium: 271mg

Marinara Poached Eggs

Prep Time: 5 minutes | **Cooking Time:** 15 minutes | **Servings:** 6

Ingredients

1 tablespoon extra-virgin olive oil
1 cup chopped onion
2 garlic cloves, minced
2 (14.5-ounce / 411-g) cans no-salt-added

Italian diced tomatoes, undrained
6 large eggs
½ cup chopped fresh flat-leaf parsley

Directions

1. Heat the olive oil in a large skillet over medium-high heat.
2. Add the onion and sauté for 5 minutes, stirring occasionally. Add the garlic and cook for 1 minute more.
3. Pour the tomatoes with their juices over the onion mixture and cook for 2 to 3 minutes until bubbling.
4. Reduce the heat to medium and use a large spoon to make six indentations in the tomato mixture. Crack the eggs, one at a time, into each indentation. Cover and simmer for 6 to 7 minutes, or until the eggs are cooked to your preference.
5. Serve with the parsley sprinkled on top.

Per Serving
calories: 89 | fat: 6.0g | protein: 4.0g | carbs: 4.0g | fiber: 1.0g | sodium: 77mg

Frittata with Feta and Spinach

Prep Time: 10 minutes | **Cooking Time:** 15 minutes | **Servings:** 2

Ingredients

4 large eggs, beaten
2 tablespoons fresh chopped herbs, such as rosemary, thyme, oregano, basil or 1 teaspoon dried herbs
¼ teaspoon salt
Freshly ground black pepper, to taste
4 tablespoons extra-virgin olive oil, divided

1 cup fresh spinach, arugula, kale, or other leafy greens
4 ounces (113 g) quartered artichoke hearts, rinsed, drained, and thoroughly dried
8 cherry tomatoes, halved
½ cup crumbled soft goat cheese

Directions

1. Preheat the broiler to Low. In a small bowl, combine the beaten eggs, herbs, salt, and pepper and whisk well with a fork
2. In an ovenproof skillet, heat 2 tablespoons of olive oil over medium heat. Add the spinach, artichoke hearts, and cherry tomatoes and sauté until just wilted, 1 to 2 minutes.
3. Pour in the egg mixture and let it cook undisturbed over medium heat for 3 to 4 minutes, until the eggs begin to set on the bottom.
4. Sprinkle the goat cheese across the top of the egg mixture and transfer the skillet to the oven.
5. Broil for 4 to 5 minutes, or until the frittata is firm in the center and golden brown on top.
6. Remove from the oven and run a rubber spatula around the edge to loosen the sides. Slice the frittata in half and serve drizzled with the remaining 2 tablespoons of olive oil.

Per Serving
calories: 529 | fat: 46.5g | protein: 21.4g | carbs: 7.1g | fiber: 3.1g | sodium: 762mg

Savory Breakfast Oatmeal

Prep Time: 5 minutes | **Cooking Time:** 15 minutes | **Servings:** 2

Ingredients

½ cup steel-cut oats
1 cup water
1 medium cucumber, chopped
1 large tomato, chopped
1 tablespoon olive oil

Pinch freshly grated Parmesan cheese
Sea salt and freshly ground pepper, to taste
Flat-leaf parsley or mint, chopped, for garnish

Directions

1. Combine the oats and water in a medium saucepan and bring to a boil over high heat, stirring continuously, or until the water is absorbed, about 15 minutes.
2. Divide the oatmeal between 2 bowls and scatter the tomato and cucumber on top. Drizzle with the olive oil and sprinkle with the Parmesan cheese.
3. Season with salt and pepper to taste. Serve garnished with the parsley.

Per Serving
calories: 197| fat: 8.9g | protein: 6.3g | carbs: 23.1g | fiber: 6.4g | sodium: 27mg

Ken's Hard-Boiled Egg (Italian)

Prep Time: 5 minutes **Cooking Time:** 15 minutes |
Servings: 8

Ingredients

1 tablespoon of salt	1/4 cup distilled white
8 eggs	vinegar
6 cups of water	

Directions

1. Mix the salt, vinegar, and water in a large saucepan and bring to a boil over high heat. Add the eggs one by one, and be careful not to split them. Lower the heat and cook over low heat and cook for 14 minutes.
2. Remove the eggs from the hot water and place them in a container filled with ice water or cold water. Cool completely, approximately 15 minutes.

Nutrition:

72 calories 5 grams of fat 0.4 g carbohydrates 6.3 g protein 186 mg of cholesterol 947 mg of sodium.

Low Carb Bagels (Italian)

Prep Time: 10 minutes | **Cooking Time:** 20 minutes |
Servings: 4

Ingredients

1 cups almond flour	2 tbsps. bagel seasoning
1 tbsp. powder for baking	3 eggs.
3 cups mozzarella cheese, shredded.	¼ cup cream cheese.

Directions

1. Heat your oven in advance at 400 ° c. Get 2 baking sheets and line them well with paper made from parchment.
2. Get a large mixing container and in it, mix the almond flour with the powder for baking.
3. Mix the mozzarella cheese and the cream cheese in a bowl that can be used in a microwave. Place the bowl in a microwave for 2 minutes when the cheese melts and combines. Get the mixture of cheese from the bowl once out of the microwave and pour it into the mixing container with the flour from almonds.
4. Take the dough when done and divide it into eight parts that are equal in measure. Using your palms, take each of the eight dough parts and roll them into balls.
5. Using your fingers, create a hole in each of the balls, and gently stretch the dough to form the shape of a bagel.
6. Take one egg and beat it in a bowl. Brush the eggs on top of each made bagel following this by sprinkling the bagel seasoning at the top as well.
7. Place the bagel dough in the oven on its rack, which is in the middle for 25 minutes when they are nice and golden in color. Remove the bagels from the oven and let them get cold for about 10 minutes before serving them.

Nutrition:

Calories: 275 g. Fat: 20 g. Fiber: 2 g. Carbs: 8 g. Protein: 20 g.

Avocado-Egg Bowls (Italian)

Prep Time: 10 minutes **Cooking Time:** 40 minutes
Servings: 3

Ingredients

1tsp. coconut oil.	2organic eggs, free-range.
1 avocado, large and ripe	Salt and pepper, to sprinkle..
For garnishing:	Chopped walnuts, as many
Balsamic pearls, to taste.	as you like.
Fresh thyme, to taste.	

Directions

1. Slice the avocado in 2, then take out the pit and remove enough of the inside so that there is enough space inside to accommodate an entire egg. Cut off a little bit of the bottom of the avocado so that the avocado will sit upright as you place it on a stable surface.
2. Open the eggs and put each of the yolks in a separate bowl or container. Place the egg whites in the same small bowl. Sprinkle some pepper and salt into the whites according to your taste, then mix them well.
3. Melt the coconut oil in a pan that has a lid that fits, and place it over medium-high heat.
4. Put the avocado "boats" meaty-side down and skin-side up in the pan, and sauté them for approx. 35 seconds, or when they become darker.
5. Turn them over, then add to the spaces inside, almost filling the inside with the egg whites.
6. Then lower the temperature and cover the pan. Let them sit covered for approx. 16–20 minutes, or until
7. Gently, add 1 yolk onto each of the avocados and keep cooking them for 4–5 minutes, or just until they get to the point of cooking you want them to.
8. Move the avocados to a dish and add toppings to each of them using the walnuts, the balsamic pearls, or/and thyme.

Nutrition: Calories: 215 g. Fats: 18 g. Protein: 9 g.

Ken's Hard-Boiled Egg (Italian)

Prep Time: 5 minutes **Cooking Time:** 15 minutes
Servings: 8

Ingredients

1 tablespoon of salt	1/4 cup distilled white
6 cups of water	vinegar
8 eggs	

Directions

1. Mix the salt, vinegar, and water in a large saucepan and bring to a boil over high heat. Add the eggs one by one, and be careful not to split them. Lower the heat and cook over low heat and cook for 14 minutes.
2. Remove the eggs from the hot water and place them in a container filled with ice water or cold water. Cool completely, approximately 15 minutes.

Nutrition: 72 calories 5 grams of fat 0.4 g carbohydrates 6.3 g protein 186 mg of cholesterol 947 mg of sodium

Avocado-Egg Bowls (Italian)

Prep Time: 10 minutes | **Cooking Time:** 40 minutes |
Servings: 3

Ingredients

1 tsp. coconut oil.

1 avocado, large and ripe.

For garnishing:

Chopped walnuts, as many as you like. Balsamic pearls to taste.

2 organic eggs, free-range.

Salt and pepper, to sprinkle.

Fresh thyme to taste.

Directions

1. Slice the avocado in 2, then take out the pit and remove enough of the inside so that there is enough space inside to accommodate an entire egg.
2. Cut off a little bit of the bottom of the avocado so that the avocado will sit upright as you place it on a stable surface.
3. Pen the eggs and put each of the yolks in a separate bowl or container. Place the egg whites in the same small bowl. Sprinkle some pepper and salt into the whites according to your taste, then mix them well.
4. Melt the coconut oil in a pan that has a lid that fits, and place it over medium-high heat. Put the avocado "boats" meaty-side down and skin-side up in the pan, and sauté them for approx. 35 seconds, or when they become darker.
5. Turn them over, then add to the spaces inside, almost filling the inside with the egg whites.
6. Then lower the temperature and cover the pan. Let them sit covered for approx. 16–20 minutes, or until the whites are just about fully cooked.
7. Gently, add 1 yolk onto each of the avocados and keep cooking them for 4–5 minutes, or just until they get to the point of cooking you want them to.
8. Move the avocados to a dish and add toppings to each of them using the walnuts, the balsamic pearls, or/and thyme.

Nutrition:
Calories: 215 g. Fats: 18 g. Protein: 9 g.

Citrus-Kissed Melon (Spanish)

Prep Time: 11 minutes | **Cooking Time:** 0 minute |
Servings: 4

Ingredients

2 cups melon, cubed

½ cup freshly squeezed orange juice

1 tbsp. orange Zest

2 cups cantaloupe, cubed

¼ cup freshly squeezed lime juice

Directions

1. In a large bowl, incorporate the melon cubes.
2. In a bowl, blend the orange juice, lime juice, and orange zest and pour over the fruit. Cover and chill for at least 4 hours, stirring occasionally. Serve chilled.

Nutrition:
Calories: 101 Fat: 11 g. Protein: 2 g

Cauliflower & Eggs (Italian)

Prep Time: 10 minutes | **Cooking Time:** 20 minutes |
Servings: 4

Ingredients

½ cauliflower head.

¼ tsp. black pepper freshly ground.

¼ tsp. cornstarch.

2 slices bacon.

2 tsps. paprika

1 tbsp. olive oil extra virgin.

¼ tsp. salt.

3 eggs.

1 cup cheddar cheese shredded.

1 tsp. fresh chives.

Directions

1. Get a box grater, and with it, grate the half head of cauliflower until it is well grated.
2. Place the grated cauliflower into a mixing container and add an egg to it together with the cheddar cheese that has been shredded, cornstarch, and salt. Mix them all well.
3. Get a large frying pan and heat the olive oil over medium heat. Using a serving spoon, scoop the cauliflower mix into the frying pan and shape it into patties.
4. Cook these patties for five minutes until they are crispy and done. Ensure to flip both sides.
5. Get a saucepan and poach the remaining 2 eggs over medium heat using boiling water.
6. Get another pan for frying and over a medium flame, let the olive oil become hot. Follow this by adding in bacon pieces and allow them to cook until they are crispy.
7. Crack the eggs and remove them from the shell. Slice them into circles.
8. Place the cooked cauliflower patties on a plate and add the sliced eggs together with the slices of crispy bacon. Sprinkle the paprika and chives and serve.

Nutrition:
Calories: 40 g. Fat: 1 g. Fiber: 2 g. Carbs: 8 g. Protein: 2 g.

Mushrooms with a Soy Sauce Glaze (Italian)

Prep Time: 5 minutes **Cooking Time:** 10 minutes
Servings: 2

Ingredients

2 tablespoons butter

2 cloves garlic, minced

2 teaspoons soy sauce

ground black pepper to taste

1(8 ounces) package sliced white mushrooms

Directions

1. Melt the butter in a frying pan over medium heat; add the mushrooms; cook and stir until the mushrooms are soft and released about 5 minutes. Stir in the garlic; keep cooking and stir for 1 minute. Pour the soy sauce; cook the mushrooms in the soy sauce until the liquid has evaporated, about 4 minutes.

Nutrition: 135 calories 11.9 g of fat 5.4 g carbohydrates 4.2 g of protein 31 mg of cholesterol 387 mg of sodium

Breakfast Skillet with Chard (Greek)

Prep Time: 10 minutes **Cooking Time:** 20 minutes
Servings: 4

Ingredients

Cherry tomatoes: 1 1/4 cups, quartered Olive oil: 3 tbsp.
Chopped yellow onion: 2 cups
4 eggs
Red wine vinegar: 1 tbsp.
2 bunches of Swiss chard
4 minced garlic cloves
Black pepper: half tsp.
Sea salt: half tsp.

Directions

1. In a bowl, toss tomatoes with vinegar.
2. Remove the stems off of chard leaves and chop the leaves and rinse them. Let them dry in a colander.
3. Slice the stems thinly.
4. In a skillet, add oil and sauté the stems and onion for ten minutes.
5. Turn the heat low and add garlic; cook for 60 seconds.
6. Add leaves and season with salt and pepper.
7. Toss on high heat until it wilts.
8. Make for wells in the pan and put one egg in each nest.
9. Cook for four minutes until yolks are set.
10. Add tomatoes to the skillet and serve.

Nutrition: 245 Cal | 11 g Fat | 17 g Carbs | 15 g Protein

Greek Omelet Casserole (Greek)

Prep Time: 10 minutes **Cooking Time:** 35-40 minutes
Servings: 12

Ingredients

12 eggs
oregano: 1 tsp.
Whole milk: 2 cups
Artichoke with olives, peppers, chopped without liquid Tomato (sun dried) feta cheese: ¾ cup, crumbled
Fresh spinach: 1 ½ cups
Lemon pepper: 1 tsp.
2 minced garlic cloves Dried
Fresh chopped dill: 1 tbsp.
Salt: 1 tsp.
Olive oil: 4 tsp.

Directions

1. Let the oven preheat to 350 F.
2. In a skillet, add oil (1 tbsp.), add garlic and spinach, sauté for three minutes.
3. Take a baking dish (9 by 13") and oil spray it.
4. Spread the spinach mixture on the bottom evenly.
5. In a bowl, whisk eggs with the rest of the except for feta cheese.
6. Pour the mixture over spinach mixture, and spread feta cheese on top.
7. Bake for 35 to 40 minutes until set.

Nutrition: 186 Cal | 13 g Fat | 5 g Carbs | 10 g Protein

Easy Breakfast Stuffed Peppers (Greek)

Prep Time: 10 minutes **Cooking Time:** 30 minutes
Servings: 5-6

Ingredients

Olive oil, as needed
3 minced garlic cloves
6 eggs
Chopped yellow onion: 1 cup Peeled potatoes: 10-12 oz., diced
Mushrooms: 6 oz., chopped
Coriander: ¾ tsp.
Chopped fresh parsley, packed: half cup
3 bell peppers, halved lengthwise and emptied
Water, as needed
Salt & black pepper, to taste
Chopped cherry tomatoes: half cup Aleppo pepper: ¾ tsp.
Organic cumin: ¾ tsp.
Turmeric: half tsp.

Directions

1. Let the oven preheat to 350 F.
2. Place the half peppers in the baking dish. Add water (1 cup) in the baking dish, cover with aluminum foil and bake for 10-15 minutes.
3. Place a cast-iron skillet on high flame, add mushrooms, salt and cook until browned. Take them out on a plate.
4. Add olive oil to the skillet (2 tbsp.) add potatoes and onion in hot oil.
5. Season with salt, pepper and other spices. Cook for five minutes and add garlic cook for 5-7 minutes on medium flame until potatoes become tender.
6. Add mushrooms, parsley and tomatoes. Mix well and turn off the heat.
7. Take peppers out from the oven, discard the water and stuff the mixture into the peppers, 3/4 of the way. Put one egg on top of the stuffing.
8. Cover with foil and bake for 18-20 minutes.
9. Serve right away.

Nutrition: 224 Cal 20 g Fat | 15.9 g Carbs | 17 g Protein

Snow Pea & Ricotta Toasts (Greek)

Prep Time: 10 minutes
Cooking Time: 0 minutes
Servings: 4

Ingredients

Snow peas: 4 oz.
Salt: half tsp.
Ricotta: 4 oz.
4 slices of toasted bread
White wine vinegar: 1 tbsp.
Olive oil: 1 tbsp.
Prepared horseradish: 2 tsp.
Honey: half tsp.

Directions

1. Cut peas in ¼ inch thick crosswise. In a bowl, whisk the rest of the with snow peas except for bread and ricotta.
2. On each toast slice, spread one oz. of ricotta and serve with snow peas mixture on top.

Nutrition: 131 Cal | 5.5 g Fat | 17 g Carbs | 8.5 g Protein

Chapter 3
Sides Recipes, Salads Recipes, & Soups Recipes

Salad with grilled Greek vegetables

Prep Time: 20 minutes | **Cooking Time:** 0 minutes |
Servings: 6

Ingredients

Salad:
1 (15-ounce / 425-g) can chickpeas, drained and rinsed
1 (14-ounce / 397-g) can artichoke hearts, drained and halved
1 head Bibb lettuce, chopped (about 2½ cups)
1 cucumber, peeled deseeded, and chopped (about 1½ cups)
1½ cups grape tomatoes, halved
¼ cup chopped basil leaves
½ cup sliced black olives
½ cup cubed feta cheese

Dressing:
1 tablespoon freshly squeezed lemon juice (from about ½ small lemon)
¼ teaspoon freshly ground black pepper
1 tablespoon chopped fresh oregano
2 tablespoons extra-virgin olive oil
1 tablespoon red wine vinegar
1 teaspoon honey

Directions
1. Combine the for the salad in a large salad bowl, then toss to combine well.
2. Combine the for the dressing in a small bowl, then stir to mix well.
3. Dress the salad and serve immediately.

Per Serving
calories: 165 | fat: 8.1g | protein: 7.2g | carbs: 17.9g | fiber: 7.0g | sodium: 337mg

Slaw with apples and Brussels sprouts

Prep Time: 15 minutes | **Cooking Time:** 0 minutes |
Servings: 4

Ingredients

Salad:
1 pound (454 g) Brussels sprouts, stem ends removed and sliced thinly
1 apple, cored and sliced thinly
½ red onion, sliced thinly

Dressing:
1 teaspoon Dijon mustard
2 teaspoons apple cider vinegar
1 tablespoon raw honey
1 cup plain coconut yogurt
1 teaspoon sea salt
For Garnish:
½ cup pomegranate seeds
½ cup chopped toasted hazelnuts

Directions
1. Combine the for the salad in a large salad bowl, then toss to combine well.
2. Combine the for the dressing in a small bowl, then stir to mix well.
3. Dress the salad let sit for 10 minutes. Serve with pomegranate seeds and toasted hazelnuts on top.

Per Serving
calories: 248 | fat: 11.2g | protein: 12.7g | carbs: 29.9g | fiber: 8.0g | sodium: 645mg

Butternut Squash and Cauliflower Soup

Prep Time: 15 minutes | **Cooking Time:** 4 hours |
Servings: 4 to 6

Ingredients

1 pound (454 g) butternut squash, peeled and cut into 1-inch cubes
1 small head cauliflower, cut into 1-inch pieces
1 onion, sliced
2 cups unsweetened coconut milk
1 tablespoon curry powder
4 cups low-sodium vegetable soup
2 tablespoons coconut oil
1 teaspoon sea salt
¼ teaspoon freshly ground white pepper
¼ cup chopped fresh cilantro, divided
½ cup no-added-sugar apple juice

Directions
1. Combine all the , except for the cilantro, in the slow cooker. Stir to mix well. Cook on high heat for 4 hours or until the vegetables are tender.
2. Pour the soup in a food processor, then pulse until creamy and smooth. Pour the puréed soup in a large serving bowl and garnish with cilantro before serving.

Per Serving
calories: 415 | fat: 30.8g | protein: 10.1g | carbs: 29.9g | fiber: 7.0g | sodium: 1386mg

Avgolemono (Lemon Chicken Soup)

Prep Time: 15 minutes | **Cooking Time:** 60 minutes | **Servings:** 2

Ingredients

½ large onion
2 medium carrots
1 celery stalk
1 garlic clove
5 cups low-sodium chicken stock
¼ cup brown rice
1½ cups (about 5 ounces / 142 g) shredded rotisserie chicken

3 tablespoons freshly squeezed lemon juice
1 egg yolk
2 tablespoons chopped fresh dill
2 tablespoons chopped fresh parsley
Salt, to taste

Directions

1. Put the onion, carrots, celery, and garlic in a food processor and pulse until the vegetables are minced.
2. Add the vegetables and chicken stock to a stockpot and bring it to a boil over high heat.
3. Reduce the heat to medium-low and add the rice, shredded chicken and lemon juice. Cover and let the soup simmer for 40 minutes, or until the rice is cooked.
4. In a small bowl, whisk the egg yolk lightly. Slowly, while whisking with one hand, pour about ½ of a ladle of the broth into the egg yolk to warm, or temper, the yolk. Slowly add another ladle of broth and continue to whisk.
5. Remove the soup from the heat and pour the whisked egg yolk–broth mixture into the pot. Stir well to combine.
6. Add the fresh dill and parsley. Season with salt to taste and serve.

Per Serving
calories: 172 | fat: 4.2g | protein: 18.2g | carbs: 16.1g | fiber: 2.1g | sodium: 232mg

Garlicky Roasted Grape Tomatoes (Spanish)

Prep Time: 10 minutes **Cooking Time:** 45 minutes
Servings: 2

Ingredients

1-pint grape tomatoes
1 fresh thyme sprig
¼ cup olive oil
1 fresh rosemary sprig

10 whole garlic cloves, skins removed
½ teaspoon salt

Directions

1. Preheat oven to 350ºF (180ºC).
2. Toss tomatoes, garlic cloves, oil, salt, and herb sprigs in a baking dish.
3. Roast tomatoes until they are soft and begin to caramelize, about 45 minutes.
4. Remove herbs before serving.

Nutrition: calories: 271 fats: 26g protein: 3g carbs: 12g fiber: 3g sodium: 593mg

Vegetables with Herbs Roasted (Italian)

Prep Time: 15 minutes **Cooking Time:** 45 minutes
Servings: 6

Ingredients

Nonstick cooking spray
1 zucchini, sliced ¼ inch thick
1 yellow summer squash, sliced ¼ inch thick 2 Roma tomatoes, sliced 1/8 inch thick
¼ teaspoon dried oregano
¼ teaspoon salt

1 eggplants, peeled and sliced 1/8 inch thick
black pepper to taste
¼ cup, plus 2 tablespoons extra-virgin olive oil, divided 1 tablespoon garlic powder
¼ teaspoon dried basil

Directions

1. Preheat the oven to 400ºF (205ºC).
2. Spray a 9-by-13-inch baking dish with cooking spray. In the dish, toss the eggplant, zucchini, squash, and tomatoes with 2 tablespoons oil, garlic powder, oregano, basil, salt, and pepper. Standing the vegetables up (like little soldiers), alternate layers of eggplant, zucchini, squash, and Roma tomato.
3. Drizzle the top with the remaining ¼ cup of olive oil.
4. Bake, uncovered, for 40 to 45 minutes, or until vegetables are golden brown.

Nutrition: calories: 186 fats: 14g protein: 3g carbs: 15g fiber: 5g sodium: 110mg

Mediterranean Bruschetta Hummus Platter(Greek)

Prep Time: 15 minutes **Cooking Time:** 0 minutes
Servings: 6

Ingredients

1/3 cup finely diced seedless English cucumber
4 warmed pitas, cut into wedges, for serving
1 (10-ounce / 283-g) container plain hummus
Carrot sticks, for serving
2 tablespoons crumbled feta cheese
Celery sticks, for serving
Purple cauliflower, for serving

½ cup finely diced fresh tomato
1 tablespoon fresh chopped parsley or basil
1 teaspoon extra-virgin olive oil
¼ cup Herbed Olive Oil
2 tablespoons balsamic glaze
Sliced bell peppers for serving
Broccoli, for serving

Directions

1. In a small bowl, mix the tomato and cucumber and toss with the olive oil. Pile the cucumber mixture over a fresh container of hummus. Drizzle the hummus and vegetables with the balsamic glaze. Top with crumbled feta and fresh parsley.
2. Put the hummus on a large cutting board. Pour the Herbed Olive Oil in a small bowl and put it on the cutting board. Surround the bowls with the pita wedges and cut carrot sticks, celery sticks, sliced bell peppers, broccoli, and cauliflower.

Nutrition: calories: 345 fats: 19g protein: 9g carbs: 32g fiber: 3g sodium: 473mg

Pumpkin Soup with Crispy Sage Leaves

Prep Time: 15 minutes | **Cooking Time:** 10 minutes | **Servings:** 4

Ingredients

1 tablespoon olive oil
2 garlic cloves, cut into ⅛-inch-thick slices
1 onion, chopped
2 cups freshly puréed pumpkin
4 cups low-sodium vegetable soup
2 teaspoons chipotle powder
1 teaspoon sea salt
½ teaspoon freshly ground black pepper
½ cup vegetable oil
12 sage leaves, stemmed

Directions

1. Heat the olive oil in a stockpot over high heat until shimmering.
2. Add the garlic and onion, then sauté for 5 minutes or until the onion is translucent.
3. Pour in the puréed pumpkin and vegetable soup in the pot, then sprinkle with chipotle powder, salt, and ground black pepper. Stir to mix well.
4. Bring to a boil. Reduce the heat to low and simmer for 5 minutes.
5. Meanwhile, heat the vegetable oil in a nonstick skillet over high heat.
6. Add the sage leaf to the skillet and sauté for a minute or until crispy. Transfer the sage on paper towels to soak the excess oil.
7. Gently pour the soup in three serving bowls, then divide the crispy sage leaves in bowls for garnish. Serve immediately.

Per Serving

calories: 380 | fat: 20.1g | protein: 8.9g | carbs: 45.2g | fiber: 18.0g | sodium: 1364mg

Green Beans with Tahini-Lemon Sauce

Prep Time: 5 minutes | **Cooking Time:** 10 minutes | **Servings:** 2

Ingredients

1 pound (454 g) green beans, washed and trimmed
2 tablespoons tahini
1 garlic clove, minced
Grated zest and juice of 1 lemon
Salt and black pepper, to taste
1 teaspoon toasted black or white sesame seeds (optional)

Directions

1. Steam the beans in a medium saucepan fitted with a steamer basket (or by adding ¼ cup water to a covered saucepan) over medium-high heat. Drain, reserving the cooking water. Mix the tahini, garlic, lemon zest and juice, and salt and pepper to taste. Use the reserved cooking water to thin the sauce as desired.
2. Toss the green beans with the sauce and garnish with the sesame seeds, if desired. Serve immediately.

Per Serving calories: 188 | fat: 8.4g | protein: 7.2g | carbs: 22.2g | fiber: 7.9g | sodium: 200mg

Soup with Barley and Mushrooms

Prep Time: 5 minutes | **Cooking Time:** 20 to 23 minutes | **Servings:** 6

Ingredients

2 tablespoons extra-virgin olive oil
1 cup chopped carrots
1 cup chopped onion
5½ cups chopped mushrooms
6 cups no-salt-added vegetable broth
1 cup uncooked pearled barley
¼ cup red wine
2 tablespoons tomato paste
4 sprigs fresh thyme or ½ teaspoon dried thyme
1 dried bay leaf
6 tablespoons grated Parmesan cheese

Directions

1. In a large stockpot over medium heat, heat the oil. Add the onion and carrots and cook for 5 minutes, stirring frequently. Turn up the heat to medium-high and add the mushrooms. Cook for 3 minutes, stirring frequently.
2. Add the broth, barley, wine, tomato paste, thyme, and bay leaf. Stir, cover, and bring the soup to a boil. Once it's boiling, stir a few times, reduce the heat to medium-low, cover, and cook for another 12 to 15 minutes, until the barley is cooked through.
3. Remove the bay leaf and serve the soup in bowls with 1 tablespoon of cheese sprinkled on top of each.

Per Serving

calories: 195 | fat: 4.0g | protein: 7.0g | carbs: 34.0g | fiber: 6.0g | sodium: 173mg

Sautéed White Beans with Rosemary

Prep Time: 10 minutes | **Cooking Time:** 12 minutes | **Servings:** 2

Ingredients

1 tablespoon olive oil
2 garlic cloves, minced
1 (15-ounce / 425-g) can white cannellini beans, drained and rinsed
1 teaspoon minced fresh rosemary plus 1 whole fresh rosemary sprig
¼ teaspoon dried sage
½ cup low-sodium chicken stock
Salt, to taste

Directions

1. Heat the olive oil in a saucepan over medium-high heat.
2. Add the garlic and sauté for 30 seconds until fragrant.
3. Add the beans, minced and whole rosemary, sage, and chicken stock and bring the mixture to a boil.
4. Reduce the heat to medium and allow to simmer for 10 minutes, or until most of the liquid is evaporated. If desired, mash some of the beans with a fork to thicken them. Season with salt to taste. Remove the rosemary sprig before serving.

Per Serving calories: 155 | fat: 7.0g | protein: 6.0g | carbs: 17.0g | fiber: 8.0g | sodium: 153mg

Mixture of Garlic Snap Peas (Greek)

Prep Time: 10 minutes **Cooking Time:** 10 minutes
Servings: 4

Ingredients

½ cup walnuts, chopped
1 and ½ teaspoons garlic, minced
1 pound sugar snap peas

¼ cup olive oil
½ cup veggie stock
2 teaspoons lime juice
Salt and black pepper to the taste
1 tablespoon chives, chopped

Directions

1. Heat up a pan with the stock over medium heat, add the snap peas and cook for 5 minutes.
2. Add the rest of the except the chives, cook for 5 minutes more and divide between plates.
3. Sprinkle the chives on top and serve as a side dish.

Nutrition: calories 200, fat 7.6, fiber 3.5, carbs 8.5, protein 4.3

Corn and Olives (Spanish)

Prep Time: 5 minutes **Cooking Time:** 0 min
Servings: 4

Ingredients

2 cups corn
2 tablespoons extra virgin olive oil
½ teaspoon balsamic vinegar
Salt and black pepper to the taste

4 ounces green olives, pitted and halved
1 teaspoon thyme, chopped
1 tablespoon oregano, chopped

Directions

1. In a bowl, combine the corn with the olives and the rest of the , toss and serve as a side dish.

Nutrition: calories 154, fat 10, fiber 3.4, carbs 17, protein 9.3

Rosemary Red Quinoa (Greek)

Prep Time: 10 minutes **Cooking Time:** 25 minutes
Servings: 6

Ingredients

4 cups chicken stock
2 tablespoons olive oil
1 teaspoon lemon zest, grated
2 tablespoons lemon juice
1 red onion, chopped

2 cups red quinoa, rinsed
1 tablespoon garlic, minced
Salt and black pepper to the taste
2 tablespoons rosemary, chopped

Directions

1. Heat up a pan with the oil over medium heat, add the onion and the garlic and sauté for 5 minutes.
2. Add the quinoa, the stock and the rest of the , bring to a simmer and cook for 20 minutes stirring from time to time.
3. Divide the mix between plates and serve.

Nutrition: calories 193, fat 7.9, fiber 1.4, carbs 5.4, protein 1.3

Thyme Corn and Cheese Mix (Greek)

Prep Time: 5 minutes **Cooking Time:** 0 min
Servings: 4

Ingredients

1 tablespoon olive oil
2 cups corn
1 cup scallions, sliced
2 tablespoons blue cheese, crumbled

1 teaspoon thyme, chopped
Salt and black pepper to the taste
1 tablespoon chives, chopped

1. In a salad bowl, combine the corn with scallions, thyme and the rest of the , toss, divide between plates and serve.

Nutrition: calories 183, fat 5.5, fiber 7.5, carbs 14.5

Olives and Carrots Sauté (Greek)

Prep Time: 10 minutes **Cooking Time:** 20 minutes
Servings: 4

Ingredients

1 tablespoon green olives, pitted and sliced
½ teaspoon lemon zest, grated
¼ teaspoon rosemary, dried
Salt and black pepper to the taste
2 pounds carrots, sliced
1 tablespoon parsley, chopped

2 teaspoons capers, drained and chopped
1 and ½ teaspoons balsamic vinegar
¼ cup veggie stock
2 spring onions, chopped
3 tablespoons olive oil

Directions

1. Heat up a pan with the oil over medium heat, add the carrots and brown for 5 minutes.
2. Add green olives, capers and the rest of the except the parsley and the chives, stir and cook over medium heat for 15 minutes.
3. Add the chives and parsley, toss, divide the mix between plates and serve as a side dish.

Nutrition: calories 244, fat 11, fiber 3.5, carbs 5.6, protein 6.3

Lemon Endives (Greek)

Prep Time: 10 minutes **Cooking Time:** 35 minutes
Servings: 4

Ingredients

Juice of 1 and ½ lemons
3 tablespoons olive oil
¼ cup veggie stock

Salt and black pepper to the taste
4 endives, halved lengthwise
1 tablespoon dill, chopped

Directions

1. In a roasting pan, combine the endives with the rest of the, introduce in the oven and cook at 375 degrees F for 35 minutes.
2. Divide the endives between plates and serve as a side dish.

Nutrition: calories 221, fat 5.4, fiber 6.4, carbs 15.4, protein 14.3

Soup with Moroccan lentils, tomatoes, and cauliflower

Prep Time: 15 minutes | **Cooking Time:** 4 hours | **Servings:** 6

Ingredients

1 cup chopped carrots
1 cup chopped onions
3 cloves garlic, minced
½ teaspoon ground coriander
1 teaspoon ground cumin
1 teaspoon ground turmeric
¼ teaspoon ground cinnamon
¼ teaspoon freshly ground black pepper
1 cup dry lentils
1 tablespoon red wine vinegar (optional)
28 ounces (794 g) tomatoes, diced, reserve the juice
1½ cups chopped cauliflower
4 cups low-sodium vegetable soup
1 tablespoon no-salt-added tomato paste
1 teaspoon extra-virgin olive oil
1 cup chopped fresh spinach
¼ cup chopped fresh cilantro

Directions

1. Put the carrots and onions in the slow cooker, then sprinkle with minced garlic, coriander, cumin, turmeric, cinnamon, and black pepper. Stir to combine well.
2. Add the lentils, tomatoes, and cauliflower, then pour in the vegetable soup and tomato paste. Drizzle with olive oil. Stir to combine well. Put the slow cooker lid on and cook on high for 4 hours or until the vegetables are tender.
3. In the last 30 minutes during the cooking time, open the lid and stir the soup, then fold in the spinach.
4. Pour the cooked soup in a large serving bowl, then spread with cilantro and drizzle with vinegar. Serve immediately.

Per Serving
calories: 131 | fat: 2.1g | protein: 5.6g | carbs: 25.0g | fiber: 5.5g | sodium: 364mg

Tricolor Summer Salad

Prep Time: 10 minutes | **Cooking Time:** 0 minutes | **Servings:** 3 to 4

Ingredients

¼ cup while balsamic vinegar
2 tablespoons Dijon mustard
1 tablespoon sugar
½ teaspoon garlic salt
½ teaspoon freshly ground black pepper
¼ cup extra-virgin olive oil
1½ cups chopped orange, yellow, and red tomatoes
½ cucumber, peeled and diced
1 small red onion, thinly sliced
¼ cup crumbled feta (optional)

Directions

1. In a small bowl, whisk the vinegar, mustard, sugar, pepper, and garlic salt. Then slowly whisk in the olive oil. In a large bowl, add the tomatoes, cucumber, and red onion. Add the dressing. Toss once or twice, and serve with the feta crumbles (if desired) sprinkled on top.

Per Serving calories: 246 | fat: 18.0g | protein: 1.0g | carbs: 19.0g | fiber: 2.0g | sodium: 483mg

Soup with Mushrooms and Soba Noodles

Prep Time: 15 minutes | **Cooking Time:** 10 minutes | **Servings:** 4

Ingredients

2 tablespoons coconut oil
8 ounces (227 g) shiitake mushrooms, stemmed and sliced thin
1 tablespoon minced fresh ginger
4 scallions, sliced thin
1 garlic clove, minced
1 teaspoon sea salt
4 cups low-sodium vegetable broth
3 cups water
4 ounces (113 g) soba noodles
1 bunch spinach, blanched, rinsed and cut into strips
1 tablespoon freshly squeezed lemon juice

Directions

1. Heat the coconut oil in a stockpot over medium heat until melted.
2. Add the mushrooms, ginger, scallions, garlic, and salt. Sauté for 5 minutes or until fragrant and the mushrooms are tender. Pour in the vegetable broth and water. Bring to a boil, then add the soba noodles and cook for 5 minutes or until al dente.
3. Turn off the heat and add the spinach and lemon juice. Stir to mix well.
4. Pour the soup in a large bowl and serve immediately.

Per Serving
calories: 254 | fat: 9.2g | protein: 13.1g | carbs: 33.9g | fiber: 4.0g | sodium: 1773mg

Parmesan Roasted Red Potatoes

Prep Time: 10 minutes | **Cooking Time:** 55 minutes | **Servings:** 2

Ingredients

12 ounces (340 g) red potatoes (3 to 4 small potatoes), scrubbed and diced into 1-inch pieces
1 tablespoon olive oil
½ teaspoon garlic powder
¼ teaspoon salt
1 tablespoon grated Parmesan cheese
1 teaspoon minced fresh rosemary (from 1 sprig)

Directions

1. Preheat the oven to 425°F (220°C). Line a baking sheet with parchment paper. In a mixing bowl, combine the potatoes, olive oil, garlic powder, and salt. Toss well to coat. Lay the potatoes on the parchment paper and roast for 10 minutes. Flip the potatoes over and roast for another 10 minutes. Check the potatoes to make sure they are golden brown on the top and bottom. Toss them again, turn the heat down to 350°F (180°C), and roast for 30 minutes more. When the potatoes are golden brown, scatter the Parmesan cheese over them and toss again. Return to the oven for 3 minutes to melt the cheese.
2. Remove from the oven and sprinkle with the fresh rosemary before serving.

Per Serving calories: 200 | fat: 8.2g | protein: 5.1g | carbs: 30.0g | fiber: 3.2g | sodium: 332mg

Quinoa and Garbanzo Salad (Spanish)

Prep Time: 10 minutes **Cooking Time:** 30 minutes
Servings: 8

Ingredients

4 cups water	2 cups red or yellow quinoa
1 cup thinly sliced onions (red or white)	1 (16-ounce / 454-g) can garbanzo beans, rinsed and drained
2 teaspoons salt, divided	1/3 cup extra-virgin olive oil
1 teaspoon freshly ground black pepper	
¼ cup lemon juice	

Directions

1. In a 3-quart pot over medium heat, bring the water to a boil.
2. Add the quinoa and 1 teaspoon of salt to the pot. Stir, cover, and let cook over low heat for 15 to 20 minutes.
3. Turn off the heat, fluff the quinoa with a fork, cover again, and let stand for 5 to 10 more minutes.
4. Put the cooked quinoa, onions, and garbanzo beans in a large bowl.
5. In a separate small bowl, whisk together the olive oil, lemon juice, remaining 1 teaspoon of salt, and black pepper.
6. Add the dressing to the quinoa mixture and gently toss everything together. Serve warm or cold.

Nutrition: calories: 318 fat: 6g protein: 9g carbs: 43g fiber: 13g sodium: 585mg

Mediterranean Salad with Peppers and Tomatoes(Greek)

Prep Time: 35 minutes **Cooking Time:** 30 minutes
Servings: 2

Ingredients

1 eggplant	1 zucchini
1 bell pepper	4 tomatoes
1 onion	4 sprigs of rosemary
3 tbsp olive oil	6 sprigs of thyme
4 stalks of sage	3 tbsp balsamic vinegar salt and pepper

Directions

1. Quarter tomatoes. Cut the remaining vegetables into bite-sized pieces, halve the onion and chop it into small pieces. Line a baking sheet with parchment paper, place the vegetables on top, drizzle with olive oil and mix well.
2. Season with salt and pepper. Scatter the herbs over the vegetables. Put the vegetables in the oven and bake at 200 degrees for about 30 minutes.
3. Remove and transfer to a large bowl and mix with olive oil with balsamic vinegar. Season with salt and pepper.
4. Let it draw covered. When the salad is still lukewarm, add the tomato quarters and mix well.
5. Serve the salad lukewarm.

Nutrition: Calories: 355 Carbohydrates: 39.43g Protein: 6.51g Fat: 21.43g

Israeli Salad (Greek)

Prep Time: 15 minutes **Cooking Time:** 6 mins
Servings: 4

Ingredients

¼ cup pine nuts	¼ cup shelled pistachios
¼ cup coarsely chopped walnuts	¼ cup shelled pumpkin seeds
¼ cup shelled sunflower seeds	2 large English cucumbers, unpeeled and finely chopped
1 pint cherry tomatoes, finely chopped	1 teaspoon salt
½ small red onion, finely chopped	½ cup finely chopped fresh flat-leaf Italian parsley
¼ cup extra-virgin olive oil	2 to 3 tablespoons freshly squeezed lemon juice
4 cups baby arugula	
¼ teaspoon freshly ground black pepper	

Directions

1. In a large dry skillet, toast the pine nuts, pistachios, walnuts, pumpkin seeds, and sunflower seeds over medium-low heat until golden and fragrant, 5 to 6 minutes, being careful not to burn them. Remove from the heat and set aside.
2. In a large bowl, combine the cucumber, tomatoes, red onion, and parsley.
3. In a small bowl, whisk together olive oil, lemon juice, salt, and pepper. Pour over the chopped vegetables and toss to coat.
4. Add the toasted nuts and seeds and arugula and toss with the salad to blend well. Serve at room temperature or chilled.

Nutrition: calories: 414 fat: 34g protein: 10g carbs: 17g fiber: 6g sodium: 642mg

Healthy Detox Salad (Italian)

Prep Time: 5 minutes **Cooking Time:** 0 minutes
Servings: 4

Ingredients

4 cups mixed greens	2 tbsp pumpkin seed oil
2 tbsp lemon juice	1 tbsp chia seeds
2 tbsp almonds, chopped	1 large carrot, coarsely grated
1 large apple, diced	1 large beet, coarsely grated

Directions

1. In a medium salad bowl, except for mixed greens, combine all thoroughly.
2. Into 4 salad plates, divide the mixed greens.
3. Evenly top mixed greens with the salad bowl mixture.
4. Serve and enjoy.

Nutrition: Calories: 141; Protein: 2.1g; Carbs: 14.7g; Fat: 8.2g

Broccoli with Artichoke Hearts and Garlic (Greek)

Prep Time: 5 minutes **Cooking Time:** 10 minutes
Servings: 4

Ingredients

1pounds (907 g) fresh broccoli rabe
1 teaspoon salt
1(13 3/4-ounce / 390-g) can artichoke hearts, drained and quartered
1 tablespoon water

½ cup extra-virgin olive oil, divided
1 tbsp red pepper flakes
2tablespoons red wine vinegar Freshly ground black pepper, to taste
3 garlic cloves, finely minced

Directions

1. Trim away any thick lower stems and yellow leaves from the broccoli rabe and discard. Cut into individual florets with a couple inches of thin stem attached.
2. In a large skillet, heat ¼ cup olive oil over medium-high heat. Add the trimmed broccoli, garlic, salt, and red pepper flakes and sauté for 5 minutes, until the broccoli begins to soften. Add the artichoke hearts and sauté for another 2 minutes.
3. Add the water and reduce the heat to low. Cover and simmer until the broccoli stems are tender, 3 to 5 minutes.
4. In a small bowl, whisk together remaining ¼ cup olive oil and the vinegar. Drizzle over the broccoli and artichokes. Season with ground black pepper, if desired.

Nutrition: calories: 358 fats: 35g protein: 11g carbs: 18g fiber: 10g sodium: 918mg

Romano Broccolini (Italian)

Prep Time: 5 minutes **Cooking Time:** 10 minutes
Servings: 2

Ingredients

1bunch broccolini (about 5 ounces / 142 g)
1 tablespoon olive oil
¼ teaspoon salt

½ teaspoon garlic powder
2 tablespoons grated Romano cheese

Directions

1. Preheat the oven to 400ºF (205ºC) and set the oven rack to the middle position. Line a sheet pan with parchment paper or foil.
2. Slice the tough ends off the broccolini and place in a medium bowl. Add the olive oil, garlic powder, and salt and toss to combine. Arrange broccolini on the lined sheet pan.
3. Roast for 7 minutes, flipping pieces over halfway through the roasting time.
4. Remove the pan from the oven and sprinkle the cheese over the broccolini. With a pair of tongs, carefully flip the pieces over to coat all sides. Return to the oven for another 2 to 3 minutes, or until the cheese melts and starts to turn golden.

Nutrition: calories: 114 fats: 9g protein: 4g carbs: 5g fiber: 2g sodium: 400mg

Roasted Parmesan Rosemary Potatoes (Italian)

Prep Time: 10 minutes
Cooking Time: 55 minutes
Servings: 2

Ingredients

12 ounces (340 g) red potatoes (3 to 4 small potatoes)
1 tablespoon olive oil
¼ teaspoon salt
1 teaspoon minced fresh rosemary (from 1 sprig)

½ teaspoon garlic powder
1 tablespoon grated Parmesan cheese

Directions

1. Preheat the oven to 425ºF (220ºC) and set the rack to the bottom position. Line a baking sheet with parchment paper. (Do not use foil, as the potatoes will stick.)
2. Scrub the potatoes and dry them well. Dice into 1-inch pieces.
3. In a mixing bowl, combine the potatoes, olive oil, garlic powder, and salt. Toss well to coat.
4. Lay the potatoes on the parchment paper and roast for 10 minutes. Flip the potatoes over and return to the oven for 10 more minutes.
5. Check the potatoes to make sure they are golden brown on the top and bottom. Toss them again, turn the heat down to 350ºF (180ºC), and roast for 30 minutes more.
6. When the potatoes are golden, crispy, and cooked through, sprinkle the Parmesan cheese over them and toss again. Return to the oven for 3 minutes to let the cheese melt a bit.
7. Remove from the oven and sprinkle with the fresh rosemary.

Nutrition: calories: 193 | fat: 8g | protein: 5g | carbs: 28g | fiber: 3g | sodium: 334mg

Cabbage and Mushrooms Mix (Greek)

Prep Time: 10 minutes **Cooking Time:** 15 minutes
Servings: 2

Ingredients

1 yellow onion, sliced
2 tablespoons olive oil
½ pound white mushrooms, sliced
1 green cabbage head, shredded

1 tablespoon balsamic vinegar
4 spring onions, chopped
Salt and black pepper to the taste

Directions

1. Heat a pan with the oil over medium heat, add the yellow onion and the spring onions and cook for 5 minutes.
2. Add the rest of the , cook everything for 10 minutes, divide between plates and serve.

Nutrition: 199 Calories 4.5g Fat 2.4g Fiber 5.6g Carbs 2.2g protein

Lemony Carrots (Italian)

Prep Time: 10 minutes **Cooking Time:** 40 minutes
Servings: 4

Ingredients

1tablespoons olive oil	2 pounds baby carrots, trimmed
1 tablespoon dill, chopped	1/3 cup Greek yogurt
½ teaspoon lemon zest, grated	1 garlic clove, minced
1 tablespoon lemon juice	Salt and black pepper to the taste
1 teaspoon cumin, ground	

Directions

1. In a roasting pan, combine the carrots with the oil, salt, pepper and the rest of the except the dill, toss and bake at 400 degrees F for 20 minutes.
2. Reduce the temperature to 375 degrees F and cook for 20 minutes more.
3. Divide the mix between plates, sprinkle the dill on top and serve.

Nutrition: calories 192, fat 5.4, fiber 3.4, carbs 7.3, protein 5.6

Oregano Potatoes (Spanish)

Prep Time: 10 minutes **Cooking Time:** 40 minutes
Servings: 4

Ingredients

6 red potatoes, peeled and cut into wedges	2 tablespoons olive oil ½ cup chicken stock
Salt and black pepper to the taste	1 teaspoon oregano, dried
1 teaspoon lemon zest, grated	1tablespoon chives, chopped

Directions

1. In a roasting pan, combine the potatoes with salt, pepper, the oil and the rest of the except the chives, toss, introduce in the oven and cook at 425 degrees F for 40 minutes.
2. Divide the mix between plates, sprinkle the chives on top and serve as a side dish.

Nutrition: calories 245, fat 4.5, fiber 2.8, carbs 7.1, protein 6.4

Chives Rice Mix (Spanish)

Prep Time: 5 minutes **Cooking Time:** 5 mins
Servings: 4

Ingredients

2tablespoons avocado oil	1 cup Arborio rice cooked
2 tablespoons chives, chopped	Salt and black pepper to the taste
	2 teaspoons lemon juice

Directions

1. Heat up a pan with the avocado oil over medium high heat, add the rice and the rest of the , toss, cook for 5 minutes, divide the mix between plates and serve as a side dish.

Nutrition: calories 236, fat 9, fiber 12.4, carbs 17.5, protein 4.5

Mixture of Baby Squash and Lentils (Greek)

Prep Time: 10 minutes **Cooking Time:** 10 minutes
Servings: 4

Ingredients

1tablespoons olive oil	½ teaspoon sweet paprika
10 ounces baby squash, sliced	15 ounces canned lentils, drained and rinsed Salt and black pepper to the taste
1 tablespoon balsamic vinegar	
1 tablespoon dill, chopped	

Directions

1. Heat up a pan with the oil over medium heat, add the squash, lentils and the rest of the , toss and cook over medium heat for 10 minutes.
2. Divide the mix between plates and serve as a side dish.

Nutrition: calories 438, fat 8.4, fiber 32.4, carbs 65.5, protein 22.4

Parmesan Quinoa and Mushrooms (Spanish)

Prep Time: 10 minutes **Cooking Time:** 20 minutes
Servings: 4

Ingredients

1cup quinoa, cooked	½ cup chicken stock
2tablespoons olive oil	6 ounces white mushrooms, sliced
1 teaspoon garlic, minced	½ cup parmesan, grated
Salt and black pepper to the taste	
2 tablespoons cilantro, chopped	

Directions

1. Heat up a pan with the oil over medium heat, add the garlic and mushrooms, stir and sauté for 10 minutes. Add the quinoa and the rest of the , toss, cook over medium heat for 10 minutes more, divide between plates and serve as a side dish.

Nutrition: calories 233, fat 9.5, fiber 6.4, carbs 27.4, protein 12.5

Green Beans and Peppers Mix (Greek)

Prep Time: 10 minutes **Cooking Time:** 10 minutes
Servings: 4

Ingredients

2 tablespoons olive oil	1and ½ pounds green beans, trimmed and halved
1 tablespoon dill, chopped	Salt and black pepper to the taste
1 tablespoon lime juice	2 tablespoons rosemary, chopped
2 red bell peppers, cut into strips	

Directions

1. Heat up a pan with the oil over medium heat, add the bell peppers and the green beans, toss and cook for 5 minutes.
2. Add the rest of the , toss, cook for 5 minutes more, divide between plates and serve as a side dish.

Nutrition: calories 222, fat 8.6, fiber 3.4, carbs 8.6, protein 3.4

Bulgur, Kale and Cheese Mix (Italian)

Prep Time: 10 minutes
Cooking Time: 10 minutes
Servings: 6

Ingredients

4 ounces bulgur
1 tablespoon mint, chopped
A pinch of allspice, ground
2 tablespoons olive oil
Zest and juice of ½ lemon

4 ounces kale, chopped
1 cucumber, chopped
4 ounces feta cheese, crumbled
3 spring onions, chopped

Directions

1. Put bulgur in a bowl, cover with hot water, aside for 10 minutes, and fluff with a fork. Heat a pan with the oil over medium heat, add the onions and the allspice and cook for 3 minutes.
2. Add the bulgur and the rest of the , cook everything for 5-6 minutes more, divide between plates, and serve.

Nutrition: 200 Calories 6.7g Fat 3.4g Fiber 15.4g Carbs 4.5g protein

Spicy Green Beans Mix (Greek)

Prep Time: 5 minutes **Cooking Time:** 15 minutes
Servings: 4

Ingredients

4 teaspoons olive oil
¾ cup veggie stock
1-pound green beans, trimmed and halved
1 garlic clove, minced

½ teaspoon hot paprika
1 yellow onion, sliced
½ cup goat cheese, shredded
2 teaspoon balsamic vinegar

Directions

1. Heat a pan with the oil over medium heat, add the garlic, stir, and cook for 1 minute.
2. Add the green beans and the rest of the , toss, cook everything for 15 minutes more, divide between plates, and serve as a side dish.

Nutrition: 188 Calories 4g Fat 3g Fiber 12.4g Carbs 4.4g protein

Beans and Rice (Spanish)

Prep Time: 10 minutes **Cooking Time:** 55 minutes
Servings: 6

Ingredients

1 tablespoon olive oil
2 celery stalks, chopped
2 garlic cloves, minced
1 and ½ cup canned black beans, rinsed and drained

1 yellow onion, chopped
2 cups brown rice
4 cups water
Salt and black pepper to the taste

Directions

1. Heat a pan with the oil over medium heat, add the celery, garlic, and onion, stir, and cook for 10 minutes.
2. Add the rest of the , stir, bring to a simmer, and cook over medium heat for 45 minutes. Divide between plates and serve.

Nutrition: 224 Calories 8.4g Fat 3.4g Fiber 15.3g Carbs 6.2g protein

Mixture of Lime and Cucumber (Greek)

Prep Time: 10 minutes
Cooking Time: 0 minute
Servings: 8

Ingredients

4 cucumbers, chopped
1 yellow onion, chopped
1 chili pepper, chopped
1 garlic clove, minced
1 tablespoon dill, chopped
1 tablespoon olive oil

½ cup green bell pepper, chopped
1 teaspoon parsley, chopped
2 tablespoons lime juice
Salt and black pepper to the taste

Directions

1. In a large bowl, mix the cucumber with the bell peppers and the rest of the , toss, and serve as a side dish.

Nutrition: 123 Calories 4.3g Fat 2.3g Fiber 5.6g Carbs 2g protein

Walnuts Cucumber Mix (Greek)

Prep Time: 5 minutes **Cooking Time:** 0 minute
Servings: 2

1cucumbers, chopped
1 tablespoon olive oil
1 tablespoon lemon juice
3 tablespoons walnuts, chopped
1 red chili pepper, dried

Salt and black pepper to the taste
1 tablespoon balsamic vinegar
1 teaspoon chives, chopped

Directions

1. In a bowl, mix the cucumbers with the oil and the rest of the , toss, and serve as a side dish.

Nutrition: 121 Calories 2.3g Fat 2g Fiber 6.7g Carbs 2.4g protein

Balsamic Asparagus (Greek)

Prep Time: 10 minutes **Cooking Time:** 15 minutes
Servings: 4

Ingredients

3 tablespoons olive oil
3 garlic cloves minced
2 tablespoons shallot chopped
1 and ½ pound asparagus trimmed

Salt and black pepper to the taste
2 teaspoons balsamic vinegar

Directions

1. Heat a pan with the oil over medium-high heat, add the garlic and the shallot and sauté for 3 minutes.
2. Add the rest of the , cook for 12 minutes more, divide between plates, and serve as a side dish.

Nutrition: 100 Calories 10.5g Fat 1.2g Fiber 2.3g Carbs 2.1g protein

Yogurt Peppers Mix (Greek)

Prep Time: 10 minutes **Cooking Time:** 15 minutes
Servings: 4

Ingredients

1red bell peppers, cut into thick strips	2shallots, chopped
3 garlic cloves, minced	2 tablespoons olive oil
1 tablespoon cilantro, chopped	Salt and black pepper to the taste
½ cup Greek yogurt	

Directions

1. Heat up a pan with the oil over medium heat, add the shallots and garlic, stir and cook for 5 minutes.
2. Add the rest of the , toss, cook for 10 minutes more, divide the mix between plates and serve as a side dish.

Nutrition: calories 274, fat 11, fiber 3.5, protein 13.3, carbs 6.5

Basil Artichokes (Italian)

Prep Time: 10 minutes **Cooking Time:** 12 minutes
Servings: 4

Ingredients

1red onion, chopped	2garlic cloves, minced
Salt and black pepper to the taste	½ cup veggie stock
10 ounces canned artichoke hearts, drained	1teaspoon lemon juice
2tablespoons basil, chopped	1 tablespoon olive oil

Directions

1. Heat up a pan with the oil over medium high heat, add the
2. onion and the garlic, stir and sauté for 2 minutes.
3. Add the artichokes and the rest of the , toss, cook for 10 minutes more, divide between plates and serve as a side dish.

Nutrition: calories 105, fat 7.6, fiber 3, carbs 6.7, protein 2.5

Broccoli and Roasted Peppers (Greek)

Prep Time: 10 minutes **Cooking Time:** 10 minutes
Servings: 4

Ingredients

1 pound broccoli florets.	2 garlic cloves, minced.
1 tablespoon olive oil	¼ cup roasted peppers, chopped.
2 tablespoons balsamic vinegar.	Salt and black pepper to the taste.
1 tablespoon cilantro, chopped	

Directions

1. Heat up a pan with the oil over medium high heat, add the garlic and the peppers and cook for 2 minutes.
2. Add the broccoli and the rest of the , toss, cook over medium heat for 8 minutes more, divide between plates and serve as a side dish.

Nutrition: calories 193, fat 5.6, fiber 3.45, carbs 8.6, protein 4.5

Quinoa Cauliflower (Greek)

Prep Time: 5 minutes **Cooking Time:** 10 minutes
Servings: 4

Ingredients

1 and ½ cups quinoa	3 tablespoons olive oil
3 cups cauliflower florets	chopped Salt and pepper to the taste
2 spring onions	
1 tablespoon red wine vinegar	chopped
1 tablespoon parsley	1 tablespoon chives chopped

Directions

1. Heat up a pan with the oil over medium-high heat, add the spring onions and cook for 2 minutes.
2. Add the cauliflower, quinoa and the rest of the , toss, cook over medium heat for 8-9 minutes, divide between plates and serve as a side dish.

Nutrition: calories 220, fat 16.7, fiber 5.6, carbs 6.8, protein 5.4

Mixed Veggies and Chard (Greek)

Prep Time: 10 minutes **Cooking Time:** 20 minutes
Servings: 4

Ingredients

½ cup celery, chopped	½ cup carrot, chopped
½ cup red onion, chopped	½ cup red bell pepper, chopped
1 cup veggie stock	½ cup black olives, pitted and chopped
1 tablespoon olive oil	10 ounces ruby chard, torn
Salt and black pepper to the taste	1 teaspoon balsamic vinegar

Directions

1. Heat up a pan with the oil over medium-high heat, add the celery, carrot, onion, bell pepper, salt and pepper, stir and sauté for 5 minutes.
2. Add the rest of the , toss, cook over medium heat for 15 minutes more, divide between plates and serve as a side dish.

Nutrition: calories 150, fat 6.7, fiber 2.6, carbs 6.8, protein 5.4

Spicy Broccoli and Almonds (Greek)

Prep Time: 10 minutes **Cooking Time:** 30 minutes
Servings: 4

Ingredients

1 broccoli head, florets separated	1 tablespoon olive oil
1tablespoon chili powder	2 garlic cloves, minced
2tablespoons almonds, toasted and chopped	Salt and black pepper to the taste
	1 tablespoon mint, chopped

Directions

1. In a roasting pan, combine the broccoli with the garlic, oil and the rest of the , toss, introduce in the oven and cook at 390 degrees F for 30 minutes.
2. Divide the mix between plates and serve as a side dish.

Nutrition: calories 156, fat 5.4, fiber 1.2, carbs 4.3, protein 2

Chapter 4
Sandwiches Recipes, Pizzas Recipes, & Wraps Recipes

Falafel Balls with Tahini

Prep Time: 2 hours 20 minutes | **Cooking Time:** 20 minutes | **Servings:** 4

Ingredients

Tahini Sauce:
½ cup tahini
2 tablespoons lemon juice
¼ cup finely chopped flat-leaf parsley
2 cloves garlic, minced
½ cup cold water, as needed

Falafel:
1 cup dried chickpeas, soaked overnight, drained
¼ cup chopped flat-leaf parsley

¼ cup chopped cilantro
1 large onion, chopped
1 teaspoon cumin
½ teaspoon chili flakes
4 cloves garlic
1 teaspoon sea salt
5 tablespoons almond flour
1½ teaspoons baking soda, dissolved in 1 teaspoon water
2 cups peanut oil
1 medium bell pepper, chopped
1 medium tomato, chopped
4 whole-wheat pita breads

Directions

Make the Tahini Sauce
1. Combine the for the tahini sauce in a small bowl. Stir to mix well until smooth.
2. Wrap the bowl in plastic and refrigerate until ready to serve.

Make the Falafel
3. Put the chickpeas, parsley, cilantro, onion, cumin, chili flakes, garlic, and salt in a food processor. Pulse to mix well but not puréed.
4. Add the flour and baking soda to the food processor, then pulse to form a smooth and tight dough.
5. Put the dough in a large bowl and wrap in plastic. Refrigerate for at least 2 hours to let it rise.
6. Divide and shape the dough into walnut-sized small balls.
7. Pour the peanut oil in a large pot and heat over high heat until the temperature of the oil reaches 375°F (190°C).
8. Drop 6 balls into the oil each time, and fry for 5 minutes or until golden brown and crispy. Turn the balls with a strainer to make them fried evenly.
9. Transfer the balls on paper towels with the strainer, then drain the oil from the balls.
10. Roast the pita breads in the oven for 5 minutes or until golden brown, if needed, then stuff the pitas with falafel balls and top with bell peppers and tomatoes. Drizzle with tahini sauce and serve immediately.

Per Serving
calories: 574 | fat: 27.1g | protein: 19.8g | carbs: 69.7g | fiber: 13.4g | sodium: 1246mg

Fajitas with Mushrooms and Vegetables in a Glaze

Prep Time: 20 minutes | **Cooking Time:** 20 minutes
Makes 6

Ingredients

Spicy Glazed Mushrooms:
1 teaspoon olive oil
1 (10- to 12-ounce / 284- to 340-g) package cremini mushrooms, rinsed and drained, cut into thin slices
to 1 teaspoon chili powder
Sea salt and freshly ground black pepper, to taste
1 teaspoon maple syrup

Fajitas:
2 teaspoons olive oil
1 onion, chopped
Sea salt, to taste
1 bell pepper, any color, deseeded and sliced into long strips
1 zucchini, cut into large matchsticks
6 whole-grain tortilla
2 carrots, grated
3 to 4 scallions, sliced
½ cup fresh cilantro, finely chopped

Directions

Make the Spicy Glazed Mushrooms
1. Heat the olive oil in a nonstick skillet over medium heat until shimmering.
2. Add the mushrooms and sauté for 10 minutes or until tender.
3. Sprinkle the mushrooms with chili powder, salt, and ground black pepper. Drizzle with maple syrup. Stir to mix well and cook for 5 to 7 minutes or until the mushrooms are glazed. Set aside until ready to use.

Make the Fajitas
4. Heat the olive oil in the same skillet over medium heat until shimmering.
5. Add the onion and sauté for 5 minutes or until translucent. Sprinkle with salt.
6. Add the bell pepper and zucchini and sauté for 7 minutes or until tender.
7. Meanwhile, toast the tortilla in the oven for 5 minutes or until golden brown.
8. Allow the tortilla to cool for a few minutes until they can be handled, then assemble the tortilla with glazed mushrooms, sautéed vegetables and remaining vegetables to make the fajitas. Serve immediately.

Per Serving
calories: 403 | fat: 14.8g | protein: 11.2g | carbs: 7.9g | fiber: 7.0g | sodium: 230mg

Wraps with Greek Salad from the Mediterranean

Prep Time: 15 minutes | **Cooking Time:** 0 minutes | Servings: 4

Ingredients

1½ cups seedless cucumber, peeled and chopped
1 cup chopped tomato
½ cup finely chopped fresh mint
¼ cup diced red onion
1 (2.25-ounce / 64-g) can sliced black olives, drained
2 tablespoons extra-virgin olive oil
1 tablespoon red wine vinegar
¼ teaspoon kosher salt
¼ teaspoon freshly ground black pepper
½ cup crumbled goat cheese
4 whole-wheat flatbread wraps or soft whole-wheat tortillas

Directions

1. In a large bowl, stir together the cucumber, tomato, mint, onion and olives.
2. In a small bowl, whisk together the oil, vinegar, salt, and pepper. Spread the dressing over the salad. Toss gently to combine.
3. On a clean work surface, lay the wraps. Divide the goat cheese evenly among the wraps. Scoop a quarter of the salad filling down the center of each wrap.
4. Fold up each wrap: Start by folding up the bottom, then fold one side over and fold the other side over the top. Repeat with the remaining wraps.
5. Serve immediately.

Per Serving

calories: 225 | fat: 12.0g | protein: 12.0g | carbs: 18.0g | fiber: 4.0g | sodium: 349mg

Pizza Pockets

Prep Time: 10 minutes | **Cooking Time:** 0 minutes | Servings: 2

Ingredients

½ cup tomato sauce
½ teaspoon oregano
½ teaspoon garlic powder
½ cup chopped black olives
2 canned artichoke hearts, drained and chopped
2 ounces (57 g) pepperoni, chopped
½ cup shredded Mozzarella cheese
1 whole-wheat pita, halved

Directions

1. In a medium bowl, stir together the tomato sauce, oregano, and garlic powder.
2. Add the olives, artichoke hearts, pepperoni, and cheese. Stir to mix.
3. Spoon the mixture into the pita halves and serve.

Per Serving

calories: 375 | fat: 23.5g | protein: 17.1g | carbs: 27.1g | fiber: 6.1g | sodium: 1080mg

Grilled Caesar Salad Sandwiches

Prep Time: 5 minutes | **Cooking Time:** 5 minutes | Servings: 2

Ingredients

¾ cup olive oil, divided
2 romaine lettuce hearts, left intact
3 to 4 anchovy fillets
Juice of 1 lemon
2 to 3 cloves garlic, peeled
1 teaspoon Dijon mustard
¼ teaspoon Worcestershire sauce
Sea salt and freshly ground pepper, to taste
2 slices whole-wheat bread, toasted
Freshly grated Parmesan cheese, for serving

Directions

1. Preheat the grill to medium-high heat and oil the grates.
2. On a cutting board, drizzle the lettuce with 1 to 2 tablespoons of olive oil and place on the grates.
3. Grill for 5 minutes, turning until lettuce is slightly charred on all sides. Let lettuce cool enough to handle.
4. In a food processor, combine the remaining olive oil with the anchovies, lemon juice, garlic, mustard, and Worcestershire sauce.
5. Pulse the until you have a smooth emulsion. Season with sea salt and freshly ground pepper to taste. Chop the lettuce in half and place on the bread.
6. Drizzle with the dressing and serve with a sprinkle of Parmesan cheese.

Per Serving

calories: 949 | fat: 85.6g | protein: 12.9g | carbs: 34.1g | fiber: 13.9g | sodium: 786mg

Chickpea Lettuce Wraps

Prep Time: 15 minutes | **Cooking Time:** 0 minutes | Servings: 2

Ingredients

1 (15-ounce / 425-g) can chickpeas, drained and rinsed well
1 celery stalk, diced
½ shallot, minced
1 green apple, cored and diced
3 tablespoons tahini (sesame paste)
2 teaspoons freshly squeezed lemon juice
1 teaspoon raw honey
1 teaspoon Dijon mustard
Dash salt
Filtered water, to thin
4 romaine lettuce leaves

Directions

1. In a medium bowl, stir together the chickpeas, celery, shallot, apple, tahini, lemon juice, honey, mustard, and salt. If needed, add some water to thin the mixture.
2. Place the romaine lettuce leaves on a plate. Fill each with the chickpea filling, using it all. Wrap the leaves around the filling. Serve immediately.

Per Serving calories: 397 | fat: 15.1g | protein: 15.1g | carbs: 53.1g | fiber: 15.3g | sodium: 409mg

Baked Parmesan Chicken Wraps

Prep Time: 10 minutes | **Cooking Time:** 18 minutes | **Servings:** 6

Ingredients

1 pound (454 g) boneless, skinless chicken breasts
1 large egg
¼ cup unsweetened almond milk
⅔ cup whole-wheat bread crumbs
½ cup grated Parmesan cheese
¾ teaspoon garlic powder, divided
1 cup canned low-sodium or no-salt-added crushed tomatoes
1 teaspoon dried oregano
6 (8-inch) whole-wheat tortillas, or whole-grain spinach wraps
1 cup fresh Mozzarella cheese, sliced
1½ cups loosely packed fresh flat-leaf (Italian) parsley, chopped
Cooking spray

Directions

1. Preheat the oven to 425°F (220°C). Line a large, rimmed baking sheet with aluminum foil. Place a wire rack on the aluminum foil, and spritz the rack with nonstick cooking spray. Set aside.
2. Place the chicken breasts into a large plastic bag. With a rolling pin, pound the chicken so it is evenly flattened, about ¼ inch thick. Slice the chicken into six portions.
3. In a bowl, whisk together the egg and milk. In another bowl, stir together the bread crumbs, Parmesan cheese and ½ teaspoon of the garlic powder.
4. Dredge each chicken breast portion into the egg mixture, and then into the Parmesan crumb mixture, pressing the crumbs into the chicken so they stick. Arrange the chicken on the prepared wire rack.
5. Bake in the preheated oven for 15 to 18 minutes, or until the internal temperature of the chicken reads 165°F (74°C) on a meat thermometer and any juices run clear.
6. Transfer the chicken to a cutting board, and cut each portion diagonally into ½-inch pieces.
7. In a small, microwave-safe bowl, stir together the tomatoes, oregano, and the remaining ¼ teaspoon of the garlic powder. Cover the bowl with a paper towel and microwave for about 1 minute on high, until very hot. Set aside.
8. Wrap the tortillas in a damp paper towel and microwave for 30 to 45 seconds on high, or until warmed through.
9. Assemble the wraps: Divide the chicken slices evenly among the six tortillas and top with the sliced Mozzarella cheese. Spread 1 tablespoon of the warm tomato sauce over the cheese on each tortilla, and top each with about ¼ cup of the parsley.
10. Wrap the tortilla: Fold up the bottom of the tortilla, then fold one side over and fold the other side over the top.
11. Serve the wraps warm with the remaining sauce for dipping.

Per Serving

calories: 358 | fat: 12.0g | protein: 21.0g | carbs: 41.0g | fiber: 7.0g | sodium: 755mg

Sandwiches with eggplant, spinach, and feta

Prep Time: 10 minutes | **Cooking Time:** 6 to 8 minutes | **Servings:** 2

Ingredients

1 medium eggplant, sliced into ½-inch-thick slices
2 tablespoons olive oil
Sea salt and freshly ground pepper, to taste
5 to 6 tablespoons hummus
4 slices whole-wheat bread, toasted
1 cup baby spinach leaves
2 ounces (57 g) feta cheese, softened

Directions

1. Preheat the grill to medium-high heat.
2. Salt both sides of the sliced eggplant, and let sit for 20 minutes to draw out the bitter juices.
3. Rinse the eggplant and pat dry with a paper towel.
4. Brush the eggplant slices with olive oil and season with sea salt and freshly ground pepper to taste.
5. Grill the eggplant until lightly charred on both sides but still slightly firm in the middle, about 3 to 4 minutes per side.
6. Spread the hummus on the bread slices and top with the spinach leaves, feta cheese, and grilled eggplant. Top with the other slice of bread and serve immediately.

Per Serving

calories: 493 | fat: 25.3g | protein: 17.1g | carbs: 50.9g | fiber: 14.7g | sodium: 789mg

Za'atar Pizza

Prep Time: 10 mins | **Cooking Time:** 10 to 12 mins | **Servings:** 4 to 6

Ingredients

1 sheet puff pastry
¼ cup extra-virgin olive oil
⅓ cup za'atar seasoning

Directions

1. Preheat the oven to 350°F (180°C). Line a baking sheet with parchment paper.
2. Place the puff pastry on the prepared baking sheet. Cut the pastry into desired slices.
3. Brush the pastry with the olive oil. Sprinkle with the za'atar seasoning.
4. Put the pastry in the oven and bake for 10 to 12 minutes, or until edges are lightly browned and puffed up.
5. Serve warm.

Per Serving

calories: 374 | fat: 30.0g | protein: 3.0g | carbs: 20.0g | fiber: 1.0g | sodium: 166mg

Green Veggie Sandwiches

Prep Time: 20 minutes | **Cooking Time:** 0 minutes | **Servings:** 2

Ingredients

Spread:

1 (15-ounce / 425-g) can cannellini beans, drained and rinsed

⅓ cup packed fresh basil leaves

⅓ cup packed fresh parsley

⅓ cup chopped fresh chives

2 garlic cloves, chopped

Zest and juice of ½ lemon

1 tablespoon apple cider vinegar

Sandwiches:

4 whole-grain bread slices, toasted

8 English cucumber slices

1 large beefsteak tomato, cut into slices

1 large avocado, halved, pitted, and cut into slices

1 small yellow bell pepper, cut into slices

2 handfuls broccoli sprouts

2 handfuls fresh spinach

Directions

Make the Spread

1. In a food processor, combine the cannellini beans, basil, parsley, chives, garlic, lemon zest and juice, and vinegar. Pulse a few times, scrape down the sides, and purée until smooth. You may need to scrape down the sides again to incorporate all the basil and parsley. Refrigerate for at least 1 hour to allow the flavors to blend. Assemble the Sandwiches

2. Build your sandwiches by spreading several tablespoons of spread on each slice of bread. Layer two slices of bread with the cucumber, tomato, avocado, bell pepper, broccoli sprouts, and spinach. Top with the remaining bread slices and press down lightly. Serve immediately.

Per Serving

calories: 617 | fat: 21.1g | protein: 28.1g | carbs: 86.1g | fiber: 25.6g | sodium: 593mg

Mushroom-Pesto Baked Pizza

Prep Time: 5 minutes | **Cooking Time:** 15 minutes | **Servings:** 2

Ingredients

1 teaspoon extra-virgin olive oil

½ cup sliced mushrooms

½ red onion, sliced

Salt and freshly ground black pepper

¼ cup store-bought pesto sauce

2 whole-wheat flatbreads

¼ cup shredded Mozzarella cheese

Directions

1. Preheat the oven to 350°F (180°C). In a small skillet, heat the oil over medium heat. Add the mushrooms and onion, and season with salt and pepper. Sauté for 3 to 5 minutes until the onion and mushrooms begin to soften. Spread 2 tablespoons of pesto on each flatbread. Divide the mushroom-onion mixture between the two flatbreads. Top each with 2 tablespoons of cheese. Place the flatbreads on a baking sheet and bake for 10 to 12 minutes until the cheese is melted and bubbly. Serve warm.

Per Serving calories: 348 | fat: 23.5g | protein: 14.2g | carbs: 28.1g | fiber: 7.1g | sodium: 792mg

Tuna and Hummus Wraps

Prep Time: 10 minutes | **Cooking Time:** 0 minutes | **Servings:** 2

Ingredients

Hummus:

1 cup from 1 (15-ounce / 425-g) can low-sodium chickpeas, drained and rinsed

2 tablespoons tahini

1 tablespoon extra-virgin olive oil

1 garlic clove

Juice of ½ lemon

2 tablespoons water

Wraps:

4 large lettuce leaves

1 (5-ounce / 142-g) can chunk light tuna packed in water, drained

1 red bell pepper, seeded and cut into strips

1 cucumber, sliced

¼ teaspoon salt

Directions

Make the Hummus

1. In a blender jar, combine the chickpeas, tahini, olive oil, garlic, lemon juice, salt, and water. Process until smooth. Taste and adjust with additional lemon juice or salt, as needed.

Make the Wraps

2. On each lettuce leaf, spread 1 tablespoon of hummus, and divide the tuna among the leaves. Top each with several strips of red pepper and cucumber slices.

3. Roll up the lettuce leaves, folding in the two shorter sides and rolling away from you, like a burrito. Serve immediately.

Per Serving calories: 192 | fat: 5.1g | protein: 26.1g | carbs: 15.1g | fiber: 4.1g | sodium: 352mg

Tuna and Olive Salad Sandwiches

Prep Time: 10 minutes | **Cooking Time:** 0 minutes | **Servings:** 4

Ingredients

3 tablespoons freshly squeezed lemon juice

2 tablespoons extra-virgin olive oil

1 garlic clove, minced

½ teaspoon freshly ground black pepper

2 (5-ounce / 142-g) cans tuna, drained

1 (2.25-ounce / 64-g) can sliced olives, any green or black variety

½ cup chopped fresh fennel, including fronds

8 slices whole-grain crusty bread

Directions

1. In a medium bowl, whisk together the lemon juice, oil, garlic, and pepper. Add the tuna, olives and fennel to the bowl. Using a fork, separate the tuna into chunks and stir to incorporate all the .

2. Divide the tuna salad equally among 4 slices of bread. Top each with the remaining bread slices.

3. Let the sandwiches sit for at least 5 minutes so the zesty filling can soak into the bread before serving.

Per Serving

calories: 952 | fat: 17.0g | protein: 165.0g | carbs: 37.0g | fiber: 7.0g | sodium: 2572mg

Wraps with a Mediterranean Greek Salad

Prep Time: 10 minutes | **Cooking Time:** 5 minutes | **Servings:** 4

Ingredients

2 (6- to 7-inch) whole-wheat submarine or hoagie rolls, sliced open horizontally

1 tablespoon extra-virgin olive oil

1 garlic clove, halved

1 large ripe tomato, cut into 8 slices

¼ teaspoon dried oregano

1 cup fresh Mozzarella, sliced

¼ cup lightly packed fresh basil leaves, torn into small pieces

¼ teaspoon freshly ground black pepper

Directions

1. Preheat the broiler to High with the rack 4 inches under the heating element. Put the sliced bread on a large, rimmed baking sheet and broil for 1 minute, or until the bread is just lightly toasted. Remove from the oven.
2. Brush each piece of the toasted bread with the oil, and rub a garlic half over each piece. Put the toasted bread back on the baking sheet. Evenly divide the tomato slices on each piece. Sprinkle with the oregano and top with the cheese.
3. Place the baking sheet under the broiler. Set the timer for 1½ minutes, but check after 1 minute. When the cheese is melted and the edges are just starting to get dark brown, remove the sandwiches from the oven. Top each sandwich with the fresh basil and pepper before serving.

Per Serving calories: 93 | fat: 2.0g | protein: 10.0g | carbs: 8.0g | fiber: 2.0g | sodium: 313mg

Zucchini Hummus Wraps

Prep Time: 15 minutes | **Cooking Time:** 6 minutes | **Servings:** 2

Ingredients

1 zucchini, ends removed, thinly sliced lengthwise

¼ teaspoon freshly ground black pepper

¼ cup hummus

2 Roma tomatoes, cut lengthwise into slices

2 tablespoons chopped red onion

½ teaspoon dried oregano

¼ teaspoon garlic powder

2 whole wheat tortillas

1 cup chopped kale

½ teaspoon ground cumin

Directions

1. In a skillet over medium heat, add the zucchini slices and cook for 3 minutes per side. Sprinkle with the oregano, pepper, and garlic powder and remove from the heat.
2. Spread 2 tablespoons of hummus on each tortilla. Lay half the zucchini in the center of each tortilla. Top with tomato slices, kale, red onion, and ¼ teaspoon of cumin. Wrap tightly and serve.

Per Serving
calories: 248 | fat: 8.1g | protein: 9.1g | carbs: 37.1g | fiber: 8.1g | sodium: mg

Panini with Roasted Vegetables

Prep Time: 10 minutes | **Cooking Time:** 15 minutes | **Servings:** 4

2 tablespoons extra-virgin olive oil, divided

1½ cups diced broccoli

1 cup diced zucchini

¼ cup diced onion

¼ teaspoon dried oregano

⅛ teaspoon kosher or sea salt

⅛ teaspoon freshly ground black pepper

1 (12-ounce / 340-g) jar roasted red peppers, drained and finely chopped

2 tablespoons grated Parmesan or Asiago cheese

1 cup fresh Mozzarella (about 4 ounces / 113 g), sliced

1 (2-foot-long) whole-grain Italian loaf, cut into 4 equal lengths Cooking spray

Directions

1. Place a large, rimmed baking sheet in the oven. Preheat the oven to 450°F (235°C) with the baking sheet inside.
2. In a large bowl, stir together 1 tablespoon of the oil, broccoli, zucchini, onion, oregano, salt and pepper.
3. Remove the baking sheet from the oven and spritz the baking sheet with cooking spray. Spread the vegetable mixture on the baking sheet and roast for 5 minutes, stirring once halfway through cooking. Remove the baking sheet from the oven. Stir in the red peppers and Parmesan cheese. In a large skillet over medium-high heat, heat the remaining 1 tablespoon of the oil.
4. Cut open each section of bread horizontally, but don't cut all the way through. Fill each with the vegetable mix (about ½ cup), and layer 1 ounce (28 g) of sliced Mozzarella cheese on top. Close the sandwiches, and place two of them on the skillet. Place a heavy object on top and grill for 2½ minutes. Flip the sandwiches and grill for another 2½ minutes. Repeat the grilling process with the remaining two sandwiches. Serve hot.

Per Serving calories: 116 | fat: 4.0g | protein: 12.0g | carbs: 9.0g | fiber: 3.0g | sodium: 569mg

Chapter 5
Beans Recipes, Grains Recipes, & Pastas Recipes

Oatmeal Baked with Pears and Pecans

Prep Time: 15 minutes | **Cooking Time:** 30 minutes | **Servings:** 6

Ingredients

2 tablespoons coconut oil, melted, plus more for greasing the pan
3 ripe pears, cored and diced
2 cups unsweetened almond milk
1 tablespoon pure vanilla extract
¼ cup pure maple syrup

2 cups gluten-free rolled oats
½ cup raisins
¾ cup chopped pecans
¼ teaspoon ground nutmeg
1 teaspoon ground cinnamon
½ teaspoon ground ginger
¼ teaspoon sea salt

Directions

1. Preheat the oven to 350°F (180°C). Grease a baking dish with melted coconut oil, then spread the pears in a single layer on the baking dish evenly.
2. Combine the almond milk, vanilla extract, maple syrup, and coconut oil in a bowl. Stir to mix well.
3. Combine the remaining in a separate large bowl. Stir to mix well. Fold the almond milk mixture in the bowl, then pour the mixture over the pears.
4. Place the baking dish in the preheated oven and bake for 30 minutes or until lightly browned and set.
5. Serve immediately.

Per Serving

calories: 479 | fat: 34.9g | protein: 8.8g | carbs: 50.1g | fiber: 10.8g | sodium: 113mg

Brown Rice Pilaf with Pistachios and Raisins

Prep Time: 5 minutes | **Cooking Time:** 15 minutes | **Servings:** 6

Ingredients

1 tablespoon extra-virgin olive oil
1 cup chopped onion
½ cup shredded carrot
½ teaspoon ground cinnamon
1 teaspoon ground cumin

2 cups brown rice
1¾ cups pure orange juice
¼ cup water
½ cup shelled pistachios
1 cup golden raisins
½ cup chopped fresh chives

Directions

1. Heat the olive oil in a saucepan over medium-high heat until shimmering.
2. Add the onion and sauté for 5 minutes or until translucent.
3. Add the carrots, cinnamon, and cumin, then sauté for 1 minutes or until aromatic.
4. Pour int the brown rice, orange juice, and water. Bring to a boil. Reduce the heat to medium-low and simmer for 7 minutes or until the liquid is almost absorbed.
5. Transfer the rice mixture in a large serving bowl, then spread with pistachios, raisins, and chives. Serve immediately.

Per Serving

calories: 264 | fat: 7.1g | protein: 5.2g | carbs: 48.9g | fiber: 4.0g | sodium: 86mg

Asparagus and Broccoli Primavera Farfalle

Prep Time: 15 minutes | **Cooking Time:** 12 minutes | **Servings:** 4

Ingredients

1 bunch asparagus, trimmed, cut into 1-inch pieces
2 cups broccoli florets
3 tablespoons olive oil
3 teaspoons salt
10 ounces (283 g) egg noodles
3 garlic cloves, minced
2½ cups vegetable stock
½ cup heavy cream
1 cup small tomatoes, halved
¼ cup chopped basil
½ cup grated Parmesan cheese

Directions

1. Pour 2 cups of water, add the noodles, 2 tablespoons of olive oil, garlic and salt. Place a trivet over the water. Combine asparagus, broccoli, remaining olive oil and salt in a bowl. Place the vegetables on the trivet.Seal the lid and cook on Steam for 12 minutes on High. Do a quick release. Remove the vegetables to a plate. Stir the heavy cream and tomatoes in the pasta. Press Sauté and simmer the cream until desired consistency.
2. Gently mix in the asparagus and broccoli. Garnish with basil and Parmesan, to serve.

Per Serving calories: 544 | fat: 23.8g | protein: 18.5g | carbs: 66.1g | fiber: 6.0g | sodium: 2354mg

Super Cheesy Tagliatelle

Prep Time: 10 minutes | **Cooking Time:** 20 minutes | **Servings:** 6

Ingredients

¼ cup goat cheese, chevre
¼ cup grated Pecorino cheese
½ cup grated Parmesan
1 cup heavy cream
½ cup grated Gouda
2 tablespoons olive oil
1 tablespoon Italian Seasoning mix
1 cup vegetable broth
1 pound (454 g) tagliatelle

Directions

1. In a bowl, mix goat cheese, pecorino, Parmesan, and heavy cream. Stir in Italian seasoning. Transfer to your instant pot. Stir in the broth and olive oil.
2. Seal the lid and cook on High Pressure for 4 minutes. Do a quick release.
1. Meanwhile, drop the tagliatelle in boiling water and cook for 6 minutes.
2. Remove the instant pot's lid and stir in the tagliatelle. Top with grated gouda and let simmer for about 10 minutes on Sauté mode.

Per Serving
calories: 511 | fat: 22.0g | protein: 14.5g | carbs: 65.7g | fiber: 9.0g | sodium: 548mg

Chickpea Curry

Prep Time: 10 minutes | **Cooking Time:** 24 minutes | **Servings:** 4

Ingredients

½ cup raw chickpeas
1½ tablespoons cooking oil
½ cup chopped onions
1 bay leaf
½ tablespoon grated garlic
¼ tablespoon grated ginger
¾ cup water
1 cup fresh tomato purée
½ green chili, finely chopped
¼ teaspoon turmeric
½ teaspoon coriander powder
1 teaspoon chili powder
1 cup chopped baby spinach
Salt, to taste
Boiled white rice, for serving

Directions

1. Add the oil and onions to the Instant Pot. Sauté for 5 minutes.
2. Stir in ginger, garlic paste, green chili and bay leaf. Cook for 1 minute, then add all the spices.
3. Add the chickpeas, tomato purée and the water to the pot.
4. Cover and secure the lid. Turn its pressure release handle to the sealing position.
5. Cook on the Manual function with High Pressure for 15 mins.
6. After the beep, do a Natural release for 20 minutes.
7. Stir in spinach and cook for 3 minutes on the Sauté setting.
8. Serve hot with boiled white rice.

Per Serving
calories: 176 | fat: 6.8g | protein: 6.7g | carbs: 24.1g | fiber: 5.1g | sodium: 185mg

Cumin Quinoa Pilaf

Prep Time: 5 minutes | **Cooking Time:** 5 minutes | **Servings:** 2

Ingredients

2 tablespoons extra virgin olive oil
2 cloves garlic, minced
3 cups water
2 cups quinoa, rinsed
2 teaspoons ground cumin
2 teaspoons turmeric
Salt, to taste
1 handful parsley, chopped

Directions

1. Press the Sauté button to heat your Instant Pot.
2. Once hot, add the oil and garlic to the pot, stir and cook for 1 minute. Add water, quinoa, cumin, turmeric, and salt, stirring well. Lock the lid. Select the Manual mode and set the cooking time for 1 minute at High Pressure.
3. When the timer beeps, perform a natural pressure release for 10 minutes, then release any remaining pressure. Carefully remove the lid.
4. Fluff the quinoa with a fork. Season with more salt, if needed.
5. Sprinkle the chopped parsley on top and serve.

Per Serving
calories: 384 | fat: 12.3g | protein: 12.8g | carbs: 57.4g | fiber: 6.9g | sodium: 448mg

Cannellini Beans in Italian Sauté

Prep Time: 10 minutes | **Cooking Time:** 15 minutes | **Servings:** 6

Ingredients

2 teaspoons extra-virgin olive oil
½ cup minced onion
¼ cup red wine vinegar
1 (12-ounce / 340-g) can no-salt-added tomato paste
2 tablespoons raw honey
½ cup water
¼ teaspoon ground cinnamon

Directions

1. 2(15-ounce / 425-g) cans cannellini beans
1. Heat the olive oil in a saucepan over medium heat until shimmering.
2. Add the onion and sauté for 5 minutes or until translucent.
3. Pour in the red wine vinegar, tomato paste, honey, and water. Sprinkle with cinnamon. Stir to mix well. Reduce the heat to low, then pour all the beans into the saucepan. Cook for 10 more minutes. Stir constantly. Serve immediately.

Per Serving

calories: 435 | fat: 2.1g | protein: 26.2g | carbs: 80.3g | fiber: 24.0g | sodium: 72mg

Lentil and Vegetable Curry Stew

Prep Time: 20 minutes | **Cooking Time:** 4 hours 7 mins | **Servings:** 8

Ingredients

1 tablespoon coconut oil
1 yellow onion, diced
¼ cup yellow Thai curry paste
2 cups unsweetened coconut milk
2 cups dry red lentils, rinsed well and drained
3 cups bite-sized cauliflower florets
2 golden potatoes, cut into chunks
2 carrots, peeled and diced
8 cups low-sodium vegetable soup, divided
1 bunch kale, stems removed and roughly chopped
Sea salt, to taste
½ cup fresh cilantro, chopped
Pinch crushed red pepper flakes

Directions

1. Heat the coconut oil in a nonstick skillet over medium-high heat until melted. Add the onion and sauté for 5 minutes or until translucent. Pour in the curry paste and sauté for another 2 minutes, then fold in the coconut milk and stir to combine well. Bring to a simmer and turn off the heat.
2. Put the lentils, cauliflower, potatoes, and carrot in the slow cooker. Pour in 6 cups of vegetable soup and the curry mixture. Stir to combine well. Cover and cook on high for 4 hours or until the lentils and vegetables are soft. Stir periodically.
3. During the last 30 minutes, fold the kale in the slow cooker and pour in the remaining vegetable soup. Sprinkle with salt. Pour the stew in a large serving bowl and spread the cilantro and red pepper flakes on top before serving hot.

Per Serving calories: 530 | fat: 19.2g | protein: 20.3g | carbs: 75.2g | fiber: 15.5g | sodium: 562mg

Veggie Chili Ritzy

Prep Time: 15 minutes | **Cooking Time:** 5 hours | **Servings:** 4

Ingredients

1 (28-ounce / 794-g) can chopped tomatoes, with the juice
1 (15-ounce / 425-g) can black beans, drained and rinsed
1 (15-ounce / 425-g) can redly beans, drained and rinsed
1 medium green bell pepper, chopped
1 yellow onion, chopped
1 tablespoon onion powder
1 teaspoon paprika
1 teaspoon cayenne pepper
1 teaspoon garlic powder
½ teaspoon sea salt
½ teaspoon ground black pepper
1 tablespoon olive oil
1 large hass avocado, pitted, peeled, and chopped, for garnish

Directions

1. Combine all the , except for the avocado, in the slow cooker. Stir to mix well.
2. Put the slow cooker lid on and cook on high for 5 hours or until the vegetables are tender and the mixture has a thick consistency.
3. Pour the chili in a large serving bowl. Allow to cool for 30 minutes, then spread with chopped avocado and serve.

Per Serving calories: 633 | fat: 16.3g | protein: 31.7g | carbs: 97.0g | fiber: 28.9g | sodium: 792mg

Walnut and Ricotta Spaghetti

Prep Time: 15 minutes | **Cooking Time:** 10 minutes | **Servings:** 6

Ingredients

1 pound (454 g) cooked whole-wheat spaghetti
2 tablespoons extra-virgin olive oil
4 cloves garlic, minced
¾ cup walnuts, toasted and finely chopped
2 tablespoons ricotta cheese
¼ cup flat-leaf parsley, chopped
½ cup grated Parmesan cheese
Sea salt and freshly ground pepper, to taste

Directions

1. Reserve a cup of spaghetti water while cooking the spaghetti.
2. Heat the olive oil in a nonstick skillet over medium-low heat or until shimmering.
3. Add the garlic and sauté for a minute or until fragrant.
4. Pour the spaghetti water into the skillet and cook for 8 more minutes.
5. Turn off the heat and mix in the walnuts and ricotta cheese.
6. Put the cooked spaghetti on a large serving plate, then pour the walnut sauce over. Spread with parsley and Parmesan, then sprinkle with salt and ground pepper. Toss to serve.

Per Serving

calories: 264 | fat: 16.8g | protein: 8.6g | carbs: 22.8g | fiber: 4.0g | sodium: 336mg

Pearl Barley Risotto with Parmesan Cheese

Prep Time: 5 minutes | **Cooking Time:** 20 minutes | **Servings:** 6

Ingredients

4 cups low-sodium or no-salt-added vegetable broth
1 tablespoon extra-virgin olive oil
1 cup chopped yellow onion
2 cups uncooked pearl barley
½ cup dry white wine

1 cup freshly grated Parmesan cheese, divided
¼ teaspoon kosher or sea salt
¼ teaspoon freshly ground black pepper
Fresh chopped chives and lemon wedges, for serving (optional)

Directions

1. Pour the broth into a medium saucepan and bring to a simmer.
2. Heat the olive oil in a large stockpot over medium-high heat. Add the onion and cook for about 4 minutes, stirring occasionally.
3. Add the barley and cook for 2 minutes, stirring, or until the barley is toasted. Pour in the wine and cook for about 1 minute, or until most of the liquid evaporates. Add 1 cup of the warm broth into the pot and cook, stirring, for about 2 minutes, or until most of the liquid is absorbed.
4. Add the remaining broth, 1 cup at a time, cooking until each cup is absorbed (about 2 minutes each time) before adding the next. The last addition of broth will take a bit longer to absorb, about 4 minutes.
5. Remove the pot from the heat, and stir in ½ cup of the cheese, and the salt and pepper.
6. Serve with the remaining ½ cup of the cheese on the side, along with the chives and lemon wedges (if desired).

Per Serving calories: 421 | fat: 11.0g | protein: 15.0g | carbs: 67.0g | fiber: 11.0g | sodium: 641mg

Cranberry and Almond Quinoa

Prep Time: 5 minutes | **Cooking Time:** 10 minutes | **Servings:** 2

Ingredients

2 cups water
1 cup quinoa, rinsed
¼ cup salted sunflower seeds

½ cup slivered almonds
1 cup dried cranberries

Directions

1. Combine water and quinoa in the Instant Pot.
2. Secure the lid. Select the Manual mode and set the cooking time for 10 minutes at High Pressure.
3. Once cooking is complete, do a quick pressure release. Carefully open the lid.
4. Add sunflower seeds, almonds, and dried cranberries and gently mix until well combined.
5. Serve hot.

Per Serving

calories: 445 | fat: 14.8g | protein: 15.1g | carbs: 64.1g | fiber: 10.2g | sodium: 113mg

Israeli Couscous with Asparagus

Prep Time: 5 minutes | **Cooking Time:** 25 minutes | **Servings:** 6

Ingredients

1½ pounds (680 g) asparagus spears, ends trimmed and stalks chopped into 1-inch pieces
1 garlic clove, minced
1 tablespoon extra-virgin olive oil
¼ teaspoon freshly ground black pepper

1¾ cups water
1 (8-ounce / 227-g) box uncooked whole-wheat or regular Israeli couscous (about 1⅓ cups)
¼ teaspoon kosher salt
1 cup garlic-and-herb goat cheese, at room temperature

Directions

1. Preheat the oven to 425ºF (220ºC).
2. In a large bowl, stir together the asparagus, garlic, oil, and pepper. Spread the asparagus on a large, rimmed baking sheet and roast for 10 minutes, stirring a few times. Remove the pan from the oven, and spoon the asparagus into a large serving bowl. Set aside.
3. While the asparagus is roasting, bring the water to a boil in a medium saucepan. Add the couscous and season with salt, stirring well.
4. Reduce the heat to medium-low. Cover and cook for 12 minutes, or until the water is absorbed.
5. Pour the hot couscous into the bowl with the asparagus. Add the goat cheese and mix thoroughly until completely melted. Serve immediately.

Per Serving calories: 103 | fat: 2.0g | protein: 6.0g | carbs: 18.0g | fiber: 5.0g | sodium: 343mg

Gouda Beef and Spinach Fettuccine

Prep Time: 10 minutes | **Cooking Time:** 15 minutes | **Servings:** 6

Ingredients

10 ounces (283 g) ground beef
1 pound (454 g) fettuccine pasta
1 cup gouda cheese, shredded
1 cup fresh spinach, torn
1 medium onion, chopped

2 cups tomatoes, diced
1 tablespoon olive oil
1 teaspoon salt
½ teaspoon ground black pepper

Directions

1. Heat the olive oil on Sauté mode in the Instant Pot. Stir-fry the beef and onion for 5 minutes. Add the pasta. Pour water enough to cover and season with salt and pepper. Cook on High Pressure for 5 minutes. Do a quick release. Press Sauté and stir in the tomato and spinach; cook for 5 minutes. Top with Gouda to serve.

Per Serving calories: 493 | fat: 17.7g | protein: 20.6g | carbs: 64.3g | fiber: 9.5g | sodium: 561mg

Freekeh Pilaf with Dates and Pistachios

Prep Time: 10 minutes | **Cooking Time:** 10 minutes | **Servings:** 4 to 6

Ingredients

2 tablespoons extra-virgin olive oil, plus extra for drizzling	1¾ cups water
1 shallot, minced	1½ cups cracked freekeh, rinsed
1½ teaspoons grated fresh ginger	3 ounces (85 g) pitted dates, chopped
¼ teaspoon ground coriander	¼ cup shelled pistachios, toasted and coarsely chopped
¼ teaspoon ground cumin	1½ tablespoons lemon juice
Salt and pepper, to taste	¼ cup chopped fresh mint

Directions

1. Set the Instant Pot to Sauté mode and heat the olive oil until shimmering. Add the shallot, ginger, coriander, cumin, salt, and pepper to the pot and cook for about 2 minutes, or until the shallot is softened. Stir in the water and freekeh.
2. Secure the lid. Select the Manual mode and set the cooking time for 4 minutes at High Pressure. Once cooking is complete, do a quick pressure release. Carefully open the lid. Add the dates, pistachios and lemon juice and gently fluff the freekeh with a fork to combine. Season to taste with salt and pepper. Transfer to a serving dish and sprinkle with the mint. Serve drizzled with extra olive oil.

Per Serving calories: 280 | fat: 8.0g | protein: 8.0g | carbs: 46.0g | fiber: 9.0g | sodium: 200mg

Black-Eyed Pea and Vegetable Stew

Prep Time: 15 minutes | **Cooking Time:** 40 minutes | **Servings:** 2

Ingredients

½ cup black-eyed peas, soaked in water overnight	¼ teaspoon turmeric
3 cups water, plus more as needed	¼ teaspoon cayenne pepper
1 large carrot, peeled and cut into ½-inch pieces (about ¾ cup)	¼ teaspoon ground cumin seeds, toasted
1 large beet, peeled and cut into ½-inch pieces	¼ cup finely chopped parsley
	¼ teaspoon salt (optional)
	½ teaspoon fresh lime juice

Directions

1. Pour the black-eyed peas and water into a large pot, then cook over medium heat for 25 minutes. Add the carrot and beet to the pot and cook for 10 minutes more, adding more water as needed. Add the turmeric, cayenne pepper, cumin, and parsley to the pot and cook for another 6 minutes, or until the vegetables are softened.
2. Stir the mixture periodically. Season with salt, if desired.
3. Serve drizzled with the fresh lime juice.

Per Serving calories: 89 | fat: 0.7g | protein: 4.1g | carbs: 16.6g | fiber: 4.5g | sodium: 367mg

Salad of Chickpeas with Tomatoes and Basil

Prep Time: 5 minutes | **Cooking Time:** 45 minutes | **Servings:** 2

Ingredients

1 cup dried chickpeas, rinsed	1 cup chopped fresh basil leaves
1 quart water, or enough to cover the chickpeas by 3 to 4 inches	2 to 3 tablespoons balsamic vinegar
1½ cups halved grape tomatoes	½ teaspoon garlic powder
	½ teaspoon salt, or more to taste

Directions

1. In your Instant Pot, combine the chickpeas and water.
2. Secure the lid. Select the Manual mode and set the cooking time for 45 minutes at High Pressure.
3. Once cooking is complete, do a natural pressure release for 20 minutes, then release any remaining pressure. Carefully open the lid and drain the chickpeas. Refrigerate to cool (unless you want to serve this warm, which is good, too).
4. While the chickpeas cool, in a large bowl, stir together the basil, tomatoes, vinegar, garlic powder, and salt. Add the beans, stir to combine, and serve.

Per Serving calories: 395 | fat: 6.0g | protein: 19.8g | carbs: 67.1g | fiber: 19.0g | sodium: 612mg

Mediterranean Lentils

Prep Time: 7 minutes | **Cooking Time:** 24 minutes | **Servings:** 2

Ingredients

1 tablespoon olive oil	½ teaspoon salt, plus more as needed
1 small sweet or yellow onion, diced	¼ teaspoon freshly ground black pepper, plus more as needed
1 garlic clove, diced	1 tomato, diced
1 teaspoon dried oregano	1 cup brown or green lentils
½ teaspoon ground cumin	2½ cups vegetable stock
½ teaspoon dried parsley	1 bay leaf

Directions

1. Set your Instant Pot to Sauté and heat the olive oil until it shimmers. Add the onion and cook for 3 to 4 minutes until soft. Turn off the Instant Pot and add the garlic, oregano, cumin, parsley, salt, and pepper. Cook until fragrant, about 1 minute.
2. Stir in the tomato, lentils, stock, and bay leaf.
3. Lock the lid. Select the Manual mode and set the cooking time for 18 minutes at High Pressure.
4. When the timer beeps, perform a natural pressure release for 10 minutes, then release any remaining pressure. Carefully open the lid. Remove and discard the bay leaf. Taste and season with more salt and pepper, as needed. If there's too much liquid remaining, select Sauté and cook until it evaporates. Serve warm.

Per Serving calories: 426 | fat: 8.1g | protein: 26.2g | carbs: 63.8g | fiber: 31.0g | sodium: 591mg

Fava and Garbanzo Bean Ful

Prep Time: 10 minutes | **Cooking Time:** 10 minutes | **Servings:** 6

Ingredients

1 (15-ounce / 425-g) can fava beans, rinsed and drained
1 (1-pound / 454-g) can garbanzo beans, rinsed and drained
3 cups water
½ cup lemon juice
3 cloves garlic, peeled and minced
1 teaspoon salt
3 tablespoons extra-virgin olive oil

Directions

1. In a pot over medium heat, cook the beans and water for 10 minutes.
2. Drain the beans and transfer to a bowl. Reserve 1 cup of the liquid from the cooked beans.
3. Add the reserved liquid, lemon juice, minced garlic and salt to the bowl with the beans. Mix to combine well. Using a potato masher, mash up about half the beans in the bowl.
4. Give the mixture one more stir to make sure the beans are evenly mixed.
5. Drizzle with the olive oil and serve.

Per Serving

calories: 199 | fat: 9.0g | protein: 10.0g | carbs: 25.0g | fiber: 9.0g | sodium: 395mg

Cherry, Apricot, and Pecan Brown Rice Bowl

Prep Time: 15 minutes | **Cooking Time:** 1 hour 1 min | **Servings:** 2

Ingredients

2 tablespoons olive oil
2 green onions, sliced
½ cup brown rice
1 cup low-sodium chicken stock
2 tablespoons dried cherries
4 dried apricots, chopped
2 tablespoons pecans, toasted and chopped
Sea salt and freshly ground pepper, to taste

Directions

1. Heat the olive oil in a medium saucepan over medium-high heat until shimmering.
2. Add the green onions and sauté for 1 minutes or until fragrant.
3. Add the rice. Stir to mix well, then pour in the chicken stock.
4. Bring to a boil. Reduce the heat to low. Cover and simmer for 50 minutes or until the brown rice is soft.
5. Add the cherries, apricots, and pecans, and simmer for 10 more minutes or until the fruits are tender.
6. Pour them in a large serving bowl. Fluff with a fork. Sprinkle with sea salt and freshly ground pepper. Serve immediately.

Per Serving

calories: 451 | fat: 25.9g | protein: 8.2g | carbs: 50.4g | fiber: 4.6g | sodium: 122mg

Curry Apple Couscous with Leeks and Pecans

Prep Time: 10 minutes | **Cooking Time:** 8 minutes | **Servings:** 4

Ingredients

2 teaspoons extra-virgin olive oil
2 leeks, white parts only, sliced
1 apple, diced
2 cups cooked couscous
2 tablespoons curry powder
½ cup chopped pecans

Directions

1. Heat the olive oil in a skillet over medium heat until shimmering.
2. Add the leeks and sauté for 5 minutes or until soft.
3. Add the diced apple and cook for 3 more minutes until tender.
4. Add the couscous and curry powder. Stir to combine.
5. Transfer them in a large serving bowl, then mix in the pecans and serve.

Per Serving

calories: 254 | fat: 11.9g | protein: 5.4g | carbs: 34.3g | fiber: 5.9g | sodium: 15mg

Lebanese Flavor Broken Thin Noodles

Prep Time: 10 minutes | **Cooking Time:** 25 minutes | **Servings:** 6

Ingredients

1 tablespoon extra-virgin olive oil
1 (3-ounce / 85-g) cup vermicelli, broken into 1- to 1½-inch pieces
3 cups shredded cabbage
1 cup brown rice
3 cups low-sodium vegetable soup
½ cup water
2 garlic cloves, mashed
¼ teaspoon sea salt
⅛ teaspoon crushed red pepper flakes
½ cup coarsely chopped cilantro
Fresh lemon slices, for serving

Directions

1. Heat the olive oil in a saucepan over medium-high heat until shimmering.
2. Add the vermicelli and sauté for 3 minutes or until toasted.
3. Add the cabbage and sauté for 4 minutes or until tender.
4. Pour in the brown rice, vegetable soup, and water. Add the garlic and sprinkle with salt and red pepper flakes.
5. Bring to a boil over high heat. Reduce the heat to medium low. Put the lid on and simmer for another 10 minutes.
6. Turn off the heat, then let sit for 5 minutes without opening the lid.
7. Pour them on a large serving platter and spread with cilantro. Squeeze the lemon slices over and serve warm.

Per Serving

calories: 127 | fat: 3.1g | protein: 4.2g | carbs: 22.9g | fiber: 3.0g | sodium: 224mg

Linguine with Parmesan Squash

Prep Time: 15 minutes | **Cooking Time:** 5 minutes | **Servings:** 4

Ingredients

1 cup flour
2 teaspoons salt
2 eggs
4 cups water
1 cup seasoned breadcrumbs
½ cup grated Parmesan cheese, plus more for garnish

1 yellow squash, peeled and sliced
1 pound (454 g) linguine
24 ounces (680 g) canned seasoned tomato sauce
2 tablespoons olive oil
1 cup shredded Mozzarella cheese
Minced fresh basil

Directions

1. Break the linguine in half. Put it in the pot and add water and half of salt. Seal the lid and cook on High Pressure for 5 minutes. Combine the flour and 1 teaspoon of salt in a bowl. In another bowl, whisk the eggs and 2 tablespoons of water. In a third bowl, mix the breadcrumbs and Mozzarella cheese.
2. Coat each squash slices in the flour. Shake off excess flour, dip in the egg wash, and dredge in the bread crumbs. Set aside. Quickly release the pressure. Remove linguine to a serving bowl and mix in the tomato sauce and sprinkle with fresh basil. Heat oil on Sauté and fry breaded squash until crispy.
3. Serve the squash topped Mozzarella cheese with the linguine on side.

Per Serving

calories: 857 | fat: 17.0g | protein: 33.2g | carbs: 146.7g | fiber: 18.1g | sodium: 1856mg

Caprese Fusilli

Prep Time: 15 minutes | **Cooking Time:** 7 minutes | **Servings:** 3

Ingredients

1 tablespoon olive oil
1 onion, thinly chopped
6 garlic cloves, minced
1 teaspoon red pepper flakes
2½ cups dried fusilli
1 (15-ounce / 425-g) can tomato sauce

1 cup tomatoes, halved
1 cup water
¼ cup basil leaves
1 teaspoon salt
1 cup Ricotta cheese, crumbled
2 tablespoons chopped fresh basil

Directions

1. Warm oil on Sauté. Add red pepper flakes, garlic and onion and cook for 3 minutes until soft.
2. Mix in fusilli, tomatoes, half of the basil leaves, water, tomato sauce, and salt. Seal the lid, and cook on High Pressure for 4 minutes. Release the pressure quickly.
3. Transfer the pasta to a serving platter and top with the crumbled ricotta and remaining chopped basil.

Per Serving

calories: 589 | fat: 17.7g | protein: 19.5g | carbs: 92.8g | fiber: 13.8g | sodium: 879mg

Red Bean Curry

Prep Time: 10 minutes | **Cooking Time:** 24 minutes | **Servings:** 4

Ingredients

½ cup raw red beans
1½ tablespoons cooking oil
½ cup chopped onions
1 bay leaf
½ tablespoon grated garlic
¼ tablespoon grated ginger
¾ cup water
1 cup fresh tomato purée
Salt, to taste

½ green chili, finely chopped
¼ teaspoon turmeric
½ teaspoon coriander powder
1 teaspoon chili powder
1 cup chopped baby spinach
Boiled white rice or quinoa, for serve

Directions

1. Add the oil and onions to the Instant Pot. Sauté for 5 minutes.
2. Stir in ginger, garlic paste, green chili and bay leaf. Cook for 1 minute, then add all the spices.
3. Add the red beans, tomato purée and water to the pot.
4. Cover and secure the lid. Turn its pressure release handle to the sealing position.
5. Cook on the Manual function with High Pressure for 15 minutes.
6. After the beep, do a Natural release for 20 minutes.
7. Stir in spinach and cook for 3 minutes on the Sauté setting.
8. Serve hot with boiled white rice or quinoa.

Per Serving

calories: 159 | fat: 5.6g | protein: 6.8g | carbs: 22.5g | fiber: 5.5g | sodium: 182mg

Easy Simple Pesto Pasta (Italian)

Prep Time: 10 minutes **Cooking Time:** 8 minutes **Servings:** 4 to 6

Ingredients

1-pound (454 g) spaghetti
3 cloves garlic
1 teaspoon salt
1/2 cup toasted pine nuts
1/4 cup lemon juice
1 cup extra-virgin olive oil

4 cups fresh basil leaves, stems removed
1/2 teaspoon freshly ground black pepper
1/2 cup grated Parmesan cheese

Directions

1. Bring a large pot of salted water to a boil. Add the spaghetti to the pot and cook for 8 minutes.
2. In a food processor, place the remaining , except for the olive oil, and pulse. While the processor is running, slowly drizzle the olive oil through the top opening. Process until all the olive oil has been added.
3. Reserve ½ cup of the cooking liquid. Drain the pasta and put it into a large bowl. Add the pesto and cooking liquid to the bowl of pasta and toss everything together.
4. Serve immediately.

Nutrition: calories: 1067 fat: 72.0g protein: 23.0g carbs: 91.0g fiber: 6.0g sodium: 817mg

Bowls of Pesto Arborio Rice and Veggies

Prep Time: 10 minutes | **Cooking Time:** 1 minute | **Servings:** 2

Ingredients

1 cup arborio rice, rinsed and drained
2 cups vegetable broth
Salt and black pepper to taste
1 potato, peeled, cubed
1 head broccoli, cut into small florets
1 bunch baby carrots, peeled
¼ cabbage, chopped
2 eggs
¼ cup pesto sauce
Lemon wedges, for serving

Directions

1. In the pot, mix broth, pepper, rice and salt. Set trivet to the inner pot on top of rice and add a steamer basket to the top of the trivet. Mix carrots, potato, eggs and broccoli in the steamer basket. Add pepper and salt for seasoning.
2. Seal the lid and cook for 1 minute on High Pressure. Quick release the pressure. Take away the trivet and steamer basket from the pot.
3. Set the eggs in a bowl of ice water. Then peel and halve the eggs. Use a fork to fluff rice.
4. Adjust the seasonings. In two bowls, equally divide rice, broccoli, eggs, carrots, sweet potatoes, and a dollop of pesto. Serve alongside a lemon wedge.

Per Serving calories: 858 | fat: 24.4g | protein: 26.4g | carbs: 136.2g | fiber: 14.1g | sodium: 985mg

Rice and Bean Stuffed Zucchini

Prep Time: 10 minutes | **Cooking Time:** 15 minutes | **Servings:** 4

Ingredients

2 small zucchinis, halved lengthwise
½ cup cooked rice
½ cup canned white beans, drained and rinsed
½ cup chopped tomatoes
½ cup chopped toasted cashew nuts
½ cup grated Parmesan cheese
1 tablespoon olive oil
½ teaspoon salt
½ teaspoon freshly ground black pepper

Directions

1. Pour 1 cup of water in the instant pot and insert a trivet. Scoop out the pulp of zucchini and chop roughly.
2. In a bowl, mix the zucchini pulp, rice, tomatoes, cashew nuts, ¼ cup of Parmesan, olive oil, salt, and black pepper. Fill the zucchini boats with the mixture, and arrange the stuffed boats in a single layer on the trivet. Seal the lid and cook for 15 minutes on Steam on High. Do a quick release and serve.

Per Serving calories: 239 | fat: 14.7g | protein: 9.4g | carbs: 19.0g | fiber: 2.6g | sodium: 570mg

Chard and Mushroom Risotto

Prep Time: 15 minutes | **Cooking Time:** 20 minutes | **Servings:** 4

Ingredients

3 tablespoons olive oil
1 onion, chopped
2 Swiss chard, stemmed and chopped
1 cup risotto rice
⅓ cup white wine
3 cups vegetable stock
½ teaspoon salt
½ cup mushrooms
4 tablespoons pumpkin seeds, toasted
⅓ cup grated Pecorino Romano cheese

Directions

1. Heat oil on Sauté, and cook onion and mushrooms for 5 minutes, stirring, until tender. Add the rice and cook for a minute. Stir in wine and cook for 2 to 3 minutes until almost evaporated.
2. Pour in stock and season with salt. Seal the lid and cook on High Pressure for 10 minutes.
3. Do a quick release. Stir in chard until wilted, mix in cheese to melt, and serve scattered with pumpkin seeds.

Per Serving calories: 420 | fat: 17.7g | protein: 11.8g | carbs: 54.9g | fiber: 4.9g | sodium: 927mg

Cheesy Tomato Linguine

Prep Time: 15 minutes | **Cooking Time:** 11 minutes | **Servings:** 4

Ingredients

2 tablespoons olive oil
1 small onion, diced
2 garlic cloves, minced
1 cup cherry tomatoes, halved
1½ cups vegetable stock
¼ cup julienned basil leaves
1 teaspoon salt
½ teaspoon ground black pepper
¼ teaspoon red chili flakes
1 pound (454 g) Linguine noodles, halved
Fresh basil leaves for garnish
½ cup Parmigiano-Reggiano cheese, grated

Directions

1. Warm oil on Sauté. Add onion and Sauté for 2 minutes until soft. Mix garlic and tomatoes and sauté for 4 minutes. To the pot, add vegetable stock, salt, julienned basil, red chili flakes and pepper.
2. Add linguine to the tomato mixture until covered. Seal the lid and cook on High Pressure for 5 minutes.
3. Naturally release the pressure for 5 minutes. Stir the mixture to ensure it is broken down.
4. Divide into plates. Top with basil and Parmigiano-Reggiano cheese and serve.

Per Serving calories: 311 | fat: 11.3g | protein: 10.3g | carbs: 42.1g | fiber: 1.9g | sodium: 1210mg

Tomato Sauce and Basil Pesto Fettuccine

Prep Time: 15 minutes | **Cooking Time:** 15 minutes | **Servings:** 4

Ingredients

4 Roma tomatoes, diced
2 teaspoons no-salt-added tomato paste
1 tablespoon chopped fresh oregano
2 garlic cloves, minced
1 cup low-sodium vegetable soup
½ teaspoon sea salt
1 packed cup fresh basil leaves
¼ cup pine nuts
¼ cup grated Parmesan cheese
2 tablespoons extra-virgin olive oil
1 pound (454 g) cooked whole-grain fettuccine

Directions

1. Put the tomatoes, tomato paste, oregano, garlic, vegetable soup, and salt in a skillet. Stir to mix well.
2. Cook over medium heat for 10 minutes or until lightly thickened. Put the remaining , except for the fettuccine, in a food processor and pulse to combine until smooth.
3. Pour the puréed basil mixture into the tomato mixture, then add the fettuccine. Cook for a few minutes or until heated through and the fettuccine is well coated. Serve immediately.

Per Serving calories: 389 | fat: 22.7g | protein: 9.7g | carbs: 40.2g | fiber: 4.8g | sodium: 616mg

Bean and Veggie Pasta

Prep Time: 10 minutes | **Cooking Time:** 15 minutes | **Servings:** 2

Ingredients

16 ounces (454 g) small whole wheat pasta, such as penne, farfalle, or macaroni
5 cups water
1 (15-ounce / 425-g) can cannellini beans, drained and rinsed
1 (14.5-ounce / 411-g) can diced (with juice) or crushed tomatoes
1 yellow onion, chopped
1 red or yellow bell pepper, chopped
2 tablespoons tomato paste
1 tablespoon olive oil
3 garlic cloves, minced
¼ teaspoon crushed red pepper (optional)
1 bunch kale, stemmed and chopped
1 cup sliced basil
½ cup pitted Kalamata olives, chopped

Directions

1. Add the pasta, water, beans, tomatoes (with juice if using diced), onion, bell pepper, tomato paste, oil, garlic, and crushed red pepper (if desired), to a large stockpot. Bring to a boil over high heat, stirring often.
2. Reduce the heat to medium-high, add the kale, and cook, continuing to stir often, until the pasta is al dente, about 10 minutes.
3. Remove from the heat and let sit for 5 minutes. Garnish with the basil and olives and serve.

Per Serving
calories: 565 | fat: 17.7g | protein: 18.0g | carbs: 85.5g | fiber: 16.5g | sodium: 540mg

Butternut Squash and Zucchini with Penne

Prep Time: 15 minutes | **Cooking Time:** 30 minutes | **Servings:** 6

Ingredients

1 large zucchini, diced
1 large butternut squash, peeled and diced
1 large yellow onion, chopped
2 tablespoons extra-virgin olive oil
1 teaspoon paprika
½ teaspoon garlic powder
½ teaspoon sea salt
½ teaspoon freshly ground black pepper
1 pound (454 g) whole-grain penne
½ cup dry white wine
2 tablespoons grated Parmesan cheese

Directions

1. Preheat the oven to 400°F (205°C). Line a baking sheet with aluminum foil. Combine the zucchini, butternut squash, and onion in a large bowl. Drizzle with olive oil and sprinkle with paprika, garlic powder, salt, and ground black pepper. Toss to coat well.
2. Spread the vegetables in the single layer on the baking sheet, then roast in the preheated oven for 25 minutes or until the vegetables are tender. Meanwhile, bring a pot of water to a boil, then add the penne and cook for 14 minutes or until al dente. Drain the penne through a colander.
3. Transfer ½ cup of roasted vegetables in a food processor, then pour in the dry white wine. Pulse until smooth.
4. Pour the puréed vegetables in a nonstick skillet and cook with penne over medium-high heat for a few minutes to heat through. Transfer the penne with the purée on a large serving plate, then spread the remaining roasted vegetables and Parmesan on top before serving.

Per Serving calories: 340 | fat: 6.2g | protein: 8.0g | carbs: 66.8g | fiber: 9.1g | sodium: 297mg

Chili Halloumi Cheese with Rice

Prep Time: 10 minutes | **Cooking Time:** 8 minutes | **Servings:** 6

Ingredients

2 cups water
2 tablespoons brown sugar
2 tablespoons rice vinegar
1 tbsp sweet chili sauce
1 tablespoon olive oil
1 tbsp fresh minced garlic
20 ounces (567 g) Halloumi cheese, cubed
1 cup rice
¼ cup chopped fresh chives, for garnish

Directions

1. Heat the oil on Sauté and fry the halloumi for 5 minutes until golden brown. Set aside. To the pot, add water, garlic, olive oil, vinegar, sugar, soy sauce, and chili sauce and mix well until smooth. Stir in rice noodles. Seal the lid and cook on High Pressure for 3 minutes. Release the pressure quickly. Split the rice between bowls. Top with fried halloumi and sprinkle with fresh chives before serving.

Per Serving
calories: 534 | fat: 34.3g | protein: 24.9g | carbs: 30.1g | fiber: 1.0g | sodium: 652mg

Beef and Bean Stuffed Pasta Shells

Prep Time: 15 minutes | **Cooking Time:** 17 minutes | **Servings:** 4

Ingredients

- 2 tablespoons olive oil
- 1 pound (454 g) ground beef
- 1 pound (454 g) pasta shells
- 2 cups water
- 15 ounces (425 g) tomato sauce
- 1 (15-ounce / 425-g) can black beans, drained and rinsed
- 15 ounces (425 g) canned corn, drained (or 2 cups frozen corn)
- 10 ounces (283 g) red enchilada sauce
- 4 ounces (113 g) diced green chiles
- 1 cup shredded Mozzarella cheese
- Salt and ground black pepper to taste
- Additional cheese for topping
- Finely chopped parsley for garnish

Directions

1. Heat oil on Sauté. Add ground beef and cook for 7 minutes until it starts to brown.
2. Mix in pasta, tomato sauce, enchilada sauce, black beans, water, corn, and green chiles and stir to coat well. Add more water if desired.
3. Seal the lid and cook on High Pressure for 10 minutes. Do a quick Pressure release. Into the pasta mixture, mix in Mozzarella cheese until melted; add black pepper and salt. Garnish with parsley to serve.

Per Serving

calories: 1006 | fat: 30.0g | protein: 53.3g | carbs: 138.9g | fiber: 24.4g | sodium: 1139mg
g Protein 23.7 g Cholesterol 55 mg

Pesto Chicken Pasta (Italian)

Prep Time: 10 minutes **Cooking Time:** 10 minutes **Servings:** 6

Ingredients

- 1 lb. chicken breast, skinless, boneless, and diced
- 3 tbsp olive oil
- 1/4 cup heavy cream
- 3 1/2 cups water Pepper
- 6 oz basil pesto
- 1/2 cup parmesan cheese, shredded
- 1 tsp Italian seasoning
- 16 oz whole wheat pasta
- Salt

Directions

1. Season chicken with Italian seasoning, pepper, and salt.
2. Add oil into the inner pot of instant pot and set the pot on sauté mode.
3. Add chicken to the pot and sauté until brown.
4. Add remaining except for parmesan cheese, heavy cream, and pesto and stir well.
5. Seal pot with lid and cook on high for 5 minutes.
6. Once done, release pressure using quick release. Remove lid.
7. Stir in parmesan cheese, heavy cream, and pesto and serve.

Nutrition: Calories 475 Fat 14.7 g Carbohydrates 57 g Sugar 2.8 g Protein 28.7 g Cholesterol 61 mg

Bolognese Chicken and Spaghetti

Prep Time: 15 minutes | **Cooking Time:** 42 minutes | **Servings:** 8

Ingredients

- 2 tablespoons olive oil
- 6 ounces (170 g) bacon, cubed
- 1 onion, minced
- 1 carrot, minced
- 1 celery stalk, minced
- 2 garlic cloves, crushed
- 1/4 cup tomato paste
- 1/4 teaspoon crushed red pepper flakes
- 1½ pounds (680 g) ground chicken
- ½ cup white wine
- 1 cup milk
- 1 cup chicken broth
- Salt, to taste
- 1 pound (454 g) spaghetti

Directions

1. Warm oil on Sauté. Add bacon and fry for 5 minutes until crispy.
2. Add celery, carrot, garlic and onion and cook for 5 minutes until fragrant. Mix in red pepper flakes and tomato paste, and cook for 2 minutes. Break chicken into small pieces and place in the pot.
3. Cook for 10 minutes, as you stir, until browned. Pour in wine and simmer for 2 minutes. Add chicken broth and milk. Seal the lid and cook for 15 minutes on High Pressure. Release the pressure quickly.
4. Add the spaghetti and stir. Seal the lid, and cook on High Pressure for another 5 minutes.
5. Release the pressure quickly. Check the pasta for doneness. Taste, adjust the seasoning and serve hot.

Per Serving calories: 477 | fat: 20.6g | protein: 28.1g | carbs: 48.5g | fiber: 5.3g | sodium: 279mg

Italian Chicken Pasta (Italian)

Prep Time: 10 minutes **Cooking Time:** 9 minutes **Servings:** 8

Ingredients

- 1 lb. chicken breast, skinless, boneless, and cut into chunks
- 1 tsp garlic, minced
- 1/2 cup cream cheese
- 2 tomatoes, diced
- 2 cups of water
- 1 cup mozzarella cheese, shredded
- 1 1/2 tsp Italian seasoning
- 1cup mushrooms, diced
- 1/2 onion, diced
- 16 oz whole wheat penne pasta Pepper, Salt

Directions

1. Add all except cheeses into the inner pot of instant pot and stir well.
2. Seal pot with lid and cook on high for 9 minutes.
3. Once done, allow to release pressure naturally for 5 minutes then release remaining using quick release. Remove lid.
4. Add cheeses and stir well and serve.

Nutrition: Calories 328 Fat 8.5 g Carbohydrates 42.7 g Sugar 1.4

Vegetarian Lasagna (Italian)

Prep Time: 15 minutes **Cooking Time:** 1 hour
Servings: 6

Ingredients

1Sweet Onion, Sliced Thick	2Zucchini, Sliced Lengthwise
1 Eggplant, Sliced Thick	2 Tablespoons Olive Oil
28 Ounces Canned tomatoes, Diced & Sodium Free	1Cup Quartered, Canned & Water Packed Artichokes, Drained
2 Teaspoons Garlic, Minced	2 Teaspoons Oregano, Fresh & Chopped
2 tbsp Basil Chopped	
12 Lasagna Noodles, Whole Grain & No-Boil	¼ Teaspoon Red Pepper Flakes
¾ Cup Asiago Cheese, Grated	

Directions

1. Start by heating your oven to 400, and then get out a baking sheet. Line it with foil before placing it to the side.
2. Get out a large bowl and toss your zucchini, yellow squash, eggplant, onion, and olive oil, making sure it's coated well.
3. Arrange your vegetables on the baking sheet, roasting for twenty minutes. They should be lightly caramelized and tender.
4. Chop your roasted vegetables before placing them in a bowl.
5. Stir in your garlic, basil, oregano, artichoke hearts, tomatoes, and red pepper flakes, spooning a quarter of this mixture in the bottom of a nine by thirteen baking dish. Arrange four lasagna noodles over this sauce, and continue by alternating it. Sprinkle with asiago cheese on top, baking for a half hour.
6. Allow it to cool for fifteen minutes before slicing to serve.

Nutrition: Calories: 386 Protein: 15 g Fat: 11 g Carbs: 59 g

Simple Pesto Pasta (Italian)

Prep Time: 10 minutes **Cooking Time:** 10 minutes
Servings: 4

Ingredients

1 lb. spaghetti	4 cups fresh basil leaves, stems removed
3 cloves garlic	
1 tsp. salt	1/2 tsp. freshly ground black pepper
1/4 cup lemon juice	
1/2 cup pine nuts, toasted	1/2 cup grated Parmesan cheese
1 cup extra-virgin olive oil	

Directions

1. Bring a large pot of salted water to a boil. Add the spaghetti to the pot and cook for 8 minutes.
2. Put basil, garlic, salt, pepper, lemon juice, pine nuts, and Parmesan cheese in a food processor bowl with chopping blade and purée.
3. While the processor is running, slowly drizzle the olive oil through the top opening. Process until all the olive oil has been added.
4. Reserve ½ cup of the pasta water. Drain the pasta and put it into a bowl. Immediately add the pesto and pasta water to the pasta and toss everything together. Serve warm.

Nutrition: Calories: 113; Protein: 12.3g; Carbs: 3.4g; Fat: 6.3g

Cake with Spaghetti Pesto (Italian)

Prep Time: 10 minutes **Cooking Time:** 40 minutes
Servings: 6

Ingredients

12 ounces ricotta	1 cup Basil Pesto, or store-bought
2 tablespoons olive oil	
¼ cup freshly grated Parmesan cheese Salt	1-pound spaghetti

Directions

1. Preheat the oven to 400°F. Set a large pot of salted water to boil over high heat.
2. In a food processor, combine the ricotta and basil pesto. Purée into a smooth cream and transfer to a large bowl. Set aside.
3. Coat a 10-cup Bundt pan with the olive oil and sprinkle with the Parmesan cheese. Set aside.
4. Once the water is boiling, add the pasta to the pot and cook for about 6 minutes until al dente.
5. Drain the pasta well and add it to the pesto cream. Mix well until all the pasta is saturated with the sauce.
6. Spoon the pasta into the prepared pan, pressing to ensure it is tightly packed. Bake for 30 minutes.
7. Place a flat serving platter on top of the cake pan. Quickly and carefully invert the pasta cake. Gently remove the pan. Cut into slices and serve topped with your favorite sauce, if desired.

Nutrition: Calories: 622; Total Fat: 30g; Saturated Fat: 7g; Carbohydrates: 67g; Fiber: 3g; Protein: 20g; Sodium: 425mg

Pasta with Lemon and Artichokes (Italian)

Prep Time: 10 minutes **Cooking Time:** 15 minutes
Servings: 4

Ingredients

16 ounces linguine or angel hair pasta	8 garlic cloves, finely minced or pressed
2 (15-ounce) jars water-packed artichoke hearts, drained and quartered	1/4 cup thinly sliced fresh basil
2 tablespoons freshly squeezed lemon juice	1 teaspoon of sea salt
Freshly ground black pepper	1/4 cup extra-virgin olive oil

Directions

1. Boil a pot of water on high heat and cook the pasta.
2. While the pasta is cooking, heat the oil in a skillet over medium heat and cook the garlic, stirring often, for 1 to 2 minutes until it just begins to brown. Toss the garlic with the artichokes in a large bowl.
3. When the pasta is cooked, drain it very carefully and add it to the artichoke mixture, then add the lemon juice, basil, salt, and pepper. Gently stir and serve.

Nutrition: Calories: 423 Protein: 15 g Fat: 14 g

Pasta with Roasted Ratatouille (Italian)

Prep Time: 10 minutes **Cooking Time:** 30 minutes
Servings: 2

Ingredients

1 small eggplant
1 portobello mushroom
1 Roma tomato, halved
½ teaspoon salt, plus additional for the pasta water
2cups farfalle pasta (about 8 ounces / 227 g)

1 small zucchini
½ medium sweet red pepper, seeded
1tablespoon olive oil
1 teaspoon Italian herb seasoning
2 tablespoons minced sun-dried tomatoes in olive oil with herbs 2 tablespoons prepared pesto

Directions

1. Slice the ends off the eggplant and zucchini. Cut them lengthwise into ½-inch slices.
1. Place the eggplant, zucchini, mushroom, tomato, and red pepper in a large bowl and sprinkle with ½ teaspoon of salt. Using your hands, toss the vegetables well so that they're covered evenly with the salt. Let them rest for about 10 minutes.
2. While the vegetables are resting, preheat the oven to 400°F (205°C). Line a baking sheet with parchment paper.
3. When the oven is hot, drain off any liquid from the vegetables and pat them dry with a paper towel. Add the Italian herb seasoning and olive oil to the vegetables and toss well to coat both sides.
4. Lay the vegetables out in a single layer on the baking sheet. Roast them for 15 to 20 minutes, flipping them over after about 10 minutes or once they start to brown on the underside. When the vegetables are charred in spots, remove them from the oven.
5. While the vegetables are roasting, fill a large saucepan with water. Add salt and cook the pasta until al dente, about 8 to 10 minutes. Drain the pasta, reserving ½ cup of the pasta water.
6. When cool enough to handle, cut the vegetables into large chunks (about 2 inches) and add them to the hot pasta.
7. Stir in the sun-dried tomatoes and pesto and toss everything well. Serve immediately.

Nutrition: calories: 613 fats: 16.0g protein: 23.1g carbs: 108.5g fiber: 23.0g sodium: 775mg

Lentil and Mushroom Pasta (Italian)

Prep Time: 10 minutes **Cooking Time:** 50 minutes
Servings: 2

Ingredients

2 tablespoons olive oil
2portobello mushrooms, trimmed and chopped finely
2½ cups water
1 (28-ounce / 794-g) can diced tomatoes with basil (with juice if diced)
1 tablespoon balsamic vinegar
Chopped basil, for garnish

1large yellow onion diced
3garlic cloves, chopped
1 teaspoon oregano
1 cup brown lentils
8 ounces (227 g) pasta of choice, cooked Salt and black pepper, to taste
2 tablespoons tomato paste

Directions

1. Place a large stockpot over medium heat. Add the oil. Once the oil is hot, add the onion and mushrooms. Cover and cook until both are soft, about 5 minutes. Add the tomato paste, garlic, and oregano and cook 2 minutes, stirring constantly.
2. Stir in the water and lentils. Bring to a boil, then reduce the heat to medium-low and cook for 5 minutes, covered.
3. Add the tomatoes (and juice if using diced) and vinegar. Replace the lid, reduce the heat to low and cook until the lentils are tender, about 30 minutes. Remove the sauce from the heat and season with salt and pepper to taste. Garnish with the basil and serve over the cooked pasta.

Nutrition: calories: 463 fats: 15.9g protein: 12.5g carbs: 70.8g fiber: 16.9g sodium: 155mg

Penne Pasta with Tomato Sauce and MitzithraCheese (Italian)

Prep Time: 15 minutes **Cooking Time:** 20 minutes
Servings: 5

Ingredients

2 tablespoons olive oil
2 green garlic stalks, minced
10 ounces penne
1/4 teaspoon cayenne pepper
1/4 teaspoon dried marjoram
2 overripe tomatoes, pureed
1/2 teaspoon dried basil

2 scallion stalks, chopped
1/3 teaspoon ground black pepper, to taste
1/2 cup marinara sauce
2 cups vegetable broth
Sea salt, to taste
1/2 teaspoon dried oregano
1 cup Mitzithra cheese, grated

Directions

1. Press the "Sauté" button to preheat your Instant Pot. Heat the oil until sizzling. Now, sauté the scallions and garlic until just tender and fragrant.Stir in the penne pasta, spices, marinara sauce, broth, and pureed tomatoes; do not stir, but your pasta should be covered with the liquid.
2. Secure the lid. Choose the "Manual" mode and cook for 7 minutes at High pressure. Once cooking is complete, use a natural pressure release for 5 minutes; carefully remove the lid.

Nutrition: 395 Calories; 15.6g Fat; 51.8g Carbs; 14.9g Protein; 2.5g Sugars; 7.5g Fiber

Chapter 6
Vegetable Recipes

Spinach Stuffed Portobello Mushrooms

Prep Time: 5 minutes | **Cooking Time:** 20 minutes | **Servings:** 4

Ingredients

8 large portobello mushrooms, stems removed
3 teaspoons extra-virgin olive oil, divided
1 medium red bell pepper, diced
4 cups fresh spinach
¼ cup crumbled feta cheese

Directions

1. Preheat the oven to 450°F (235°C).
2. Using a spoon to scoop out the gills of the mushrooms and discard them. Brush the mushrooms with 2 teaspoons of olive oil.
3. Arrange the mushrooms (cap-side down) on a baking sheet. Roast in the preheated oven for 20 minutes.
4. Meantime, in a medium skillet, heat the remaining olive oil over medium heat until it shimmers.
5. Add the bell pepper and spinach and sauté for 8 to 10 minutes, stirring occasionally, or until the spinach is wilted.
6. Remove the mushrooms from the oven to a paper towel-lined plate. Using a spoon to stuff each mushroom with the bell pepper and spinach mixture. Scatter the feta cheese all over. Serve immediately.

Per Serving (2 mushrooms)

calories: 115 | fat: 5.9g | protein: 7.2g | carbs: 11.5g | fiber: 4.0g | sodium: 125mg

Chickpea Lettuce Wraps with Celery

Prep Time: 10 minutes | **Cooking Time:** 0 minutes | **Servings:** 4

Ingredients

1 (15-ounce / 425-g) can low-sodium chickpeas, drained and rinsed
1 celery stalk, thinly sliced
2 tablespoons finely chopped red onion
2 tablespoons unsalted tahini
3 tablespoons honey mustard
1 tablespoon capers, undrained
12 butter lettuce leaves

Directions

1. In a bowl, mash the chickpeas with a potato masher or the back of a fork until mostly smooth.
2. Add the celery, red onion, tahini, honey mustard, and capers to the bowl and stir until well incorporated.
3. For each serving, place three overlapping lettuce leaves on a plate and top with ¼ of the mashed chickpea filling, then roll up. Repeat with the remaining lettuce leaves and chickpea mixture.

Per Serving

calories: 182 | fat: 7.1g | protein: 10.3g | carbs: 19.6g | fiber: 3.0g | sodium: 171mg

Pesto Zoodles with Walnuts

Prep Time: 10 minutes | **Cooking Time:** 10 minutes | **Servings:** 4

Ingredients

4 medium zucchinis, spiralized
¼ cup extra-virgin olive oil, divided
1 tbsp minced garlic, divided
½ teaspoon crushed red pepper
¼ teaspoon freshly ground black pepper, divided
¼ teaspoon kosher salt, divided
2 tablespoons grated Parmesan cheese, divided
1 cup packed fresh basil leaves
¾ cup walnut pieces, divided

Directions

1. In a large bowl, stir together the zoodles, 1 tablespoon of the olive oil, ½ teaspoon of the minced garlic, red pepper, ⅛ teaspoon of the black pepper and ⅛ teaspoon of the salt. Set aside.
2. Heat ½ tablespoon of the oil in a large skillet over medium-high heat. Add half of the zoodles to the skillet and cook for 5 minutes, stirring constantly. Transfer the cooked zoodles into a bowl. Repeat with another ½ tablespoon of the oil and the remaining zoodles. When done, add the cooked zoodles to the bowl.
3. Make the pesto: In a food processor, combine the remaining ½ teaspoon of the minced garlic, ⅛ teaspoon of the black pepper and ⅛ teaspoon of the salt, 1 tablespoon of the Parmesan, basil leaves and ¼ cup of the walnuts. Pulse until smooth and then slowly drizzle the remaining 2 tablespoons of the oil into the pesto. Pulse again until well combined.
4. Add the pesto to the zoodles along with the remaining 1 tablespoon of the Parmesan and the remaining ½ cup of the walnuts. Toss to coat well. Serve immediately.

Per Serving

calories: 166 | fat: 16.0g | protein: 4.0g | carbs: 3.0g | fiber: 2.0g | sodium: 307mg

Mushroom and Spinach Stuffed Peppers

Prep Time: 15 minutes | **Cooking Time:** 8 minutes | **Servings:** 7

Ingredients

7 mini sweet peppers	½ teaspoon coarse sea salt
1 cup button mushrooms, minced	¼ teaspoon cracked mixed pepper
5 ounces (142 g) organic baby spinach	2 tablespoons water
½ teaspoon fresh garlic	1 tablespoon olive oil
	Organic Mozzarella cheese, diced

Directions

1. Put the sweet peppers and water in the instant pot and Sauté for 2 minutes.
2. Remove the peppers and put the olive oil into the pot.
3. Stir in the mushrooms, garlic, spices and spinach.
4. Cook on Sauté until the mixture is dry.
5. Stuff each sweet pepper with the cheese and spinach mixture.
6. Bake the stuffed peppers in an oven for 6 minutes at 400ºF (205ºC). Once done, serve hot.

Per Serving

calories: 81 | fat: 2.4g | protein: 4.1g | carbs: 13.2g | fiber: 2.4g | sodium: 217mg

Black Bean and Corn Tortilla Bowls

Prep Time: 10 minutes | **Cooking Time:** 8 minutes | **Servings:** 4

Ingredients

1½ cups vegetable broth	2 small potatoes, cubed
½ cup tomatoes, undrained diced	½ cup bell pepper, chopped
1 small onion, diced	½ can black beans, drained and rinsed
2 garlic cloves, finely minced	1 cup frozen corn kernels
1 teaspoon chili powder	½ tablespoon lime juice
1 teaspoon cumin	2 tablespoons cilantro for topping, chopped
½ teaspoon paprika	Whole-wheat tortilla chips
½ teaspoon ground coriander	
Salt and pepper to taste	
½ cup carrots, diced	

Directions

1. Add the oil and all the vegetables into the instant pot and Sauté for 3 minutes.
2. Add all the spices, corn, lime juice, and broth, along with the beans, to the pot.
3. Seal the lid and cook on Manual setting at High Pressure for 5 minutes.
4. Once done, natural release the pressure when the timer goes off. Remove the lid.
5. To serve, put the prepared mixture into a bowl.
6. Top with tortilla chips and fresh cilantro. Serve.

Per Serving

calories: 183 | fat: 0.9g | protein: 7.1g | carbs: 39.8g | fiber: 8.3g | sodium: 387mg

Medley of Potatoes, Corn, and Spinach

Prep Time: 10 minutes | **Cooking Time:** 10 minutes | **Servings:** 6

Ingredients

1 tablespoon olive oil	1 tablespoon fish sauce
3 scallions, chopped	2 tablespoons light soy sauce
½ cup onion, chopped	2 large cloves garlic, diced
2 large white potatoes, peeled and diced	⅓ teaspoon white pepper
1 tablespoon ginger, grated	1 teaspoon salt
3 cups frozen corn kernels	3-4 handfuls baby spinach leaves
1 cup vegetable stock	Juice of ½ lemon

Directions

1. Put the oil, ginger, garlic and onions in the instant pot and Sauté for 5 minutes. Add all the remaining except the spinach leaves and lime juice Secure the lid and cook on the Manual setting for 5 minutes at High Pressure. After the beep, Quick release the pressure and remove the lid.
2. Add the spinach and cook for 3 minutes on Sauté
3. Drizzle the lime juice over the dish and serve hot.

Per Serving

calories: 217 | fat: 3.4g | protein: 6.5g | carbs: 44.5g | fiber: 6.3g | sodium: 892mg

Mushroom and Potato Oat Burgers

Prep Time: 20 minutes | **Cooking Time:** 21 minutes | **Servings:** 5

Ingredients

½ cup minced onion	2 tablespoons chopped cilantro
1 teaspoon grated fresh ginger	1 tablespoon curry powder
½ cup minced mushrooms	1 cup quick oats
½ cup red lentils, rinsed	Brown rice flour, optional
¾ sweet potato, peeled and diced	5 tomato slices
1 cup vegetable stock	Lettuce leaves
2 tablespoons hemp seeds	5 whole-wheat buns
	2 tablespoons chopped parsley

Directions

1. Add the oil, ginger, mushrooms and onion into the instant pot and Sauté for 5 minutes.
2. Stir in the lentils, stock, and the sweet potatoes.
3. Secure the lid and cook on the Manual function for 6 minutes at High Pressure. After the beep, natural release the pressure and remove the lid. Meanwhile, heat the oven to 375ºF (190ºC) and line a baking tray with parchment paper.
4. Mash the prepared lentil mixture with a potato masher.
5. Add the oats and the remaining spices. Put in some brown rice flour if the mixture is not thick enough.
6. Wet your hands and prepare 5 patties, using the mixture, and place them on the baking tray.
7. Bake the patties for 10 minutes in the preheated oven.
8. Slice the buns in half and stack each with a tomato slice, a vegetable patty and lettuce leaves. Serve and enjoy.

Per Serving calories: 266 | fat: 5.3g | protein: 14.5g | carbs: 48.7g | fiber: 9.6g | sodium: 276mg

Honey-Glazed Baby Carrots

Prep Time: 5 minutes | **Cooking Time:** 6 minutes |
Servings: 2

Ingredients

⅔ cup water
1½ pounds (680 g) baby carrots
4 tablespoons almond butter
½ cup honey
1 teaspoon dried thyme
1½ teaspoons dried dill
Salt, to taste

Directions

1. Pour the water into the Instant Pot and add a steamer basket. Place the baby carrots in the basket.
2. Secure the lid. Select the Manual mode and set the cooking time for 4 minutes at High Pressure.
3. Once cooking is complete, do a quick pressure release. Carefully open the lid.
4. Transfer the carrots to a plate and set aside.
5. Pour the water out of the Instant Pot and dry it.
6. Press the Sauté button on the Instant Pot and heat the almond butter.
7. Stir in the honey, thyme, and dill.
8. Return the carrots to the Instant Pot and stir until well coated. Sauté for another 1 minute.
9. Taste and season with salt as needed. Serve warm.

Per Serving

calories: 575 | fat: 23.5g | protein: 2.8g | carbs: 90.6g | fiber: 10.3g | sodium: 547mg

Garlic-Butter Asparagus with Parmesan

Prep Time: 5 minutes | **Cooking Time:** 8 minutes |
Servings: 2

Ingredients

1 cup water
1 pound (454 g) asparagus, trimmed
2 cloves garlic, chopped
3 tablespoons almond butter
Salt and ground black pepper, to taste
3 tablespoons grated Parmesan cheese

Directions

1. Pour the water into the Instant Pot and insert a trivet.
2. Put the asparagus on a tin foil add the butter and garlic. Season to taste with salt and pepper.
3. Fold over the foil and seal the asparagus inside so the foil doesn't come open. Arrange the asparagus on the trivet.
4. Secure the lid. Select the Manual mode and set the cooking time for 8 minutes at High Pressure.
5. Once cooking is complete, do a quick pressure release. Carefully open the lid. Unwrap the foil packet and serve sprinkled with the Parmesan cheese.

Per Serving calories: 243 | fat: 15.7g | protein: 12.3g | carbs: 15.3g | fiber: 7.3g | sodium: 435mg

Ratatouille

Prep Time: 10 minutes | **Cooking Time:** 6 minutes |
Servings: 4

Ingredients

2 large zucchinis, sliced
2 medium eggplants, sliced
4 medium tomatoes, sliced
2 small red onions, sliced
4 cloves garlic, chopped
2 tablespoons thyme leaves
2 teaspoons sea salt
1 teaspoon black pepper
2 tablespoons balsamic vinegar
4 tablespoons olive oil
2 cups water

Directions

1. Line a springform pan with foil and place the chopped garlic in the bottom.
2. Now arrange the vegetable slices, alternately, in circles.
3. Sprinkle the thyme, pepper and salt over the vegetables. Top with oil and vinegar.
4. Pour a cup of water into the instant pot and place the trivet inside. Secure the lid and cook on Manual function for 6 minutes at High Pressure.
5. Release the pressure naturally and remove the lid.
6. Remove the vegetables along with the tin foil.
7. Serve on a platter and enjoy.

Per Serving calories: 240 | fat: 14.3g | protein: 4.7g | carbs: 27.5g | fiber: 10.8g | sodium: 1181mg

Mushroom and Potato Teriyaki

Prep Time: 10 minutes | **Cooking Time:** 18 minutes |
Servings: 4

Ingredients

¾ large yellow or white onion, chopped
1½ medium carrots, diced
1½ ribs celery, chopped
1 medium portabella mushroom, diced
¾ tablespoon garlic, chopped
2 cups water
1 pound (454 g) white potatoes, peeled and diced
¼ cup tomato paste
½ tablespoon sesame oil
2 teaspoons sesame seeds
½ tablespoon paprika
1 teaspoon fresh rosemary
¾ cups peas
¼ cup fresh parsley for garnishing, chopped

Directions

1. Add the oil, sesame seeds, and all the vegetables in the instant pot and Sauté for 5 minutes.
2. Stir in the remaining and secure the lid.
3. Cook on Manual function for 13 minutes at High Pressure.
4. After the beep, natural release the pressure and remove the lid.
5. Garnish with fresh parsley and serve hot.

Per Serving

calories: 160 | fat: 3.0g | protein: 4.7g | carbs: 30.6g | fiber: 5.5g | sodium: 52mg

Sautéed Cabbage (Spanish)

Prep Time: 10 minutes
Cooking Time: 12 to 14 minutes
Servings: 4 to 6

Ingredients

1 small head green cabbage (about 1¼ pounds / 567 g), cored and sliced thin
1½ teaspoons lemon juice
3/4 teaspoon salt, divided
¼ cup chopped fresh parsley
2 tablespoons extra-virgin olive oil, divided
1 onion, halved and sliced thin
¼ teaspoon black pepper

Directions

1. Place the cabbage in a large bowl with cold water. Let sit for 3 minutes. Drain well.
2. Heat 1 tablespoon of the oil in a skillet over medium-high heat until shimmering. Add the onion and ¼ teaspoon of the salt and cook for 5 to 7 minutes, or until softened and lightly browned. Transfer to a bowl.
3. Heat the remaining 1 tablespoon of the oil in now-empty skillet over medium-high heat until shimmering. Add the cabbage and sprinkle with the remaining ½ teaspoon of the salt and black pepper. Cover and cook for about 3 minutes, without stirring, or until cabbage is wilted and lightly browned on bottom.
4. Stir and continue to cook for about 4 minutes, uncovered, or until the cabbage is crisp-tender and lightly browned in places, stirring once halfway through cooking. Off heat, stir in the cooked onion, parsley and lemon juice.
5. Transfer to a plate and serve.

Nutrition: calories: 117 fat: 7g protein: 3g carbs: 13g fiber: 5g sodium: 472mg

Quick Spinach Focaccia (Italian)

Prep Time: 10 minutes **Cooking Time:** 25 minutes
Servings: 12

Ingredients

10 eggs
¼ tsp garlic powder
½ tsp dried basil
2 cups spinach, chopped
¼ tsp onion powder
1 ½ cups parmesan cheese, grated Salt

Directions

1. Preheat the oven to 400 F. Grease muffin tin and set aside.
2. In a large bowl, whisk eggs with basil, garlic powder, onion powder, and salt.
3. Add cheese and spinach and stir well.
4. Pour egg mixture into the prepared muffin tin and bake 15 minutes.
5. Serve and enjoy.

Nutrition: 110 Calories 7g Fat 9g Protein

Ratatouille (Italian)

Prep Time: 15 minutes
Cooking Time: 40 minutes
Servings: 6

Ingredients

2 russet potatoes, cubed
1 eggplant, cubed
1 zucchini, cubed
1 red bell pepper, chopped
1 teaspoon dried parsley
1 teaspoon dried oregano
½ teaspoon black pepper
1/3 cup olive oil
1 (8-ounce / 227-g) can tomato paste
¼ cup water
½ cup Roma tomatoes, cubed
1 red onion, chopped
1 teaspoon dried mint
½ teaspoon salt
2 garlic cloves, minced
¼ teaspoon red pepper flakes
¼ cup vegetable broth

Directions

1. Preheat the air fryer to 320°F (160°C).
2. In a large bowl, combine the potatoes, tomatoes, eggplant, zucchini, onion, bell pepper, garlic, mint, parsley, oregano, salt, black pepper, and red pepper flakes.
3. In a small bowl, mix together the olive oil, tomato paste, broth, and water.
4. Pour the oil-and-tomato-paste mixture over the vegetables and toss until everything is coated.
5. Pour the coated vegetables into the air fryer basket in an even layer and roast for 20 minutes. After 20 minutes, stir well and spread out again. Roast for an additional 10 minutes, then repeat the process and cook for another 10 minutes.

Nutrition: calories: 280 fat: 13g protein: 6g carbs: 40g fiber: 7g sodium: 264mg

Triumph of Cucumbers and Avocados (Spanish)

Prep Time: 10 minutes **Cooking Time:** 15 minutes
Servings: 4

Ingredients

12 oz cherry tomatoes, cut in half
½ tsp ground black pepper
¼ cup fresh cilantro, chopped
3 small avocados, chopped
5 small cucumbers, chopped
2 tbsp fresh lemon juice
1 tsp sea salt
2 tbsp olive oil

Directions

1. Add cherry tomatoes, cucumbers, avocados, and cilantro into the large mixing bowl and mix well.
2. Mix olive oil, lemon juice, black pepper, and salt and pour over salad.
3. Toss well and serve immediately.

Nutrition: 442 Calories 37g Fat 6.2g Protein

Veggie-Stuffed Portabello Mushrooms

Prep Time: 5 minutes | **Cooking Time:** 24 to 25 minutes | **Servings:** 6

Ingredients

3 tablespoons extra-virgin olive oil, divided
1 cup diced onion
2 garlic cloves, minced
1 large zucchini, diced
3 cups chopped mushrooms
1 cup chopped tomato
1 teaspoon dried oregano
¼ teaspoon kosher salt
¼ teaspoon crushed red pepper
6 large portabello mushrooms, stems and gills removed
Cooking spray
4 ounces (113 g) fresh Mozzarella cheese, shredded

Directions

1. In a large skillet over medium heat, heat 2 tablespoons of the oil. Add the onion and sauté for 4 minutes. Stir in the garlic and sauté for 1 minute. Stir in the zucchini, mushrooms, tomato, oregano, salt and red pepper. Cook for 10 minutes, stirring constantly. Remove from the heat.
2. Meanwhile, heat a grill pan over medium-high heat.
3. Brush the remaining 1 tablespoon of the oil over the portabello mushroom caps. Place the mushrooms, bottom-side down, on the grill pan. Cover with a sheet of aluminum foil sprayed with nonstick cooking spray. Cook for 5 minutes. Flip the mushroom caps over, and spoon about ½ cup of the cooked vegetable mixture into each cap. Top each with about 2½ tablespoons of the Mozzarella.
4. Cover and grill for 4 to 5 minutes, or until the cheese is melted. Using a spatula, transfer the portabello mushrooms to a plate. Let cool for about 5 minutes before serving.

Per Serving

calories: 111 | fat: 4.0g | protein: 11.0g | carbs: 11.0g | fiber: 4.0g | sodium: 314mg

Cauliflower and Broccoli Bowls

Prep Time: 5 minutes | **Cooking Time:** 7 minutes | **Servings:** 3

Ingredients

½ medium onion, diced
2 teaspoons olive oil
1 garlic clove, minced
½ cup tomato paste
½ pound (227 g) frozen cauliflower
½ pound (227 g) broccoli florets
½ cup vegetable broth
½ teaspoon paprika
¼ teaspoon dried thyme
2 pinches sea salt

Directions

1. Add the oil, onion and garlic into the instant pot and Sauté for 2 minutes. Add the broth, tomato paste, cauliflower, broccoli, and all the spices, to the pot. Secure the lid. Cook on the Manual setting at with pressure for 5 minutes.
2. After the beep, Quick release the pressure and remove the lid. Stir well and serve hot.

Per Serving

calories: 109 | fat: 3.8g | protein: 6.1g | carbs: 16.7g | fiber: 6.1g | sodium: 265mg

Stir-Fried Eggplant

Prep Time: 25 minutes | **Cooking Time:** 15 minutes | **Servings:** 2

Ingredients

1 cup water, plus more as needed
½ cup chopped red onion
1 tablespoon finely chopped garlic
1 tablespoon dried Italian herb seasoning
1 teaspoon ground cumin
1 small eggplant (about 8 ounces / 227 g), peeled and cut into ½-inch cubes
1 medium carrot, sliced
2 cups green beans, cut into 1-inch pieces
2 ribs celery, sliced
1 cup corn kernels
2 tablespoons almond butter
2 medium tomatoes, chopped

Directions

1. Heat 1 tablespoon of water in a large soup pot over medium-high heat until it sputters.
2. Cook the onion for 2 minutes, adding a little more water as needed.
3. Add the garlic, Italian seasoning, cumin, and eggplant and stir-fry for 2 to 3 minutes, adding a little more water as needed.
4. Add the carrot, green beans, celery, corn kernels, and ½ cup of water and stir well. Reduce the heat to medium, cover, and cook for 8 to 10 minutes, stirring occasionally, or until the vegetables are tender.
5. Meanwhile, in a bowl, stir together the almond butter and ½ cup of water. Remove the vegetables from the heat and stir in the almond butter mixture and chopped tomatoes. Cool for a few minutes before serving.

Per Serving

calories: 176 | fat: 5.5g | protein: 5.8g | carbs: 25.4g | fiber: 8.6g | sodium: 198mg

Radish and Cabbage Congee

Prep Time: 5 minutes | **Cooking Time:** 20 minutes | **Servings:** 3

Ingredients

1 cup carrots, diced
½ cup radish, diced
6 cups vegetable broth
Salt, to taste
1½ cups short grain rice, rinsed
1 tablespoon grated fresh ginger
4 cups cabbage, shredded
Green onions for garnishing, chopped

Directions

1. Add all the , except the cabbage and green onions, into the instant pot.
2. Select the Porridge function and cook on the default time and settings.
3. After the beep, Quick release the pressure and remove the lid Stir in the shredded cabbage and cover with the lid.
4. Serve after 10 minutes with chopped green onions on top.

Per Serving calories: 438 | fat: 0.8g | protein: 8.7g | carbs: 98.4g | fiber: 6.7g | sodium: 1218mg

Potato and Broccoli Medley

Prep Time: 10 minutes | **Cooking Time:** 20 minutes | **Servings:** 3

Ingredients

½ white onion, diced
1½ cloves garlic, finely chopped
1 pound (454 g) potatoes, cut into chunks
1 pound (454 g) broccoli florets, diced
1 pound (454 g) baby carrots, cut in half
¼ cup vegetable broth
½ tbsp Italian seasoning
½ tbsp Spike original seasoning
Fresh parsley for garnishing
1 tablespoon olive oil

Directions

1. Put the oil and onion into the instant pot and Sauté for 5 minutes. Stir in the carrots, and garlic and stir-fry for 5 minutes. Add the remaining and secure the lid.
2. Cook on the Manual function for 10 minutes at High Pressure. After the beep, Quick release the pressure and remove the lid. Stir gently and garnish with fresh parsley , then serve.

Per Serving calories: 256 | fat: 5.6g | protein: 9.1g | carbs: 46.1g | fiber: 12.2g | sodium: 274mg

Italian Zucchini Pomodoro

Prep Time: 10 minutes | **Cooking Time:** 12 minutes | **Servings:** 4

Ingredients

1 tablespoon avocado oil
1 large onion, peeled and diced
3 cloves garlic, minced
1 (28-ounce / 794-g) can diced tomatoes, including juice
½ cup water
1 tbsp Italian seasoning
1 teaspoon sea salt
½ teaspoon ground black pepper
2 medium zucchini, spiraled

Directions

1. Press Sauté button on the Instant Pot. Heat avocado oil. Add onions and stir-fry for 3 to 5 minutes until translucent. Add garlic and cook for an additional minute. Add tomatoes, water, Italian seasoning, salt, and pepper. Add zucchini and toss to combine. Lock lid.
2. Press the Manual button and adjust time to 1 minute. When timer beeps, let pressure release naturally for 5 minutes. Quick release any additional pressure until float valve drops and then unlock lid.
3. Transfer zucchini to four bowls. Press Sauté button, press Adjust button to change the temperature to Less, and simmer sauce in the Instant Pot unlidded for 5 minutes. Ladle over zucchini and serve immediately.

Per Serving calories: 92 | fat: 4.1g | protein: 2.5g | carbs: 13.1g | fiber: 5.1g | sodium: 980mg

Parmesan Stuffed Zucchini Boats

Prep Time: 5 minutes | **Cooking Time:** 15 minutes | **Servings:** 4

Ingredients

1 cup canned low-sodium chickpeas, drained and rinsed
1 cup no-sugar-added spaghetti sauce
2 zucchinis
¼ cup shredded Parmesan cheese

Directions

1. Preheat the oven to 425ºF (220ºC).
2. In a medium bowl, stir together the chickpeas and spaghetti sauce.
3. Cut the zucchini in half lengthwise and scrape a spoon gently down the length of each half to remove the seeds.
4. Fill each zucchini half with the chickpea sauce and top with one-quarter of the Parmesan cheese.
5. Place the zucchini halves on a baking sheet and roast in the oven for 15 minutes.
6. Transfer to a plate. Let rest for 5 minutes before serving.

Per Serving
calories: 139 | fat: 4.0g | protein: 8.0g | carbs: 20.0g | fiber: 5.0g | sodium: 344mg

Mushroom Swoodles

Prep Time: 5 minutes | **Cooking Time:** 3 minutes | **Servings:** 4

Ingredients

2 tablespoons coconut aminos
1 tablespoon white vinegar
2 teaspoons olive oil
1 teaspoon sesame oil
1 tablespoon honey
¼ teaspoon red pepper flakes
3 cloves garlic, minced
1 large sweet potato, peeled and spiraled
1 pound (454 g) shiitake mushrooms, sliced
1 cup vegetable broth
¼ cup chopped fresh parsley

Directions

1. In a large bowl, whisk together coconut aminos, vinegar, olive oil, sesame oil, honey, red pepper flakes, and garlic.
2. Toss sweet potato and shiitake mushrooms in sauce. Refrigerate covered for 30 minutes.
3. Pour vegetable broth into Instant Pot. Add trivet. Lower steamer basket onto trivet and add the sweet potato mixture to the basket. Lock lid.
4. Press the Manual button and adjust time to 3 minutes. When timer beeps, let pressure release naturally for 5 minutes. Quick release any additional pressure until float valve drops and then unlock lid.
5. Remove basket from the Instant Pot and distribute sweet potatoes and mushrooms evenly among four bowls; pour liquid from the Instant Pot over bowls and garnish with chopped parsley.

Per Serving calories: 127 | fat: 4.0g | protein: 4.2g | carbs: 20.9g | fiber: 4.1g | sodium: 671mg

Stuffed Peppers with Rice, Corn, and Beans

Prep Time: 15 minutes | **Cooking Time:** 15 minutes | **Servings:** 4

Ingredients

4 large bell peppers
2 cups cooked white rice
1 medium onion, peeled and diced
3 small Roma tomatoes, diced
¼ cup marinara sauce
1 cup corn kernels (cut from the cob is preferred)
¼ cup sliced black olives
¼ cup canned cannellini beans, rinsed and drained
¼ cup canned black beans, rinsed and drained
1 teaspoon sea salt
1 teaspoon garlic powder
½ cup vegetable broth
2 tablespoons grated Parmesan cheese

Directions

1. Cut off the bell pepper tops as close to the tops as possible. Hollow out and discard seeds. Poke a few small holes in the bottom of the peppers to allow drippings to drain.
2. In a medium bowl, combine remaining except for broth and Parmesan cheese. Stuff equal amounts of mixture into each of the bell peppers.
3. Place trivet into the Instant Pot and pour in the broth. Set the peppers upright on the trivet. Lock lid.
4. Press the Manual button and adjust time to 15 minutes. When timer beeps, let pressure release naturally until float valve drops and then unlock lid.
5. Serve immediately and garnish with Parmesan cheese.

Per Serving calories: 265 | fat: 3.0g | protein: 8.1g | carbs: 53.1g | fiber: 8.0g | sodium: 834mg

Carrot and Turnip Purée

Prep Time: 10 minutes | **Cooking Time:** 10 minutes | **Servings:** 6

Ingredients

2 tablespoons olive oil, divided
3 large turnips, peeled and quartered
4 large carrots, peeled and cut into 2-inch pieces
2 cups vegetable broth
1 teaspoon salt
½ teaspoon ground nutmeg
2 tablespoons sour cream

Directions

1. Press the Sauté button on Instant Pot. Heat 1 tablespoon olive oil. Toss turnips and carrots in oil for 1 minute. Add broth. Lock lid. Press the Manual button and adjust time to 8 minutes. When timer beeps, quick release pressure until float valve drops and then unlock lid.
2. Drain vegetables and reserve liquid; set liquid aside. Add 2 tablespoons of reserved liquid plus remaining to vegetables in the Instant Pot.
3. Use an immersion blender to blend until desired smoothness. If too thick, add more liquid 1 tablespoon at a time. Serve warm.

Per Serving calories: 95 | fat: 5.2g | protein: 1.4g | carbs: 11.8g | fiber: 3.0g | sodium: 669mg

Brussels Sprouts Linguine

Prep Time: 5 minutes | **Cooking Time:** 25 minutes | **Servings:** 4

Ingredients

8 ounces (227 g) whole-wheat linguine
⅓ cup plus 2 tablespoons extra-virgin olive oil, divided
1 medium sweet onion, diced
2 to 3 garlic cloves, smashed
8 ounces (227 g) Brussels sprouts, chopped
½ cup chicken stock
⅓ cup dry white wine
½ cup shredded Parmesan cheese
1 lemon, quartered

Directions

1. Bring a large pot of water to a boil and cook the pasta for about 5 minutes, or until al dente. Drain the pasta and reserve 1 cup of the pasta water. Mix the cooked pasta with 2 tablespoons of the olive oil. Set aside.
2. In a large skillet, heat the remaining ⅓ cup of the olive oil over medium heat. Add the onion to the skillet and sauté for about 4 minutes, or until tender. Add the smashed garlic cloves and sauté for 1 minute, or until fragrant.
3. Stir in the Brussels sprouts and cook covered for 10 minutes. Pour in the chicken stock to prevent burning. Once the Brussels sprouts have wilted and are fork-tender, add white wine and cook for about 5 minutes, or until reduced.
4. Add the pasta to the skillet and add the pasta water as needed.
5. Top with the Parmesan cheese and squeeze the lemon over the dish right before eating.

Per Serving
calories: 502 | fat: 31.0g | protein: 15.0g | carbs: 50.0g | fiber: 9.0g | sodium: 246mg

Baby Kale and Cabbage Salad

Prep Time: 10 minutes | **Cooking Time:** 0 minutes | **Servings:** 6

Ingredients

2 bunches baby kale, thinly sliced
½ head green savoy cabbage, cored and thinly sliced
1 medium red bell pepper, thinly sliced
1 garlic clove, thinly sliced
Dressing:
Juice of 1 lemon
¼ cup apple cider vinegar
1 teaspoon ground cumin
¼ teaspoon smoked paprika
1 cup toasted peanuts

Directions

1. In a large mixing bowl, toss together the kale and cabbage.
2. Make the dressing: Whisk together the lemon juice, vinegar, cumin and paprika in a small bowl.
3. Pour the dressing over the greens and gently massage with your hands. Add the pepper, garlic and peanuts to the mixing bowl. Toss to combine. Serve immediately.

Per Serving calories: 199 | fat: 12.0g | protein: 10.0g | carbs: 17.0g | fiber: 5.0g | sodium: 46mg

The Acorn Squash

Prep Time: 15 minutes | **Cooking Time:** 23 minutes | **Servings:** 4

Ingredients

½ tablespoon olive oil
2 medium Acorn squashes
¼ small yellow onion, chopped
1 jalapeño pepper, chopped
½ cup green onions
½ cup carrots, chopped
¼ cup cabbage, chopped
1 garlic clove, minced

½ (6-ounce / 170-g) can sugar-free tomato sauce
½ tablespoon chili powder
½ tablespoon ground cumin
Salt and freshly ground black pepper to taste
2 cups water
¼ cup Cheddar cheese, shredded

Directions

1. Pour the water into the instant pot and place the trivet inside. Slice the squash into 2 halves and remove the seeds.
2. Place over the trivet, skin side down, and sprinkle some salt and pepper over it. Secure the lid and cook on Manual for 15 minutes at High Pressure. Release the pressure naturally and remove the lid. Empty the pot into a bowl.
3. Now add the oil, onion, and garlic in the instant pot and Sauté for 5 minutes. Stir in the remaining vegetables and stir-fry for 3 minutes. Add the remaining and secure the lid.
4. Cook on Manual function for 2 minutes at High Pressure.
5. After the beep, natural release the pressure and remove the lid. Stuff the squashes with the prepared mixture and serve warm.

Per Serving

calories: 163 | fat: 5.1g | protein: 4.8g | carbs: 28.4g | fiber: 4.9g | sodium: 146mg

Potato Curry

Prep Time: 10 minutes | **Cooking Time:** 30 minutes | **Servings:** 2

Ingredients

2 large potatoes, peeled and diced
1 small onion, peeled, diced
8 ounces (227 g) fresh tomatoes
1 tablespoon olive oil
1 cup water

2 tablespoons garlic cloves, grated
½ tablespoon rosemary
½ tablespoon cayenne pepper
1½ tablespoons thyme
Salt and pepper, to taste

Directions

1. Pour a cup of water into the instant pot and place the steamer trivet inside. Place the potatoes and half the garlic over the trivet and sprinkle some salt and pepper on top.
2. Secure the lid and cook on Steam function for 20 minutes.
3. After the beep, natural release the pressure and remove the lid. Put the potatoes to one side and empty the pot.
4. Add the remaining to the cooker and Sauté for 10 minutes.
5. Use an immerse blender to purée the cooked mixture.
6. Stir in the steamed potatoes and serve hot.

Per Serving

calories: 398 | fat: 7.6g | protein: 9.6g | carbs: 76.2g | fiber: 10.9g | sodium: 111mg

Veggie Chili

Prep Time: 15 minutes | **Cooking Time:** 10 minutes | **Servings:** 3

Ingredients

½ tablespoon olive oil
1 small yellow onion, chopped
4 garlic cloves, minced
¾ (15-ounce / 425-g) can diced tomatoes
1 ounce (28 g) sugar-free tomato paste
½ (4-ounce / 113-g) can green chilies with liquid
1 tablespoon Worcestershire sauce

2 tablespoons red chili powder
½ cup carrots, diced
½ cup scallions, chopped
½ cup green bell pepper, chopped
¼ cup peas
1 tablespoon ground cumin
½ tablespoon dried oregano, crushed
Salt and freshly ground black pepper to taste

Directions

1. Add the oil, onion, and garlic into the instant pot and Sauté for 5 minutes.
2. Stir in the remaining vegetables and stir-fry for 3 minutes.
3. Add the remaining and secure the lid.
4. Cook on Manual function for 2 minutes at High Pressure.
5. After the beep, natural release the pressure and remove the lid.
6. Stir well and serve warm.

Per Serving

calories: 106 | fat: 3.9g | protein: 3.4g | carbs: 18.0g | fiber: 6.2g | sodium: 492mg

Creamy Potato Curry

Prep Time: 10 minutes | **Cooking Time:** 18 minutes | **Servings:** 4

Ingredients

¾ large yellow or white onion, chopped
1½ ribs celery, chopped
¼ cup carrots, diced
¼ cup green onions
½ cup coconut milk
¾ tablespoon garlic, chopped
1½ cups water

¼ cup heavy cream
¼ teaspoon thyme
¼ teaspoon rosemary
½ tablespoon black pepper
¾ cup peas Salt, to taste
2 tablespoons fresh cilantro for garnishing, chopped
1 pound (454 g) white potatoes, peeled and diced

Directions

1. Add the oil and all the vegetables in the instant pot and Sauté for 5 minutes.
2. Stir in the remaining and secure the lid.
3. Cook on Manual function for 13 minutes at High Pressure.
4. Once it beeps, natural release the pressure and remove the lid.
5. Garnish with fresh cilantro and serve hot.

Per Serving

calories: 210 | fat: 10.1g | protein: 4.1g | carbs: 27.6g | fiber: 4.7g | sodium: 74mg

Kate's Warm Mediterranean Farro Bowl (Italian)

Prep Time: 15 minutes **Cooking Time:** 10 minutes
Servings: 4

Ingredients

1/3 cup extra-virgin olive oil	½ cup chopped red bell pepper
2 garlic cloves, minced	1cup zucchini, cut in ½-inch slices
1/3 cup chopped red onions	3 cups cooked farro
½ cup canned chickpeas, drained and rinsed	½ cup coarsely chopped artichokes
Salt	Freshly ground black pepper
¼ cup sliced olives, for serving (optional)	½ cup crumbled feta cheese, for serving (optional)
2tablespoons fresh basil, chiffonade, for serving (optional)	3 tablespoons balsamic reduction, for serving (optional)

Directions

1. In a large sauté pan or skillet, heat the oil over medium heat and sauté the pepper, onions, and garlic for about 5 minutes, until tender.
2. Add the zucchini, chickpeas, and artichokes, then stir and continue to sauté vegetables, approximately 5 more minutes, until just soft.
3. Stir in the cooked farro, tossing to combine and cooking enough to heat through. Season with salt and pepper and remove from the heat.
4. Transfer the contents of the pan into the serving vessels or bowls.
5. Top with olives, feta, and basil (if using). Drizzle with balsamic reduction (if using) to finish.

Nutrition: Calories: 530; Carbs: 95.4g; Protein: 8.0g; Fat: 13.5g

Slow Cooked Buttery Mushrooms (Spanish)

Prep Time: 10 minutes **Cooking Time:** 10 minutes
Servings: 2

Ingredients

2 tablespoons butter	2tablespoons olive oil
3cloves of garlic, minced	16 ounces fresh brown mushrooms, sliced sliced
7 ounces fresh shiitake mushrooms,	A dash of thyme
Salt and pepper to taste	

Directions

1. Heat the butter and oil in a pot.
2. Sauté the garlic until fragrant, around 1 minute.
3. Stir in the rest of the and cook until soft, around 9 minutes.

Nutrition: Calories: 192; Carbs: 12.7g; Protein: 3.8g; Fat: 15.5g

Steamed Zucchini-Paprika (Italian)

Prep Time: 15 minutes **Cooking Time:** 30 minutes
Servings: 2

Ingredients

4 tablespoons olive oil	3 cloves of garlic, minced
3 medium-sized zucchinis, sliced thinly	Salt and pepper to taste
A dash of paprika	1 onion, chopped

Directions

1. Place all in the Instant Pot.
2. Give a good stir to combine all .
3. Close the lid and make sure that the steam release valve is set to "Venting."
4. Press the "Slow Cook" button and adjust the cooking time to 4 hours.
5. Halfway through the cooking time, open the lid and give a good stir to brown the other side.

Nutrition: Calories: 93; Carbs: 3.1g; Protein: 0.6g; Fat: 10.2g

Steamed Squash Chowder (Spanish)

Prep Time: 20 minutes **Cooking Time:** 40 minutes
Servings: 4

Ingredients

3 cups chicken broth	1teaspoon chili powder
½ teaspoon cumin 1 ½ teaspoon salt	2teaspoon cinnamons
2 tablespoon ghee	3 tablespoon olive oil
1 small yellow onion, chopped	2 carrots, chopped
1 green apple, sliced and cored	1 large butternut squash, peeled, seeded, and chopped to ½-inch cubes

Directions

1. In a large pot on medium high fire, melt ghee.
2. Once ghee is hot, sauté onions for 5 minutes or until soft and translucent.
3. Add olive oil, chili powder, cumin, salt, and cinnamon. Sauté for half a minute.
4. Add chopped squash and apples.
5. Sauté for 10 minutes while stirring once in a while.
6. Add broth, cover and cook on medium fire for twenty minutes or until apples and squash are tender.
7. With an immersion blender, puree chowder. Adjust consistency by adding more water.
8. Add more salt or pepper depending on desire.
9. Serve and enjoy.

Nutrition: Calories: 228; Carbs: 17.9g; Protein: 2.2g; Fat: 18.0g

Zoodles with Beet Pesto

Prep Time: 10 minutes | **Cooking Time:** 50 minutes |
Servings: 2

Ingredients

1 medium red beet, peeled, chopped	2 tablespoons plus 2 teaspoons extra-virgin olive oil, divided
½ cup walnut pieces	¼ teaspoon salt
½ cup crumbled goat cheese	4 small zucchinis, spiralized
squeezed lemon juice	3 garlic cloves
	2 tablespoons freshly

Directions

1. Preheat the oven to 375°F (190°C).
2. Wrap the chopped beet in a piece of aluminum foil and seal well.
3. Roast in the preheated oven for 30 to 40 minutes until tender.
4. Meanwhile, heat a skillet over medium-high heat until hot. Add the walnuts and toast for 5 to 7 minutes, or until fragrant and lightly browned.
5. Remove the cooked beets from the oven and place in a food processor. Add the toasted walnuts, goat cheese, garlic, lemon juice, 2 tablespoons of olive oil, and salt. Pulse until smoothly blended. Set aside.
6. Heat the remaining 2 teaspoons of olive oil in a large skillet over medium heat. Add the zucchini and toss to coat in the oil. Cook for 2 to 3 minutes, stirring gently, or until the zucchini is softened. Transfer the zucchini to a serving plate and toss with the beet pesto, then serve.

Per Serving

calories: 423 | fat: 38.8g | protein: 8.0g | carbs: 17.1g | fiber: 6.0g | sodium: 338mg

Cauliflower Hash with Carrots

Prep Time: 10 minutes | **Cooking Time:** 10 minutes |
Servings: 4

Ingredients

3 tablespoons extra-virgin olive oil	2 cups diced carrots
1 large onion, chopped	4 cups cauliflower florets
1 tablespoon minced garlic	½ teaspoon ground cumin
	1 teaspoon salt

Directions

1. In a large skillet, heat the olive oil over medium heat.
2. Add the onion and garlic and sauté for 1 minute. Stir in the carrots and stir-fry for 3 minutes.
3. Add the cauliflower florets, cumin, and salt and toss to combine.
4. Cover and cook for 3 minutes until lightly browned. Stir well and cook, uncovered, for 3 to 4 minutes, until softened.
5. Remove from the heat and serve warm.

Per Serving

calories: 158 | fat: 10.8g | protein: 3.1g | carbs: 14.9g | fiber: 5.1g | sodium: 656mg

Rolls with Fried Eggplant

Prep Time: 20 minutes | **Cooking Time:** 10 minutes |
Servings: 4 to 6

Ingredients

1 large eggplants, trimmed and cut lengthwise into ¼-inch-thick slices	4 ounces (113 g) goat cheese, shredded
1 teaspoon salt	¼ cup finely chopped fresh basil
1 cup ricotta cheese	½ teaspoon freshly ground black pepper
Olive oil spray	

Directions

1. Add the eggplant slices to a colander and season with salt. Set aside for 15 to 20 minutes.
2. Mix together the ricotta and goat cheese, basil, and black pepper in a large bowl and stir to combine. Set aside.
3. Dry the eggplant slices with paper towels and lightly mist them with olive oil spray.
4. Heat a large skillet over medium heat and lightly spray it with olive oil spray.
5. Arrange the eggplant slices in the skillet and fry each side for 3 minutes until golden brown.
6. Remove from the heat to a paper towel-lined plate and rest for 5 minutes.
7. Make the eggplant rolls: Lay the eggplant slices on a flat work surface and top each slice with a tablespoon of the prepared cheese mixture. Roll them up and serve immediately.

Per Serving

calories: 254 | fat: 14.9g | protein: 15.3g | carbs: 18.6g | fiber: 7.1g | sodium: 745mg

Zoodles

Prep Time: 10 minutes | **Cooking Time:** 5 minutes |
Servings: 2

Ingredients

2 tablespoons avocado oil	¼ teaspoon salt
2 medium zucchini, spiralized	Freshly ground black pepper

Directions

1. Heat the avocado oil in a large skillet over medium heat until it shimmers.
2. Add the zucchini noodles, salt, and black pepper to the skillet and toss to coat. Cook for 1 to 2 minutes, stirring constantly, until tender.
3. Serve warm.

Per Serving

calories: 128 | fat: 14.0g | protein: 0.3g | carbs: 0.3g | fiber: 0.1g | sodium: 291mg

Zucchini Crisp

Prep Time: 10 minutes | **Cooking Time:** 20 minutes | **Servings:** 2

Ingredients

4 zucchinis, sliced into ½-inch rounds	½ cup whole wheat bread crumbs
½ cup unsweetened almond milk	¼ cup nutritional yeast
1 teaspoon fresh lemon juice	¼ cup hemp seeds
1 teaspoon arrowroot powder	½ teaspoon garlic powder
½ teaspoon salt, divided	¼ teaspoon crushed red pepper
	¼ teaspoon black pepper

Directions

1. Preheat the oven to 375°F (190°C). Line two baking sheets with parchment paper and set aside. Put the zucchini in a medium bowl with the almond milk, lemon juice, arrowroot powder, and ¼ teaspoon of salt. Stir to mix well.
2. In a large bowl with a lid, thoroughly combine the bread crumbs, nutritional yeast, hemp seeds, garlic powder, crushed red pepper and black pepper. Add the zucchini in batches and shake until the slices are evenly coated.
3. Arrange the zucchini on the prepared baking sheets in a single layer. Bake in the preheated oven for about 20 minutes, or until the zucchini slices are golden brown. Season with the remaining ¼ teaspoon of salt before serving.

Per Serving

calories: 255 | fat: 11.3g | protein: 8.6g | carbs: 31.9g | fiber: 3.8g | sodium: 826mg

Roasted Root Veggies (Spanish)

Prep Time: 20 minutes **Cooking Time:** 1 hour 30 minutes

Servings: 6

Ingredients

2 tablespoon olive oil	1 head garlic, cloves separated and peeled
1 large turnip, peeled and cut into ½-inch pieces	1 ½ lbs. beets, trimmed but not peeled, scrubbed and cut into ½-inch pieces
1 medium sized red onion, cut into ½-inch pieces	butternut squash, peeled, seeded, cut into ½-inch pieces
1 ½ lbs. Yukon gold potatoes, unpeeled, cut into ½-inch pieces 2 ½ lbs. pieces	

Directions

1. Grease 2 rimmed and large baking sheets. Preheat oven to 425oF.
2. In a large bowl, mix all thoroughly.
3. Into the two baking sheets, evenly divide the root vegetables, spread in one layer.
4. Season generously with pepper and salt.
5. Pop into the oven and roast for 1 hour and 15 minute or until golden brown and tender. Remove from oven and let it cool for at least 15 minutes before serving.

Nutrition: Calories: 298; Carbs: 61.1g; Protein: 7.4g; Fat: 5.0g

Creamy Sweet Potatoes and Collards

Prep Time: 20 minutes | **Cooking Time:** 35 minutes | **Servings:** 2

Ingredients

1 tablespoon avocado oil	1-inch squares
3 garlic cloves, chopped	1 (14.5-ounce / 411-g) can diced tomatoes with juice
1 yellow onion, diced	1 (15-ounce / 425-g) can red kidney beans or chickpeas, drained and rinsed
½ teaspoon crushed red pepper flakes	
1 large sweet potato, peeled and diced	1½ cups water
2 bunches collard greens (about 2 pounds/907 g), stemmed, leaves chopped int	½ cup unsweetened coconut milk
	Salt and black pepper, to taste

Directions

1. In a large, deep skillet over medium heat, melt the avocado oil.
2. Add the garlic, onion, and red pepper flakes and cook for 3 minutes. Stir in the sweet potato and collards.
3. Add the tomatoes with their juice, beans, water, and coconut milk and mix well. Bring the mixture just to a boil.
4. Reduce the heat to medium-low, cover, and simmer for about 30 minutes, or until softened.
5. Season to taste with salt and pepper and serve.

Per Serving calories: 445 | fat: 9.6g | protein: 18.1g | carbs: 73.1g | fiber: 22.1g | sodium: 703mg

Celeriac Mix with Cauliflower (Italian)

Prep Time: 10 minutes **Cooking Time:** 12 minutes **Servings:** 6

Ingredients

1 head cauliflower	¼ cup butter
1 small celery root	1 tablespoon. chopped thyme
1 tablespoon. chopped rosemary	1 cup cream cheese

Directions

1. Skin the celery root and cut it into small pieces.
2. Cut the cauliflower into similar sized pieces and combine.
3. Toast the herbs in the butter in a large pan, until they become fragrant.
4. Add the cauliflower and celery root and stir to combine.
5. Season and cook at medium-high until moisture in the vegetables releases itself, then cover and cook on low for 10-12 minutes.
6. Once the vegetables are soft, remove them from the heat and place them in the blender.
7. Make it smooth, then put the cream cheese and puree again.
8. Season and serve.

Nutrition: 225 Calories 20g Fat 5g Protein

Mediterranean Baked Chickpeas (Spanish)

Prep Time: 15 minutes **Cooking Time:** 15 minutes
Servings: 6

Ingredients

1tablespoon extra-virgin olive oil
2teaspoons smoked paprika
4 cups halved cherry tomatoes
1 cup crumbled feta, for serving
½ cup plain, unsweetened, full-fat Greek yogurt

½ medium onion, chopped
3 garlic cloves, chopped
¼ teaspoon ground cumin
2 (15-ounce) cans chickpeas, drained and rinsed

Directions

1. Preheat the oven to 425°F.
2. In an oven-safe sauté pan or skillet, heat the oil over medium heat and sauté the onion and garlic. Cook for about 5 minutes, until softened and fragrant. Stir in the paprika and cumin and cook for 2 minutes. Stir in the tomatoes and chickpeas. Bring to a simmer for 5 to 10 minutes before placing in the oven.
3. Roast in oven for 25 to 30 minutes, until bubbling and thickened. To serve, top with Greek yogurt and feta.

Nutrition: Calories: 330; Carbs: 75.4g; Protein: 9.0g; Fat: 18.5g

Falafel Bites (Italian)

Prep Time: 10 minutes **Cooking Time:** 15 minutes
Servings: 4

Ingredients

1 2/3 cups falafel mix
1 tablespoon Pickled Onions (optional)
1 tablespoon Pickled Turnips (optional)

Extra-virgin olive oil spray
2 tablespoons Tzatziki Sauce (optional)
1¼ cups water

Directions

1. In a large bowl, carefully stir the falafel mix into the water. Mix well. Let stand 15 minutes to absorb the water. Form mixes into 1-inch balls and arrange on a baking sheet.
2. Preheat the broiler to high.
3. Take the balls and flatten slightly with your thumb (so they won't roll around on the baking sheet). Spray with olive oil, and then broil for 2 to 3 minutes on each side, until crispy and brown.
4. To fry the falafel, fill a pot with ½ inch of cooking oil and heat over medium-high heat to 375°F. Fry the balls for about 3 minutes, until brown and crisp. Drain on paper towels and serve with pickled onions, pickled turnips, and tzatziki sauce (if using).

Nutrition: Calories: 530; Carbs: 95.4g; Protein: 8.0g; Fat: 18.5g

Quick Vegetable Kebabs (Spanish)

Prep Time: 15 minutes **Cooking Time:** 20 minutes
Servings: 6

Ingredients

4 medium red onions, peeled and sliced into 6
2yellow bell peppers, cut into 2-inch squares
2 orange bell peppers, cut into 2-inch squares
2 beefsteak tomatoes, cut into quarters

4 bell peppers, cut into 2-inch squares
3tablespoons Herbed Oil
4 medium zucchinis, cut into 1-inch-thick slices

Directions

1. Preheat the oven or grill to medium-high or 350°F.
2. Thread 1-piece red onion, zucchini, different colored bell peppers, and tomatoes onto a skewer. Repeat until the skewer is full of vegetables, up to 2 inches away from the skewer end, and continue until all skewers are complete.
3. Put the skewers on a baking sheet and cook in the oven for 10 minutes or grill for 5 minutes on each side. The vegetables will be done with they reach your desired crunch or softness.
4. Remove the skewers from heat and drizzle with Herbed Oil.

Nutrition: Calories: 235; Carbs: 30.4g; Protein: 8.0g; Fat: 14.5g

Sautéed Collard Greens (Spanish)

Prep Time: 10 minutes **Cooking Time:** 0 minute
Servings: 4

Ingredients

1-pound fresh collard greens, cut into 2-inch pieces
1teaspoon salt
1 large onion, chopped
1 tablespoon olive oil

3 cups chicken broth
1 teaspoon pepper
1 pinch red pepper flakes
2cloves garlic, minced
3 slices bacon

Directions

1. Using a large skillet, heat oil on medium-high heat. Sauté bacon until crisp. Remove it from the pan and crumble it once cooled. Set it aside.
2. Using the same pan, sauté onion and cook until tender. Add garlic until fragrant. Add the collard greens and cook until they start to wilt.
3. Pour in the chicken broth and season with pepper, salt and red pepper flakes. Reduce the heat to low and simmer for 45 minutes.

Nutrition: Calories: 20; Carbs: 3.0g; Protein: 1.0g; Fat: 1.0g

Zucchini Fritters

Prep Time: 15 minutes | **Cooking Time:** 5 minutes | Makes 14 fritters

Ingredients

4 cups grated zucchini
Salt, to taste
2 large eggs, lightly beaten
⅓ cup sliced scallions (green and white parts)

⅔ all-purpose flour
⅛ teaspoon black pepper
2 tablespoons olive oil

Directions

1. Put the grated zucchini in a colander and lightly season with salt. Set aside to rest for 10 minutes. Squeeze out as much liquid from the grated zucchini as possible.
2. Pour the grated zucchini into a bowl. Fold in the beaten eggs, scallions, flour, salt, and pepper and stir until everything is well combined.
3. Heat the olive oil in a large skillet over medium heat until hot.
4. Drop 3 tablespoons mounds of the zucchini mixture onto the hot skillet to make each fritter, pressing them lightly into rounds and spacing them about 2 inches apart.
5. Cook for 2 to 3 minutes. Flip the zucchini fritters and cook for 2 minutes more, or until they are golden brown and cooked through.
6. Remove from the heat to a plate lined with paper towels. Repeat with the remaining zucchini mixture. Serve hot.

Per Serving (2 fritters)

calories: 113 | fat: 6.1g | protein: 4.0g | carbs: 12.2g | fiber: 1.0g | sodium: 25mg

Stuffed Portobello Mushroom with Tomatoes

Prep Time: 10 minutes | **Cooking Time:** 15 minutes | **Servings:** 4

Ingredients

4 large portobello mushroom caps
3 tablespoons extra-virgin olive oil
Salt and freshly ground black pepper, to taste

4 sun-dried tomatoes
1 cup shredded mozzarella cheese, divided
½ to ¾ cup low-sodium tomato sauce

Directions

1. Preheat the broiler to High.
2. Arrange the mushroom caps on a baking sheet and drizzle with olive oil.
1. Sprinkle with salt and pepper.
2. Broil for 1o minutes, flipping the mushroom caps halfway through, until browned on the top.
3. Remove from the broil. Spoon 1 tomato, 2 tablespoons of cheese, and 2 to 3 tablespoons of sauce onto each mushroom cap.
4. Return the mushroom caps to the broiler and continue broiling for 2 to 3 minutes.
5. Cool for 5 minutes before serving.

Per Serving

calories: 217 | fat: 15.8g | protein: 11.2g | carbs: 11.7g | fiber: 2.0g | sodium: 243mg

Moroccan Tagine with Vegetables

Prep Time: 20 minutes | **Cooking Time:** 40 minutes | **Servings:** 2

Ingredients

2 tablespoons olive oil
½ onion, diced
1 garlic clove, minced
2 cups cauliflower florets
1 medium carrot, cut into 1-inch pieces
1 cup diced eggplant
1 (28-ounce / 794-g) can whole tomatoes with their juices
1 (15-ounce / 425-g) can chickpeas, drained, rinsed

2 small red potatoes, cut into 1-inch pieces
1 cup water
1 teaspoon pure maple syrup
½ teaspoon cinnamon
½ teaspoon turmeric
1 teaspoon cumin
½ teaspoon salt
1 to 2 teaspoons harissa paste

Directions

1. In a Dutch oven, heat the olive oil over medium-high heat. Sauté the onion for 5 minutes, stirring occasionally, or until the onion is translucent.
2. Stir in the garlic, cauliflower florets, carrot, eggplant, tomatoes, and potatoes. Using a wooden spoon or spatula to break up the tomatoes into smaller pieces.
3. Add the chickpeas, water, maple syrup, cinnamon, turmeric, cumin, and salt and stir to incorporate. Bring the mixture to a boil. Once it starts to boil, reduce the heat to medium-low. Stir in the harissa paste, cover, allow to simmer for about 40 minutes, or until the vegetables are softened. Taste and adjust seasoning as needed.
4. Let the mixture cool for 5 minutes before serving.

Per Serving

calories: 293 | fat: 9.9g | protein: 11.2g | carbs: 45.5g | fiber: 12.1g | sodium: 337mg

Lentil and Tomato Collard Wraps

Prep Time: 15 minutes | **Cooking Time:** 0 minutes | **Servings:** 4

Ingredients

2 cups cooked lentils
5 Roma tomatoes, diced
½ cup crumbled feta cheese
10 large fresh basil leaves, thinly sliced
¼ cup extra-virgin olive oil
1 tablespoon balsamic vinegar

2 garlic cloves, minced
½ teaspoon raw honey
½ teaspoon salt
¼ teaspoon freshly ground black pepper
4 large collard leaves, stems removed

Directions

1. Combine the lentils, tomatoes, cheese, basil leaves, olive oil, vinegar, garlic, honey, salt, and black pepper in a large bowl and stir until well blended.
2. Lay the collard leaves on a flat work surface. Spoon the equal-sized amounts of the lentil mixture onto the edges of the leaves. Roll them up and slice in half to serve.

Per Serving

calories: 318 | fat: 17.6g | protein: 13.2g | carbs: 27.5g | fiber: 9.9g | sodium: 475mg

Sweet Potato Chickpea Buddha Bowl

Prep Time: 10 minutes | **Cooking Time:** 10 to 15 mins | **Servings:** 2

Ingredients

Sauce:
1 tablespoon tahini
2 tablespoons plain Greek yogurt
2 tablespoons hemp seeds
1 garlic clove, minced Pinch salt
Freshly ground black pepper, to taste

Bowl:
1 small sweet potato, peeled and finely diced
1 teaspoon extra-virgin olive oil
1 cup from 1 (15-ounce / 425-g) can low-sodium chickpeas, drained and rinsed
2 cups baby kale

Directions

Make the Sauce
1. Whisk together the tahini and yogurt in a small bowl.
2. Stir in the hemp seeds and minced garlic. Season with salt pepper. Add 2 to 3 tablespoons water to create a creamy yet pourable consistency and set aside.

Make the Bowl
3. Preheat the oven to 425°F (220°C). Line a baking sheet with parchment paper.
4. Place the sweet potato on the prepared baking sheet and drizzle with the olive oil. Toss well
5. Roast in the preheated oven for 10 to 15 minutes, stirring once during cooking, or until fork-tender and browned.
6. In each of 2 bowls, place ½ cup of chickpeas, 1 cup of baby kale, and half of the cooked sweet potato. Serve drizzled with half of the prepared sauce.

Per Serving
calories: 323 | fat: 14.1g | protein: 17.0g | carbs: 36.0 g | fiber: 7.9g | sodium: 304mg

Roasted Vegetables and Zucchini Pasta (Italian)

Prep Time: 10 minutes
Cooking Time: 7 minutes
Servings: 2

¼ cup raw pine nuts
1 tablespoon extra-virgin olive oil
2 garlic cloves, minced

4 cups leftover vegetables
4 medium zucchinis, cut into long strips resembling noodles

Directions
1. Heat oil in a large skillet over medium heat and sauté the garlic for 2 minutes.
2. Add the leftover vegetables and place the zucchini noodles on top. Let it cook for five minutes. Garnish with pine nuts.

Nutrition: Calories: 288; Carbs: 23.6g; Protein: 8.2g; Fat: 19.2g

Patties made with zucchini

Prep Time: 15 minutes | **Cooking Time:** 5 minutes | **Servings:** 2

Ingredients

2 medium zucchinis, shredded
1 teaspoon salt, divided
2 eggs
2 tablespoons chickpea flour

1 tbsp chopped fresh mint
1 scallion, chopped
2 tablespoons extra-virgin olive oil

Directions
1. Put the shredded zucchini in a fine-mesh strainer and season with ½ teaspoon of salt. Set aside.
2. Beat together the eggs, chickpea flour, mint, scallion, and remaining ½ teaspoon of salt in a medium bowl.
3. Squeeze the zucchini to drain as much liquid as possible. Add the zucchini to the egg mixture and stir until well incorporated.
4. Heat the olive oil in a large skillet over medium-high heat.
5. Drop the zucchini mixture by spoonfuls into the skillet. Gently flatten the zucchini with the back of a spatula.
6. Cook for 2 to 3 minutes or until golden brown. Flip and cook for an additional 2 minutes.
7. Remove from the heat and serve on a plate.

Per Serving
calories: 264 | fat: 20.0g | protein: 9.8g | carbs: 16.1g | fiber: 4.0g | sodium: 1780mg

Creamy Cauliflower Chickpea Curry

Prep Time: 5 minutes | **Cooking Time:** 15 minutes | **Servings:** 4

Ingredients

3 cups fresh or frozen cauliflower florets
2 cups unsweetened almond milk
1 (15-ounce / 425-g) can low-sodium chickpeas, drained and rinsed

1 tablespoon curry powder
¼ teaspoon garlic powder
¼ teaspoon ground ginger
⅛ teaspoon onion powder
¼ teaspoon salt
1 (15-ounce / 425-g) can coconut milk

Directions
1. Add the cauliflower florets, almond milk, chickpeas, coconut milk, curry powder, garlic powder, ginger, and onion powder to a large stockpot and stir to combine.
2. Cover and cook over medium-high heat for 10 minutes, stirring occasionally.
3. Reduce the heat to low and continue cooking uncovered for 5 minutes, or until the cauliflower is tender.
4. Sprinkle with the salt and stir well. Serve warm.

Per Serving
calories: 409 | fat: 29.6g | protein: 10.0g | carbs: 29.8g | fiber: 9.1g | sodium: 117mg

Grilled Eggplant Rolls (Spanish)

Prep Time: 30 minutes **Cooking Time:** 10 minutes
Servings: 5

Ingredients

1large eggplants	4 ounces goat cheese
¼ cup fresh basil, finely chopped	1 cup ricotta

Directions

1. Slice the tops of the eggplants off and cut the eggplants lengthwise into
1. ¼-inch-thick slices. Sprinkle the slices with the salt and place the eggplant in a colander for 15 to 20 minutes.
2. In a large bowl, combine the goat cheese, ricotta, basil, and pepper.
3. Preheat a grill, grill pan, or lightly oiled skillet on medium heat. Pat the eggplant slices dry using paper towel and lightly spray with olive oil spray. Place the eggplant on the grill, grill pan or skillet and cook for 3 minutes on each side.
4. Take out the eggplant from the heat and let cool for 5 minutes.
5. To roll, lay one eggplant slice flat, place a tablespoon of the cheese mixture at the base of the slice, and roll up. Serve immediately or chill until serving.

Nutrition: 255 Calories 15g Protein 19g Carbohydrates

Instant Pot Jackfruit Curry (Spanish)

Prep Time: 1 hour **Cooking Time:** 16 minutes
Servings: 2

Ingredients

1 tbsp. oil	Cumin seeds, Mustard seeds
20 oz. can green jackfruit (drained and rinsed)	1 tbsp. coriander powder, turmeric.
2 tomatoes (purred)	

Directions

1. Turn the instant pot to sauté mode. Add cumin seeds, mustard, ten nigella seeds and allow them to sizzle.
2. Add 2 red chilies and 2 bay leaves and allow cooking for a few seconds.
3. Add chopped 1 onion, 5 garlic cloves, ginger and salt, and pepper to taste. Stir cook for five minutes.
4. Add other and a cup of water then lid the instant pot. Set time for seven minutes on high pressure.
5. When the time has elapsed release pressure naturally, shred the jackfruit and serve.

Nutrition: 369 Calories 3g Fat 6g Fiber

Mozzarella Eggplants (Italian)

Prep Time: 20 minutes **Cooking Time:** 40 minutes
Servings: 4

Ingredients

1large eggplants	2tomatoes
3Mozzarella balls	1 tablespoon olive oil
	1 teaspoon salt

Directions

1. Trim the eggplants and make the cross cuts to get the Hasselback eggplants.
2. Sprinkle the vegetables with salt.
3. After this, slice the tomatoes and Mozzarella balls.
4. Fill the eggplant cuts with Mozzarella and tomatoes and sprinkle with olive oil.
5. Then wrap every eggplant in foil.
6. Bake the vegetables for 40 minutes at 375F.
7. Discard the foil from the eggplants and cut them on 4
8. **Servings:** (1/2 part of eggplant = 1 serving).

Nutrition: calories 195, fat 11.2, fiber 10.8, carbs 19.7, protein 8.5

Greek Style Beans (Greek)

Prep Time: 10 minutes **Cooking Time:** 10 hours and 40 minutes
Servings: 8

Ingredients

3 cups white beans	1 onion, diced
1 clove garlic, peeled	28 oz. canned crushed tomatoes
1/4 cup olive oil	

Directions

1. Pour 8 cups of water into the Instant Pot. Add the white beans.
2. Season with a pinch of salt.
3. Let the beans soak for up to 10 hours.
4. Seal the pot. Set it to manual. Choose bean/chili function.
5. Adjust time to 15 minutes at high pressure. Release the pressure naturally.
6. Transfer the white beans into a bowl and set aside.
7. Take 1 cup of the cooking liquid and set aside.
8. Drain the remaining liquid.
9. Press the sauté setting. Heat the olive oil.
10. Cook the onion, garlic and tomatoes for 5 minutes.
11. Add the reserved cooking liquid and the tomatoes.
12. Put the beans back. Stir well. Secure the pot.
13. Choose bean/chili function for 5 minutes at high pressure. Release the pressure naturally. Season with salt and pepper.

Nutrition: Calories 352; Total Fat 7g; Saturated Fat 1.1g; Cholesterol 0mg; Sodium 203mg; Total Carbohydrate 55g; Dietary Fiber 15g; Total Sugars 7.7g; Protein 20.3g; Potassium 1381mg

Colorful Vegetable Medley (Spanish)

Prep Time: 10 minutes **Cooking Time:** 3 minutes
Servings: 4

Ingredients

1 small head broccoli, broken into florets
16 asparagus, trimmed
2 carrots, peeled and cut on the bias
1 cup of water

1 small head cauliflower, broken into florets
5 ounces green beans
Salt to taste

Directions

1. Add water and set trivet on top of the water
2. Place steamer basket on top
3. Spread green beans, cauliflower, asparagus, carrots, broccoli in a steamer basket
4. Close the lid
5. Steam for 3 minutes on High
6. Release the pressure quickly
7. Season with salt
8. Serve and enjoy!

Nutrition Calories: 223 Fat: 21g Carbohydrates: 8g Protein: 3g

Veggie Ramen Miso Soup (Italian)

Prep Time: 5 minutes **Cooking Time:** 20 minutes
Servings: 1

Ingredients

2 teaspoons thinly sliced green onion
2 tablespoon mellow white miso
½ cup thinly sliced cremini mushrooms
2¼ cups water
1/2 cup baby spinach leaves – optional

½ teaspoon shoyu
A pinch of salt
1 cup zucchini, cut into angel hair spirals
½ medium carrot, cut into angel hair spirals
½ box of medium firm tofu, cut into ¼-inch cubes
1 hardboiled egg

Directions

1. In a small bowl, mix ¼ cup of water and miso. Set aside.
2. In a small saucepan on medium high fire, bring to a boil 2 cups water, mushrooms, tofu and carrots. Add salt, shoyu and miso mixture. Allow to boil for 5 minutes. Remove from fire and add green onion, zucchini and baby spinach leaves if using.
3. Let soup stand for 5 minutes before transferring to individual bowls. Garnish with ½ of hardboiled egg per bowl, serve and enjoy.

Nutrition: Calories: 335; Carbs: 19.0g; Protein: 30.6g; Fat: 17.6g

Yummy Cauliflower Fritters (Greek)

Prep Time: 10 minutes **Cooking Time:** 15 minutes
Servings: 6

Ingredients

1 large cauliflower head, cut into florets
½ teaspoon salt

½ teaspoon turmeric
2 eggs, beaten
¼ teaspoon black pepper
6 tablespoons coconut oil

Directions

1. Place the cauliflower florets in a pot with water.
2. Bring to a boil and drain once cooked.
3. Place the cauliflower, eggs, turmeric, salt, and pepper into the food processor.
4. Pulse until the mixture becomes coarse.
5. Transfer into a bowl. Using your hands, form six small flattened balls and place in the fridge for at least 1 hour until the mixture hardens.
6. Heat the oil in a skillet and fry the cauliflower patties for 3 minutes on each side Place in individual containers.
7. Put a label and store in the fridge. Allow to thaw at room temperature before heating in the microwave oven.

Nutrition: Calories per
Servings: 157; Carbs: 2.8g; Protein: 3.9g; Fat: 15.3g; Fiber: 0.9g

Vegetable Stew (Spanish)

Prep Time: 10 minutes
Cooking Time: 45 minutes
Servings: 4

Ingredients

1-pound potatoes, peeled and cut into bite-sized pieces
2 carrots, peeled and chopped
1 zucchini, cut into ½ inch thick slices
1 teaspoon black pepper
1 tablespoon paprika

3 tablespoons olive oil
2 cups vegetable broth
2 tbsp coconut oil, unsalted
2 onions, peeled and chopped
1 tablespoon salt
3 celery stalks, chopped
A handful of fresh celery leaves

Directions

1. Warm oil on Sauté mode
2. Stir-fry onions for 3-4 minutes
3. Add celery, zucchini, carrots, and ¼ cup broth
4. Cook for 10 minutes more and keep stirring continuously
5. Stir in potatoes, cayenne pepper, bay leaves, remaining broth, celery leaves, salt and pepper
6. Close the lid
7. Cook at Meat/Stew for 30 minutes on High
8. Quick-release the pressure
9. Serve and enjoy!

Nutrition: Calories: 331 Fat: 14g Carbohydrates: 44g Protein: 17g

Chapter 7
Poultry Recipes & Meats Recipes

Pork Tenderloin with Herbed Mustard Coating
Prep Time: 10 minutes | **Cooking Time:** 15 minutes | **Servings:** 4

Ingredients
3 tablespoons fresh rosemary leaves
¼ cup Dijon mustard
½ cup fresh parsley leaves
6 garlic cloves
½ teaspoon sea salt
¼ teaspoon freshly ground black pepper
1 tablespoon extra-virgin olive oil
1 (1½-pound / 680-g) pork tenderloin

Directions
1. Preheat the oven to 400°F (205°C).
2. Put all the , except for the pork tenderloin, in a food processor. Pulse until it has a thick consistency.
3. Put the pork tenderloin on a baking sheet, then rub with the mixture to coat well.
4. Put the sheet in the preheated oven and bake for 15 minutes or until the internal temperature of the pork reaches at least 165°F (74°C). Flip the tenderloin halfway through the cooking time.
5. Transfer the cooked pork tenderloin to a large plate and allow to cool for 5 minutes before serving.

Per Serving calories: 363 | fat: 18.1g | protein: 2.2g | carbs: 4.9g | fiber: 2.0g | sodium: 514mg

Grilled Pork Chops
Prep Time: 20 minutes | **Cooking Time:** 10 minutes | **Servings:** 4

Ingredients
¼ cup extra-virgin olive oil
2 tablespoons fresh thyme leaves
1 teaspoon smoked paprika
1 teaspoon salt
4 pork loin chops, ½-inch-thick

Directions
1. In a small bowl, mix together the olive oil, thyme, paprika, and salt. Put the pork chops in a plastic zip-top bag or a bowl and coat them with the spice mix. Let them marinate for 15 minutes.
2. Preheat the grill to high heat. Cook the pork chops for 4 minutes on each side until cooked through. Serve warm.

Per Serving calories: 282 | fat: 23.0g | protein: 21.0g | carbs: 1.0g | fiber: 0g | sodium: 832mg

Pork with Macadamias
Prep Time: 10 minutes | **Cooking Time:** 10 minutes | **Servings:** 4

Ingredients
1 (1-pound / 454-g) pork tenderloin, cut into ½-inch slices and pounded thin
1 teaspoon sea salt, divided
1 tablespoon extra-virgin olive oil
¼ teaspoon freshly ground black pepper, divided
½ cup macadamia nuts
1 cup unsweetened coconut milk

Directions
1. Preheat the oven to 400°F (205°C).
2. On a clean work surface, rub the pork with ½ teaspoon of the salt and ⅛ teaspoon of the ground black pepper. Set aside. Ground the macadamia nuts in a food processor, then combine with remaining salt and black pepper in a bowl. Stir to mix well and set aside.
3. Combine the coconut milk and olive oil in a separate bowl. Stir to mix well. Dredge the pork chops into the bowl of coconut milk mixture, then dunk into the bowl of macadamia nut mixture to coat well. Shake the excess off.
4. Put the well-coated pork chops on a baking sheet, then bake for 10 minutes or until the internal temperature of the pork reaches at least 165°F (74°C). Transfer the pork chops to a serving plate and serve immediately.

Per Serving calories: 436 | fat: 32.8g | protein: 33.1g | carbs: 5.9g | fiber: 3.0g | sodium: 310mg

Beef, Tomato, and Lentils Stew
Prep Time: 10 minutes | **Cooking Time:** 10 minutes | **Servings:** 4

Ingredients
1 tablespoon extra-virgin olive oil
1 onion, chopped
1 (14-ounce / 397-g) can chopped tomatoes with garlic and basil, drained
1 (14-ounce / 397-g) can lentils, drained
½ teaspoon sea salt
⅛ tbsp. freshly ground black pepper
1 pound (454 g) extra-lean ground beef

Directions
1. Heat the olive oil in a pot over medium-high heat until shimmering.
2. Add the beef and onion to the pot and sauté for 5 minutes or until the beef is lightly browned.
3. Add the remaining. Bring to a boil. Reduce the heat to medium and cook for 4 more minutes or until the lentils are tender. Keep stirring during the cooking.
4. Pour them in a large serving bowl and serve immediately.

Per Serving calories: 460 | fat: 14.8g | protein: 44.2g | carbs: 36.9g | fiber: 17.0g | sodium: 320mg

Slow Cook Lamb Shanks with Cannellini Beans Stew

Prep Time: 20 minutes | **Cooking Time:** 10 hours 15 minutes
Servings: 12

Ingredients

1 (19-ounce / 539-g) can cannellini beans, rinsed and drained
1 large yellow onion, chopped
2 medium-sized carrots, diced
1 large stalk celery, chopped
2 cloves garlic, thinly sliced
4 (1½-pound / 680-g) lamb shanks, fat trimmed
2 teaspoons tarragon
½ teaspoon sea salt
¼ teaspoon ground black pepper
1 (28-ounce / 794-g) can diced tomatoes, with the juice

Directions

1. Combine the beans, onion, carrots, celery, and garlic in the slow cooker. Stir to mix well.
2. Add the lamb shanks and sprinkle with tarragon, salt, and ground black pepper. Pour in the tomatoes with juice, then cover the lid and cook on high for an hour.
3. Reduce the heat to low and cook for 9 hours or until the lamb is super tender.
4. Transfer the lamb on a plate, then pour the bean mixture in a colander over a separate bowl to reserve the liquid.
5. Let the liquid sit for 5 minutes until set, then skim the fat from the surface of the liquid. Pour the bean mixture back to the liquid. Remove the bones from the lamb heat and discard the bones. Put the lamb meat and bean mixture back to the slow cooker. Cover and cook to reheat for 15 minutes or until heated through.
6. Pour them on a large serving plate and serve immediately.

Per Serving
calories: 317 | fat: 9.7g | protein: 52.1g | carbs: 7.0g | fiber: 2.1g | sodium: 375mg

Slow Cooker Mediterranean Beef Stew (Greek)

Prep Time: 10 minutes **Cooking Time:** 10 hours
Servings: 10

Ingredients

Beef meat (for stew) 3 pounds
Beef broth 2 cups
Dried rosemary 2 tablespoons Tomato sauce 15 ounces Balsamic vinegar ½ cup
Salt ½ tbsp. Pepper ½ tbsp
Baby mushrooms 16 ounces
Garlic, minced 10 cloves
Chopped onion 1 large
Diced tomatoes in a can 14½ ounces Jar capers, drained 2 ounces Drained black olives 6 ounces

Directions

1. Put all the except the for garnishing in a 6-quart slow cooker and combine. Cover the cooker and slow cook for 10 hours. Add pepper and salt as required.
2. Garnish with parmesan and chopped parsley while serving.

Nutrition: Calories: 273 Carbohydrate: 16g Protein: 33g Sugars: 6gFat: 9g Sodium: 931mg

Burgers with Lamb in Greek Style

Prep Time: 10 minutes | **Cooking Time:** 10 minutes |
Servings: 4

Ingredients

1 pound (454 g) ground lamb
½ teaspoon salt
½ teaspoon freshly ground black pepper
4 tablespoons crumbled feta cheese
Buns, toppings, and tzatziki, for serving (optional)

Directions

1. Preheat the grill to high heat. In a large bowl, using your hands, combine the lamb with the salt and pepper.
2. Divide the meat into 4 portions. Divide each portion in half to make a top and a bottom. Flatten each half into a 3-inch circle. Make a dent in the center of one of the halves and place 1 tablespoon of the feta cheese in the center. Place the second half of the patty on top of the feta cheese and press down to close the 2 halves together, making it resemble a round burger. Grill each side for 3 minutes, for medium-well. Serve on a bun with your favorite toppings and tzatziki sauce, if desired.

Per Serving calories: 345 | fat: 29.0g | protein: 20.0g | carbs: 1.0g | fiber: 0g | sodium: 462mg

Beef Kebabs with Onion and Pepper

Prep Time: 15 minutes | **Cooking Time:** 10 minutes |
Servings: 6

Ingredients

2 pounds (907 g) beef fillet
1½ teaspoons salt
1 teaspoon freshly ground black pepper
½ teaspoon ground nutmeg
½ teaspoon ground allspice
⅓ cup extra-virgin olive oil
1 large onion, cut into 8 quarters
1 large red bell pepper, cut into 1-inch cubes

Directions

1. Preheat the grill to high heat.
2. Cut the beef into 1-inch cubes and put them in a large bowl.
3. In a small bowl, mix together the salt, black pepper, allspice, and nutmeg.
4. Pour the olive oil over the beef and toss to coat. Evenly sprinkle the seasoning over the beef and toss to coat all pieces.
5. Skewer the beef, alternating every 1 or 2 pieces with a piece of onion or bell pepper.
6. To cook, place the skewers on the preheated grill, and flip every 2 to 3 minutes until all sides have cooked to desired doneness, 6 minutes for medium-rare, 8 minutes for well done. Serve hot.

Per Serving calories: 485 | fat: 36.0g | protein: 35.0g | carbs: 4.0g | fiber: 1.0g | sodium: 1453mg

Tender Chicken Quesadilla (Spanish)

Prep Time: 10 minutes **Cooking Time:** 20 minutes
Servings: 4

Ingredients

bread tortillas	1 teaspoon butter
2 teaspoons olive oil	1 teaspoon Taco seasoning
6 oz chicken breast, skinless, boneless, sliced	1 bell pepper, cut on the wedges
1/3 cup Cheddar cheese, shredded	

Directions

1. Pour 1 teaspoon of olive oil in the skillet and add chicken.
2. Sprinkle the meat with Taco seasoning and mix up well.
3. Roast chicken for 10 minutes over the medium heat. Stir it from time to time.
4. Then transfer the cooked chicken in the plate.
5. Add remaining olive oil in the skillet.
6. Then add bell pepper and roast it for 5 minutes. Stir it all the time.
7. Mix up together bell pepper with chicken.
8. Toss butter in the skillet and melt it.
9. Put 1 tortilla in the skillet.
10. Put Cheddar cheese on the tortilla and flatten it.
11. Then add chicken-pepper mixture and cover it with the second tortilla. Roast the quesadilla for 2 minutes from each side.
12. Cut the cooked meal on the halves and transfer in the serving plates.

Nutrition: Calories 167, Fat 8.2 g, Fiber 0.8 g, Carbs 16.4 g, Protein 24.2 g

Crack Chicken (Greek)

Prep Time: 10 minutes **Cooking Time:** 30 minutes
Servings: 4

Ingredients

4 chicken thighs, skinless, boneless	½ teaspoon salt
1 tablespoon cream cheese	1 teaspoon ground black pepper
1 teaspoon paprika	¼ cup Cheddar cheese, shredded
1 tablespoon butter	
½ teaspoon garlic powder	1 tbsp fresh dill, chopped
1 teaspoon olive oil	½ teaspoon ground nutmeg

Directions

1. Grease the baking dish with butter. Then heat up olive oil in the skillet. Meanwhile, rub the chicken thighs with ground nutmeg, garlic powder, paprika, and salt. Add ground black pepper.
2. Roast the chicken thighs in the hot oil over the high heat for 2 minutes from each side.
3. Then transfer the chicken thighs in the prepared baking dish.
4. Mix up together Cheddar cheese, cream cheese, and dill.
5. Top every chicken thigh with cheese mixture and bake for 25 minutes at 365F.

Nutrition: Calories 79, Fat 7.3 g, Fiber 0.1, Carbs 1 g, Protein 2.4 g

Salad with chicken and bacon (Italian)

Prep Time: 10 minutes **Cooking Time:** 5 minutes
Servings: 3

Ingredients

1 cups cooked chicken, shredded	1/2 cup sour cream
1 cup celery, chopped	1 cup cheddar cheese, shredded
/4 cup mayonnaise	1/2 cup bacon, crumbles
Salt	3 green onions, sliced
	1/4 cup onion, chopped
	Pepper

Directions

1. Add all ingredients into the large bowl and mix until well combined.
2. Serve and enjoy.

Nutrition: Calories 482 Fat 31.3 g Carbohydrates 9.9 g Sugar 2.7 g Protein 39.6 g Cholesterol 137 mg

Green Salsa Chicken (Italian)

Prep Time: 10 minutes **Cooking Time:** 3 hours
Servings: 6

Ingredients

1 lb. chicken breasts, skinless and boneless	15 oz green salsa Pepper
Salt	

Directions

1. Add all ingredients into the crock pot.
2. Cover and cook on high for 3 hours.
3. Shred the chicken using fork.
4. Serve and enjoy.

Nutrition: Calories 166 Fat 6 g Carbohydrates 3 g Sugar 1.4 g Protein 22 g Cholesterol 67 mg

Chicken Chili (Greek)

Prep Time: 10 minutes **Cooking Time:** 6 hours
Servings: 4

Ingredients

1 lb. chicken breasts, skinless and boneless	14 oz can tomato, diced
	2 cups of water
1 jalapeno pepper, chopped	1/2 teaspoon paprika
1 poblano pepper, chopped	1/2 teaspoon dried sage
12 oz can green chilies	1/2 teaspoon cumin
1 teaspoon dried oregano	1 teaspoon sea salt
1/2 cup dried chives	

Directions

1. Add all ingredients into the crockpot and stir well.
2. Cover and cook on low for 6 hours.
3. Shred the chicken using a fork.
4. Stir well and serve.

Nutrition: Calories 265 Fat 8.9 g Carbohydrates 11.1 g Sugar 4.2 g Protein 34.9 g Cholesterol 101 mg

Chicken Parm (Italian)

Prep Time: 10 minutes **Cooking Time:** 30 minutes
Servings: 4

Ingredients

4 chicken steaks (4 oz each steak)	½ cup crushed tomatoes
¼ cup fresh cilantro	1 onion, diced
1 teaspoon olive oil	½ cup of water
3 tablespoon Panko breadcrumbs	3 oz Parmesan, grated
2 eggs, beaten	1 teaspoon ground black pepper
	1 garlic clove, diced

Directions

1. Pour olive oil in the saucepan.
2. Add garlic and onion. Roast the vegetables for 3 minutes.
3. Then add fresh cilantro, crushed tomatoes, and water.
4. Simmer the mixture for 5 minutes.
5. Meanwhile, mix up together ground black pepper and eggs. Dip the chicken steaks in the egg mixture.
6. Then coat them in Panko breadcrumbs and again in the egg mixture. Coat the chicken steaks in grated Parmesan.
7. Place the prepared chicken steaks in the crushed tomato mixture.
8. Close the lid and cook chicken Parm for 20 minutes. Flip the chicken steaks after 10 minutes of cooking.
9. Serve the chicken Parm with crushed tomatoes sauce.

Nutrition: Calories 354, Fat 21.3 g, Fiber 2.1, Carbs 12 g, Protein 32.4 g

Chicken Bolognese (Greek)

Prep Time: 7 minutes **Cooking Time:** 25 minutes
Servings: 4

Ingredients

2 tbsp fresh parsley, chopped	1 teaspoon paprika
½ teaspoon dried oregano	1 tbsp chili pepper
½ teaspoon dried thyme	¼ teaspoon garlic, minced
1/3 cup crushed tomatoes	1cup ground chicken
	2 oz Parmesan, grated
	1 tablespoon olive oil

Directions

1. Heat up olive oil in the skillet.
2. Add ground chicken and sprinkle it with chili pepper, paprika, dried oregano, dried thyme, and parsley. Mix up well.
3. Cook the chicken for 5 minutes and add crushed tomatoes. Mix up well.
4. Close the lid and simmer the chicken mixture for 10 minutes over the low heat.
5. Then add grated Parmesan and mix up.
6. Cook chicken Bolognese for 5 minutes more over the medium heat.

Nutrition: Calories 154, Fat 9.3 g, Fiber 1.1, Carbs 3 g, Protein 15.4 g

Cashew Broccoli Chicken (Greek)

Prep Time: 25 minutes **Cooking Time:** 30 minutes
Servings: 5

Ingredients

½ cup carrots, chopped	1 red bell pepper, chopped
1/3 cup unsalted cashews	2 cups broccoli florets
3 green onions, chopped	1 cup sugar snap peas
1 pound chicken breasts, cubed 1 tablespoon olive oil	3 cloves garlic, crushed
1 teaspoon sesame oil	Sauce:
2 tablespoons honey	3 tablespoons peanut butter
1 tablespoon crushed ginger	3 tablespoons water
4 tablespoons soy sauce	

Directions

1. In a mixing bowl, add the sauce and mix them together.
2. Over medium stove flame, heat the oil in a skillet or saucepan (preferably of medium size)..
3. Add the chicken and cook it until evenly brown; season with garlic, salt, and black pepper.
4. Add the broccoli, snap peas, bell pepper, and carrots and fry for 5-6 minutes, stirring often.
5. Add the sauce and combine well. Add in the cashews, mix and serve warm.

Nutrition: Calories 235 Fat 9g Carbohydrates 21g Fiber 4g Protein 26g

Turkey And Asparagus Mix (Greek)

Prep Time: 10 minutes **Cooking Time:** 30 minutes
Servings: 4

Ingredients

1 bunch asparagus, trimmed and halved	1big turkey breast, skinless, boneless, and cut into strips
2tbsps. olive oil	A pinch of salt, and black pepper
1 tsp basil, dried	
½ cup tomato sauce	1 tbsp. chives, chopped

Directions

1. In a skillet, pour a drizzle of oil, and heat over medium-high heat. Add the turkey, and brown for 3 minutes per side.
2. Add the asparagus, and the rest of the (except the chives), and bring to a boil. When it boils, decrease the heat, and cook over medium-low heat for 25 minutes.
3. Add the chives, divide the mixture among plates, and serve.

Nutrition: Calories: 337 Carbs: 21.4g Fat: 21.2g Protein: 17.6g Fiber: 10.2g

66

Apricot Pork Meat (Spanish)

Prep Time: 5 minutes **Cooking Time:** 60 minutes
Servings: 8

Ingredients

3 pounds boneless rolled pork	½ cup ketchup
½ cup teriyaki sauce	1 teaspoon of paprika
¼ cup cider vinegar	1/3 Cup of canned apricots
1 large onion sliced	¼ cup dark brown sugar, packaged
1 teaspoon dried mustard	2 cups of water
¼ teaspoon black pepper	

Directions

1. Put the creed meat in a large plastic bag or glass dish. Combine ketchup, teriyaki sauce, canned food, vinegar, brown sugar, paprika, mustard and pepper. Mix together and pour over pork. Refrigerate overnight.
2. Remove the pork from the marinade and keep the marinade. Brown pork on both sides in the pressure cooker over medium heat. Remove pork from the pot.
3. Put the cooking rack, half of the sliced onion and the water inside the pot. Put the pork on the rack of the pot and distribute the remaining onion evenly over the meat. Close and secure the lid.
4. Place the pressure regulator on the vent tube and cook 60 minutes once the pressure regulator begins to rock slowly.
5. Let the pressure decrease on its own. Put in a saucepan the marinade that it kept and boil until it thickens, stirring occasionally.
6. Remove the meat and onions from the pressure cooker. Add onions to the thickened marinade and serve with sliced pork. Onions can be stepped on before adding to the sauce and served with rice, if desired.

Nutrition: Calories: 332, Carbohydrates: 0g, Fat: 13g, Protein: 47g, Sugar: 0g, Cholesterol: 77mg

Pork Cacciatore (Italian)

Prep Time: 10 minutes **Cooking Time:** 6 hours
Servings: 6

Ingredients

1 ½ lbs. pork chops	1 teaspoon dried oregano
3 tablespoon tomato paste	2 cups mushrooms, sliced
14 oz can tomato, diced	1 small onion, diced
1 garlic clove, minced	¼ teaspoon pepper
2 tablespoon olive oil	1 cup beef broth
½ teaspoon salt	

Directions

1. Heat oil in a pan over medium-high heat. Add pork chops in pan and cook until brown on both the sides. Transfer pork chops into the crock pot. Pour remaining over the pork chops. Cover and cook on low for 6 hours. Serve and enjoy.

Nutrition: Calories 440 Fat 33 g Carbohydrates 6 g Sugar 3 g Protein 28 g Cholesterol 97 mg

Pork Loin with Pineapple Glaze (Spanish)

Prep Time: 10 minutes **Cooking Time:** 35 minutes
Servings: 8

Ingredients

Mix to macerate:	½ cup kosher salt
½ cup light brown sugar, compact	1 tablespoon black peppercorns
1 tablespoon coriander seeds	1pork loin (clean and fat free (approx. 3½ pounds, 1¾ kg)
4 bay leaves	5 garlic cloves finely chopped
2 teaspoons chopped fresh thyme	
2tablespoons olive oil	1 pound (½ kg) peeled pearl onion
½ tbsp ground black pepper	½ cup dry white wine
2 teaspoons chopped fresh rosemary	1½ cups of pineapple juice

Directions

1. To macerate the pork, mix the kosher salt, brown sugar, peppercorns, coriander seeds and bay leaves with 2 cups of warm water, in a bowl, until the salt dissolves. Pour 6 cups of cold water. Add the pork (it must be completely submerged in the liquid), cover and refrigerate overnight.
2. Mix the garlic, 2 tablespoons of olive oil, rosemary, and thyme and ground black pepper in the 1-Quart Mixing Bowl. Remove the pork from the mixture where you mashed it and dry it with paper towels (discard the liquid). Cover it completely with the herbal mixture.
3. Preheat the pot at medium-high temperature for about 3 minutes. The temperature is correct when, when spraying a few drops of water, they bounce off the surface without evaporating. Place the pork, reduce the temperature to medium and seal for about 4 minutes, or until golden brown. Turn it carefully and seal for another 4 minutes, or until it is golden.
1. Reduce the temperature to low, cover with the closed valve, and cook for about 20 minutes, or until the pork is fully cooked. Transfer it to a tray and set aside.
2. Pour the wine into the same pot and let it boil at high temperature for 1 minute, or until it almost evaporates. Stir constantly with the Balloon Whisk, to peel off the pork pieces attached to the base.
3. Add the pineapple juice and onion. Continue cooking at medium-high temperature for about 3 minutes. Reduce the temperature to medium, put the pork back in the pot and bathe it with the sauce. Let it cook uncovered for 3 more minutes. Turn off the stove.
4. Carefully remove the pork from the pot and slice it. Top with onions and sauce, and serve immediately with your favorite rice and vegetables.

Nutrition: Calories: 258.6, Carbohydrates: 22.9g, Fat: 6.2g, Protein: 28.4g, Sugar: 19.4g, Cholesterol: 80.6mg

Chicken with Spanish Rice (Spanish)

Prep Time: 15 minutes **Cooking Time:** 25 minutes
Servings: 12

Ingredients

6 chicken breast fillets, sliced into cubes

4 cloves garlic, minced

1 onion, chopped

4 cups brown rice

28 oz. canned diced tomatoes with green chili

Directions

1. Season the chicken with salt and pepper.
2. Pour 1 tablespoon into the Instant Pot.
3. Set it to sauté.
4. Brown the chicken and set aside.
5. Add the garlic, onion and rice.
6. Cook for 2 minutes.
7. Add the canned tomatoes with green chili and 4 ½ cups of water.
8. Seal the pot.
9. Set it to manual.
10. Cook at high pressure for 24 minutes.
11. Release the pressure naturally.
12. Fluff the rice and top with the chicken.
13. Serving Suggestion: Garnish with chopped fresh parsley.

Nutrition: Calories 383 Total Fat 7.2g Saturated Fat 1.8g Cholesterol 65mg Sodium 331mg Total Carbohydrate 51.8g Dietary Fiber 2.4g Total Sugars 0.4g Protein 26.5g Potassium 435mg

Turkey Meatloaf (Greek)

Prep Time: 15 minutes **Cooking Time:** 35 minutes
Servings: 6

Ingredients

1/2 cup bread crumbs

1/4 cup onion, chopped

1 lb. lean ground turkey

1/4 cup sun dried tomatoes, diced

1/2 cup feta cheese, crumbled

Directions

1. Mix all the ingredients in a bowl.
2. Form a loaf and cover with foil.
3. Pour 1 cup of water into the Instant Pot.
4. Add the steamer basket inside.
5. Place the wrapped turkey mixture on top of basket.
6. Cover the pot. Set it to manual.
7. Cook at high pressure for 35 minutes.
8. Release the pressure quickly.
9. Serving Suggestion: Let cool before slicing and serving.

Tip: You can also add a tablespoon of almond milk to the mixture.

Nutrition: Calories 226 Total Fat 11g Saturated Fat 4.5g Cholesterol 78mg Sodium 330mg Total Carbohydrate 10.2g Dietary Fiber 0.9g Total Sugars 1.5g Protein 21.7g Potassium 424mg

Chicken Sauté (Spanish)

Prep Time: 10 minutes **Cooking Time:** 25 minutes
Servings: 2

Ingredients

4 oz chicken fillet

4 tomatoes, peeled

1 cup of water

1 tbsp salt

½ teaspoon saffron

1 bell pepper, chopped

1 teaspoon olive oil

1 chili pepper, chopped

Directions

1. Pour water in the pan and bring it to boil.
2. Meanwhile, chop the chicken fillet.
3. Add the chicken fillet in the boiling water and cook it for 10 minutes or until the chicken is tender.
4. After this, put the chopped bell pepper and chili pepper in the skillet.
5. Add olive oil and roast the vegetables for 3 minutes.
6. Add chopped tomatoes and mix up well.
7. Cook the vegetables for 2 minutes more.
8. Then add salt and a ¾ cup of water from chicken.
9. Add chopped chicken fillet and mix up.
10. Cook the sauté for 10 minutes over the medium heat.

Nutrition: Calories 192, Fat 7.2 g, Fiber 3.8 g, Carbs 14.4 g, Protein 19.2 g

Grilled Marinated Chicken (Greek)

Prep Time: 35 minutes **Cooking Time:** 20 minutes
Servings: 6

Ingredients

1-pound chicken breast, skinless, boneless

½ teaspoon ground nutmeg

1 teaspoon onion powder

2 tablespoons olive oil

1 tbsp apple cider vinegar

1 teaspoon sage

2 tablespoons lemon juice

½ teaspoon dried oregano

1 teaspoon chili flakes

1 teaspoon salt

1 tbsp paprika

Directions

1. Make the marinade: whisk together apple cider vinegar, salt, chili flakes, olive oil, onion powder, paprika, dried oregano, ground nutmeg, sage, and lemon juice.
2. Then rub the chicken with marinade carefully and leave for 25 minutes to marinate.
3. Meanwhile, preheat grill to 385F.
4. Place the marinated chicken breast in the grill and cook it for 10 minutes from each side.
5. Cut the cooked chicken on the Serving:.

Nutrition: Calories 218 Fat 8.2 g, Fiber 0.8 g, Carbs 0.4 g, Protein 32.2 g

Turkey With Green Sauce (Greek)

Prep Time: 5 minutes **Cooking Time:** 50 minutes
Servings: 4

Ingredients

1 big turkey breast, skinless, boneless, and cubed	Salt, and black pepper to the taste
1 ½ cups Salsa Verde	1 tbsp. olive oil
1 ½ cups feta cheese, crumbled	¼ cup cilantro, chopped

Directions

1. Preheat the oven to 400°F.
2. Grease a baking dish with olive oil, add the turkey with the gravy, salt, and pepper, and bake for 50 minutes.
3. Remove from the oven, add the cheese, and cilantro, and toss gently. Divide among plates, and serve.

Nutrition: Calories: 332 Carbs: 22.1g Fat: 15.4g Protein: 34.5g Fiber: 10g

Turkey With Herbs and Almonds (Greek)

Prep Time: 10 minutes **Cooking Time:** 40 minutes
Servings: 4

Ingredients

1 big turkey breast, skinless, boneless, and cubed	½ cup chicken stock
1 tbsp. rosemary, chopped	1 tbsp. basil, chopped
1 tbsp. oregano, chopped	3 garlic cloves, minced
½ cup almonds, toasted, and chopped	1 tbsp. olive oil
3 cups tomatoes, chopped	1 tbsp. parsley, chopped

Directions

1. Heat a skillet with the oil over medium-high heat. Add the turkey, and garlic, and brown for 3 minutes per side. Add the broth, and the rest of the ingredients, and bring to a boil over medium heat. Cook for 35 minutes covered.
2. Divide the mixture among plates, and serve.

Nutrition: Calories: 297 Carbs: 19.4g Fat: 11.2g Protein: 23.6g Fiber: 9.2g

Turkey With Lemon and Pine Nuts (Greek)

Prep Time: 10 minutes **Cooking Time:** 30 minutes
Servings: 4

Ingredients

2 turkey breasts, boneless, skinless, and halved	2 tbsps. avocado oil Juice of 2 lemons
1tbsp. rosemary, chopped	¼ cup pine nuts, chopped
3 garlic cloves, minced	1 cup chicken stock
A pinch of salt, and black pepper	

Directions

1. Heat an oiled skillet over medium-high heat. Add the garlic, and turkey, and brown for 4 minutes on each side.
2. Add the rest of the ingredients, and bring to a boil. When it boils, lower the heat to medium, and cook for 20 minutes.
3. Divide the mixture among plates, and serve with a side salad.

Nutrition: Calories: 293 Carbs: 17.8g Fat: 12.4g Protein: 24.5g Fiber: 9.3g

Chapter 8
Fish Recipes & Seafood Recipes

Ceviche with Avocado and Shrimp

Prep Time: 15 minutes | **Cooking Time:** 0 minutes | **Servings:** 4

Ingredients

1 pound (454 g) fresh shrimp, peeled, deveined, and cut in half lengthwise
1 small red or yellow bell pepper, cut into ½-inch chunks
½ small red onion, cut into thin slivers
½ English cucumber, peeled and cut into ½-inch chunks
¼ cup chopped fresh cilantro
½ cup extra-virgin olive oil
⅓ cup freshly squeezed lime juice
2 tablespoons freshly squeezed clementine juice
2 tablespoons freshly squeezed lemon juice
1 teaspoon salt
½ teaspoon freshly ground black pepper
2 ripe avocados, peeled, pitted, and cut into ½-inch chunks

Directions

1. Place the shrimp, bell pepper, red onion, cucumber, and cilantro in a large bowl and toss to combine.
2. In a separate bowl, stir together the olive oil, lime, clementine, and lemon juice, salt, and black pepper until smooth. Pour the mixture into the bowl of shrimp and vegetable mixture and toss until they are completely coated.
3. Cover the bowl with plastic wrap and transfer to the refrigerator to marinate for at least 2 hours, or up to 8 hours.
4. When ready, stir in the avocado chunks and toss to incorporate. Serve immediately.

Per Serving

calories: 496 | fat: 39.5g | protein: 25.3g | carbs: 13.8g | fiber: 6.0g | sodium: 755mg

Cioppino (Seafood Tomato Stew)

Prep Time: 10 minutes | **Cooking Time:** 20 minutes | **Servings:** 2

Ingredients

2 tablespoons olive oil
½ small onion, diced
½ green pepper, diced
2 teaspoons dried basil
2 teaspoons dried oregano
½ cup dry white wine
1 (14.5-ounce / 411-g) can diced tomatoes with basil
1 (8-ounce / 227-g) can no-salt-added tomato sauce
1 (6.5-ounce / 184-g) can minced clams with their juice
8 ounces (227 g) peeled, deveined raw shrimp
4 ounces (113 g) any white fish (a thick piece works best)
3 tablespoons fresh parsley
Salt and freshly ground black pepper, to taste

Directions

1. In a Dutch oven, heat the olive oil over medium heat.
2. Sauté the onion and green pepper for 5 minutes, or until tender. Stir in the basil, oregano, wine, diced tomatoes, and tomato sauce and bring to a boil.
3. Once boiling, reduce the heat to low and bring to a simmer for 5 minutes.
4. Add the clams, shrimp, and fish and cook for about 10 minutes, or until the shrimp are pink and cooked through.
5. Scatter with the parsley and add the salt and black pepper to taste. Remove from the heat and serve warm.

Per Serving calories: 221 | fat: 7.7g | protein: 23.1g | carbs: 10.9g | fiber: 4.2g | sodium: 720mg

Slow Cooker Salmon in Foil

Prep Time: 5 minutes | **Cooking Time:** 2 hours | **Servings:** 2

Ingredients

2 (6-ounce / 170-g) salmon fillets
1 tablespoon olive oil
2 cloves garlic, minced
½ tablespoon lime juice
1 teaspoon finely chopped fresh parsley
¼ teaspoon black pepper

Directions

1. Spread a length of foil onto a work surface and place the salmon fillets in the middle. Mix together the olive oil, garlic, lime juice, parsley, and black pepper in a small bowl. Brush the mixture over the fillets. Fold the foil over and crimp the sides to make a packet.
2. Place the packet into the slow cooker, cover, and cook on High for 2 hours, or until the fish flakes easily with a fork.
3. Serve hot.

Per Serving calories: 446 | fat: 20.7g | protein: 65.4g | carbs: 1.5g | fiber: 0.2g | sodium: 240mg

Spicy Haddock Stew

Prep Time: 15 minutes | **Cooking Time:** 35 minutes | **Servings:** 6

Ingredients

¼ cup coconut oil
1 tablespoon minced garlic
1 onion, chopped
2 celery stalks, chopped
½ fennel bulb, thinly sliced
1 carrot, diced
1 sweet potato, diced
1 (15-ounce / 425-g) can low-sodium diced tomatoes
1 cup coconut milk
1 cup low-sodium chicken broth
¼ teaspoon red pepper flakes
12 ounces (340 g) haddock, cut into 1-inch chunks
2 tablespoons chopped fresh cilantro, for garnish

Directions

1. In a large saucepan, heat the coconut oil over medium-high heat.
2. Add the garlic, onion, and celery and sauté for about 4 minutes, stirring occasionally, or until they are tender.
3. Stir in the fennel bulb, carrot, and sweet potato and sauté for 4 minutes more.
4. Add the diced tomatoes, coconut milk, chicken broth, and red pepper flakes and stir to incorporate, then bring the mixture to a boil.
5. Once it starts to boil, reduce the heat to low, and bring to a simmer for about 15 minutes, or until the vegetables are fork-tender.
6. Add the haddock chunks and continue simmering for about 10 minutes, or until the fish is cooked through.
7. Sprinkle the cilantro on top for garnish before serving.

Per Serving

calories: 276 | fat: 20.9g | protein: 14.2g | carbs: 6.8g | fiber: 3.0g | sodium: 226mg

Balsamic-Honey Glazed Salmon

Prep Time: 2 minutes | **Cooking Time:** 8 minutes | **Servings:** 4

Ingredients

½ cup balsamic vinegar
1 tablespoon honey
4 (8-ounce / 227-g) salmon fillets
Sea salt and freshly ground pepper, to taste
1 tablespoon olive oil

Directions

1. Heat a skillet over medium-high heat. Combine the vinegar and honey in a small bowl.
2. Season the salmon fillets with the sea salt and freshly ground pepper; brush with the honey-balsamic glaze.
3. Add olive oil to the skillet, and sear the salmon fillets, cooking for 3 to 4 minutes on each side until lightly browned and medium rare in the center.
4. Let sit for 5 minutes before serving.

Per Serving calories: 454 | fat: 17.3g | protein: 65.3g | carbs: 9.7g | fiber: 0g | sodium: 246mg

Canned Sardine Donburi (Rice Bowl)

Prep Time: 10 mins | **Cooking Time:** 40 to 50 mins | **Servings:** 4 to 6

Ingredients

4 cups water
2 cups brown rice, rinsed well
½ teaspoon salt
3 (4-ounce / 113-g) cans sardines packed in water, drained
3 scallions, sliced thin
1-inch piece fresh ginger, grated
4 tablespoons sesame oil

Directions

1. Place the water, brown rice, and salt to a large saucepan and stir to combine. Allow the mixture to boil over high heat.
2. Once boiling, reduce the heat to low, and cook covered for 45 to 50 minutes, or until the rice is tender.
3. Meanwhile, roughly mash the sardines with a fork in a medium bowl.
4. When the rice is done, stir in the mashed sardines, scallions, and ginger.
5. Divide the mixture into four bowls. Top each bowl with a drizzle of sesame oil. Serve warm.

Per Serving

calories: 603 | fat: 23.6g | protein: 25.2g | carbs: 73.8g | fiber: 4.0g | sodium: 498mg

Orange Flavored Scallops

Prep Time: 10 minutes | **Cooking Time:** 10 minutes | **Servings:** 4

Ingredients

2 pounds (907 g) sea scallops, patted dry
Sea salt and freshly ground black pepper, to taste
2 tablespoons extra-virgin olive oil
1 tablespoon minced garlic
¼ cup freshly squeezed orange juice
1 teaspoon orange zest
2 teaspoons chopped fresh thyme, for garnish

Directions

1. In a bowl, lightly season the scallops with salt and pepper. Set aside.
2. Heat the olive oil in a large skillet over medium-high heat until it shimmers.
3. Add the garlic and sauté for about 3 minutes, or until fragrant.
4. Stir in the seasoned scallops and sear each side for about 4 minutes, or until the scallops are browned.
5. Remove the scallops from the heat to a plate and set aside.
6. Add the orange juice and zest to the skillet, scraping up brown bits from bottom of skillet.
7. Drizzle the sauce over the scallops and garnish with the thyme before serving.

Per Serving

calories: 266 | fat: 7.6g | protein: 38.1g | carbs: 7.9g | fiber: 0g | sodium: 360mg

Easy Seafood French Stew (Italian)

Prep Time: 10 minutes **Cooking Time:** 45 minutes
Servings: 12

Ingredients

Pepper and Salt
1lb. shrimp, peeled and deveined
1 large lobster
1/2 lb. mussels
2tablespoon garlic, chopped
3cups tomatoes, peeled, seeded, and chopped
1 cup white wine Water
1 cup leeks, julienned
8 peppercorns
3 cloves garlic Salt and pepper

1/2 lb. littleneck clams
2lbs. assorted small whole fresh fish, scaled and cleaned
2 tbsp parsleys fine chopped
Juice and zest of one orange
Pinch of Saffron Stew
1 cup fennel, julienned
1 lb. fish bones
2 sprigs thyme
1 bay leaf
1/2 cup chopped celery
1/2 cup chopped onion
2 tablespoon olive oil

Directions

1. Do the stew: Heat oil in a large saucepan. Sauté the celery and onions for 3 minutes. Season with pepper and salt. Stir in the garlic and cook for about a minute. Add the thyme, peppercorns, and bay leaves. Stir in the wine, water and fish bones. Let it boil then before reducing to a simmer. Take the pan off the fire and strain broth into another container.
2. For the Bouillabaisse: Bring the strained broth to a simmer and stir in the parsley, leeks, orange juice, orange zest, garlic, fennel, tomatoes and saffron. Sprinkle with pepper and salt. Stir in the lobsters and fish. Let it simmer for eight minutes before stirring in the clams, mussels and shrimps. For six minutes, allow to cook while covered before seasoning again with pepper and salt.
3. Assemble in a shallow dish all the seafood and pour the broth over it.

Nutrition: Calories: 348; Carbs: 20.0g; Protein: 31.8g; Fat: 15.2g

Fresh and No-Cook Oysters (Spanish)

Prep Time: 10 minutes **Cooking Time:** 5 minutes
Servings: 4

Ingredients

1 lemons

24 medium oysters tabasco sauce

Directions

1. If you are a newbie when it comes to eating oysters, then I suggest that you blanch the oysters before eating.
2. For some, eating oysters raw is a great way to enjoy this dish because of the consistency and juiciness of raw oysters. Plus, adding lemon juice prior to eating the raw oysters cooks it a bit. So, to blanch oysters, bring a big pot of water to a rolling boil. Add oysters in batches of 6-10 pieces. Leave on boiling pot of water between 3-5 minutes and remove oysters right away. To eat oysters, squeeze lemon juice on oyster on shell, add tabasco as desired and eat.

Nutrition: Calories: 247; Protein: 29g; Fat: 7g; Carbs: 17g

Chowder with Bacon and Fish (Greek)

Prep Time: 10 minutes **Cooking Time:** 30 minutes
Servings: 8

Ingredients

1 1/2 lbs. cod
1 medium carrot, coarsely chopped
1 large onion, chopped
31/2 cups baking potato, peeled and cubed 3 slices uncooked bacon
4bay leaves
4 1/2 cups water

1 1/2 teaspoon dried thyme
1 tablespoon butter, cut into small pieces
1 teaspoon salt, divided
3/4 teaspoon freshly ground black pepper, divided
4 cups 2% reduced-fat milk

Directions

1. In a large skillet, add the water and bay leaves and let it simmer. Add the fish. Cover and let it simmer some more until the flesh flakes easily with fork. Remove the fish from the skillet and cut into large pieces. Set aside the cooking liquid. Place Dutch oven in medium heat and cook the bacon until crisp. Remove the bacon and reserve the bacon drippings. Crush the bacon and set aside.
2. Stir potato, onion and carrot in the pan with the bacon drippings, cook over medium heat for 10 minutes. Add the cooking liquid, bay leaves, 1/2 teaspoon salt, 1/4 teaspoon pepper and thyme, let it boil. Lower the heat and let simmer for 10 minutes. Add the milk and butter, simmer until the potatoes becomes tender, but do not boil. Add the fish, 1/2 teaspoon salt, 1/2 teaspoon pepper. Remove the bay leaves. Serve sprinkled with the crushed bacon.

Nutrition: Calories: 400; Carbs: 34.5g; Protein: 20.8g; Fat: 19.7g

Simple Cod Piccata (Italian)

Prep Time: 10 minutes **Cooking Time:** 15 minutes
Servings: 3

Ingredients

¼ cup capers, drained
¾ cup chicken stock
1/3 cup almond flour
2tablespoon fresh parsley, chopped
2 tablespoon grapeseed oil

½ teaspoon salt
1-pound cod fillets, patted dry
3tablespoon extra-virgin oil
3 tablespoon lemon juice

Directions

1. In a bowl, combine the almond flour and salt.
2. Dredge the fish in the almond flour to coat. Set aside.
3. Heat a little bit of olive oil to coat a large skillet. Heat the skillet over medium high heat. Add grapeseed oil. Cook the cod for 3 minutes on each side to brown. Remove from the plate and place on a paper towel- lined plate.
4. In a saucepan, mix together the chicken stock, capers and lemon juice. Simmer to reduce the sauce to half. Add the remaining grapeseed oil.
5. Drizzle the fried cod with the sauce and sprinkle with parsley.

Nutrition: Calories: 277.1; Fat: 28.3 g; Protein: 1.9 g; Carbs: 3.7 g

Teriyaki Salmon

Prep Time: 10 minutes | **Cooking Time:** 8 minutes | **Servings:** 4

Ingredients

4 (8-ounce / 227-g) thick salmon fillets.	4 teaspoons sesame seeds
1 cup soy sauce	2 cloves garlic, minced
2 cups water	2 tablespoons freshly grated ginger
½ cup mirin	4 tablespoons brown sugar
2 tablespoons sesame oil	1 tablespoon corn starch
	4 green onions, minced

Directions

1. Add the soy sauce, sesame oil, sesame seeds, mirin, ginger, water, garlic, green onions, and brown sugar to a small bowl. Mix them well. In a shallow dish place the salmon fillets and pour half of the prepared mixture over the fillets. Let it marinate for 30 minutes in a refrigerator.
2. Pour 1 cup of water into the insert of your Instant pot and place trivet inside it. Arrange the marinated salmon fillets over the trivet and secure the lid.
3. Select the Manual settings with High Pressure and 8 minutes cooking time. Meanwhile, take a skillet and add the remaining marinade mixture in it.
4. Let it cook for 2 minutes, then add the corn starch mixed with water. Stir well and cook for 1 minute.
5. Check the pressure cooker, do a Quick release if it is done.
6. Transfer the fillets to a serving platter and pour the sesame mixture over it. Garnish with chopped green chilies then serve hot.

Per Serving calories: 622 | fat: 28.6g | protein: 51.3g | carbs: 29.6g | fiber: 2.0g | sodium: 1086mg

Coconut Tangy Cod Curry

Prep Time: 5 minutes | **Cooking Time:** 3 minutes | **Servings:** 6

1 (28-ounce / 794-g) can coconut milk	2 teaspoons ground turmeric
Juice of 2 lemons	2 teaspoons ground ginger
2 tablespoons red curry paste	1 teaspoon sea salt
2 teaspoons fish sauce	1 teaspoon white pepper
2 teaspoons honey	2 pounds (907 g) codfish, cut into 1-inch cubes
4 teaspoons Sriracha	½ cup chopped fresh cilantro, for garnish
4 cloves garlic, minced	4 lime wedges, for garnish

Directions

1. Add all the , except the cod cubes and garnish, to a large bowl and whisk them well. Arrange the cod cube at the base of the Instant Pot and pour the coconut milk mixture over it. Secure the lid and hit the Manual key, select High Pressure with 3 minutes cooking time.
2. After the beep, do a Quick release then remove the lid.
3. Garnish with fresh cilantro and lemon wedges then serve.

Per Serving calories: 396 | fat: 29.1g | protein: 26.6g | carbs: 11.4g | fiber: 2.0g | sodium: 1024mg

Broccoli with Shrimp

Prep Time: 5 minutes | **Cooking Time:** 10 minutes | **Servings:** 2

Ingredients

2 teaspoons vegetable oil	¼ cup water
2 tablespoons corn starch	¼ cup sliced carrots
1 cup broccoli florets	3 tablespoons rice vinegar
¼ cup chicken broth	2 teaspoons sesame oil
8 ounces (227 g) large shrimp, peeled and deveined	1 tablespoon chili garlic sauce
¼ cup soy sauce	Coriander leaves to garnish Boiled rice or noodles, for serving

Directions

1. Add 1 tablespoon of corn starch and shrimp to a bowl. Mix them well then set it aside.
2. In a small bowl, mix the remaining corn starch, chicken broth, carrots, chili garlic sauce, rice vinegar and soy sauce together. Keep the mixture aside.
3. Select the Sauté function on your Instant pot, add the sesame oil and broccoli florets to the pot and sauté for 5 minutes. Add the water to the broccoli, cover the lid and cook for 5 minutes. Stir in shrimp and vegetable oil to the broccoli, sauté it for 5 minutes. Garnish with coriander leaves on top. Serve with rice or noodles.

Per Serving calories: 300 | fat: 16.5g | protein: 19.6g | carbs: 17.1g | fiber: 2.2g | sodium: 1241mg

Mahi-Mahi and Tomato Bowls

Prep Time: 5 minutes | **Cooking Time:** 14 minutes | **Servings:** 3

Ingredients

3 (4-ounce / 113-g) mahi-mahi fillets	1 tablespoon fresh lemon juice
1½ tablespoons olive oil	Salt and freshly ground black pepper, to taste
½ yellow onion, sliced	
½ teaspoon dried oregano	1 (14-ounce / 397-g) can sugar-free diced tomatoes

Directions

1. Add the olive oil to the Instant Pot. Select the Sauté function on it. Add all the ingredient to the pot except the fillets. Cook them for 10 minutes. Press the Cancel key, then add the mahi-mahi fillets to the sauce.
2. Cover the fillets with sauce by using a spoon.
3. Secure the lid and set the Manual function at High Pressure for 4 minutes. After the beep, do a Quick release then remove the lid. Serve the fillets with their sauce, poured on top.

Per Serving calories: 265 | fat: 8.6g | protein: 39.1g | carbs: 7.0g | fiber: 3.1g | sodium: 393mg

Salmon with Lemon Pesto Grilled

Prep Time: 5 minutes | **Cooking Time:** 6 to 10 minutes | **Servings:** 2

Ingredients

10 ounces (283 g) salmon fillet (1 large piece or 2 smaller ones)
Salt and freshly ground black pepper, to taste
2 tbsp prepared pesto sauce
1 large fresh lemon, sliced
Cooking spray

Directions

1. preheat the grill to medium-high heat. Spray the grill grates with cooking spray. Season the salmon with salt and black pepper. Spread the pesto sauce on top.
2. Make a bed of fresh lemon slices about the same size as the salmon fillet on the hot grill, and place the salmon on top of the lemon slices. Put any additional lemon slices on top of the salmon. Grill the salmon for 6 to 10 minutes, or until the fish is opaque and flakes apart easily. Serve hot.

Per Serving calories: 316 | fat: 21.1g | protein: 29.0g | carbs: 1.0g | fiber: 0g | sodium: 175mg

Lemon Rosemary Roasted Branzino

Prep Time: 15 minutes | **Cooking Time:** 30 minutes | **Servings:** 2

Ingredients

4 tablespoons extra-virgin olive oil, divided
2 (8-ounce / 227-g) branzino fillets, preferably at least 1 inch thick
1 garlic clove, minced
1 bunch scallions (white part only), thinly sliced
10 to 12 small cherry tomatoes, halved
1 large carrot, cut into ¼-inch rounds
½ cup dry white wine
2 tablespoons paprika
2 teaspoons kosher salt
½ tablespoon ground chili pepper
2 rosemary sprigs or 1 tablespoon dried rosemary
1 small lemon, thinly sliced
½ cup sliced pitted kalamata olives

Directions

1. Heat a large ovenproof skillet over high heat until hot, about 2 minutes. Add 1 tablespoon of olive oil and heat for 10 to 15 seconds until it shimmers.
2. Add the branzino fillets, skin-side up, and sear for 2 minutes. Flip the fillets and cook for an additional 2 minutes. Set aside. Swirl 2 tablespoons of olive oil around the skillet to coat evenly.
3. Add the garlic, scallions, tomatoes, and carrot, and sauté for 5 minutes, or until softened.
4. Add the wine, stirring until all are well combined. Carefully place the fish over the sauce. Preheat the oven to 450ºF (235ºC).
5. Brush the fillets with the remaining 1 tablespoon of olive oil and season with paprika, salt, and chili pepper. Top each fillet with a rosemary sprig and lemon slices. Scatter the olives over fish and around the skillet. Roast for about 10 minutes until the lemon slices are browned. Serve hot.

Per Serving calories: 724 | fat: 43.0g | protein: 57.7g | carbs: 25.0g | fiber: 10.0g | sodium: 2950mg

Breaded Shrimp

Prep Time: 10 minutes | **Cooking Time:** 4 to 6 minutes | **Servings:** 4

Ingredients

2 large eggs
1 tablespoon water
2 cups seasoned Italian bread crumbs
1 teaspoon salt
1 cup flour
1 pound (454 g) large shrimp (21 to 25), peeled and deveined
Extra-virgin olive oil, as needed

Directions

1. In a small bowl, beat the eggs with the water, then transfer to a shallow dish. Add the bread crumbs and salt to a separate shallow dish, then mix well.
2. Place the flour into a third shallow dish.
3. Coat the shrimp in the flour, then the beaten egg, and finally the bread crumbs. Place on a plate and repeat with all of the shrimp. Heat a skillet over high heat. Pour in enough olive oil to coat the bottom of the skillet. Cook the shrimp in the hot skillet for 2 to 3 minutes on each side. Remove and drain on a paper towel. Serve warm.

Per Serving
calories: 714 | fat: 34.0g | protein: 37.0g | carbs: 63.0g | fiber: 3.0g | sodium: 1727mg

Roasted Trout Stuffed with Veggies

Prep Time: 10 minutes | **Cooking Time:** 25 minutes | **Servings:** 2

Ingredients

2 (8-ounce / 227-g) whole trout fillets, dressed (cleaned but with bones and skin intact)
1 tablespoon extra-virgin olive oil
¼ teaspoon salt
⅛ teaspoon freshly ground black pepper
1 small onion, thinly sliced
½ red bell pepper, seeded and thinly sliced
1 poblano pepper, seeded and thinly sliced
2 or 3 shiitake mushrooms, sliced
1 lemon, sliced
Nonstick cooking spray

Directions

1. Preheat the oven to 425ºF (220ºC). Spray a baking sheet with nonstick cooking spray. Rub both trout fillets, inside and out, with the olive oil. Season with salt and pepper.
2. Mix together the onion, bell pepper, poblano pepper, and mushrooms in a large bowl. Stuff half of this mixture into the cavity of each fillet. Top the mixture with 2 or 3 lemon slices inside each fillet.
3. Place the fish on the prepared baking sheet side by side. Roast in the preheated oven for 25 minutes, or until the fish is cooked through and the vegetables are tender.
4. Remove from the oven and serve on a plate.

Per Serving
calories: 453 | fat: 22.1g | protein: 49.0g | carbs: 13.8g | fiber: 3.0g | sodium: 356mg

Lemon Grilled Shrimp

Prep Time: 20 minutes | **Cooking Time:** 4 to 6 minutes | **Servings:** 4

Ingredients

2 tablespoons garlic, minced
3 tablespoons fresh Italian parsley, finely chopped
¼ cup extra-virgin olive oil
½ cup lemon juice
1 teaspoon salt
2 pounds (907 g) jumbo shrimp (21 to 25), peeled and deveined
Special Equipment:
4 wooden skewers, soaked in water for at least 30 minutes

Directions

1. Whisk together the garlic, parsley, olive oil, lemon juice, and salt in a large bowl.
2. Add the shrimp to the bowl and toss well, making sure the shrimp are coated in the marinade. Set aside to sit for 15 minutes.
3. When ready, skewer the shrimps by piercing through the center. You can place about 5 to 6 shrimps on each skewer.
4. Preheat the grill to high heat.
5. Grill the shrimp for 4 to 6 minutes, flipping the shrimp halfway through, or until the shrimp are pink on the outside and opaque in the center. Serve hot.

Per Serving

calories: 401 | fat: 17.8g | protein: 56.9g | carbs: 3.9g | fiber: 0g | sodium: 1223mg

Garlic Shrimp with Mushrooms

Prep Time: 10 minutes | **Cooking Time:** 15 minutes | **Servings:** 4

Ingredients

1 pound (454 g) fresh shrimp, peeled, deveined, and patted dry
1 teaspoon salt
1 cup extra-virgin olive oil
8 large garlic cloves, thinly sliced
4 ounces (113 g) sliced mushrooms (shiitake, baby bella, or button)
½ teaspoon red pepper flakes
¼ cup chopped fresh flat-leaf Italian parsley

Directions

1. In a bowl, season the shrimp with salt. Set aside.
2. Heat the olive oil in a large skillet over medium-low heat.
3. Add the garlic and cook for 3 to 4 minutes until fragrant, stirring occasionally.
4. Sauté the mushrooms for 5 minutes, or until they start to exude their juices. Stir in the shrimp and sprinkle with red pepper flakes and sauté for 3 to 4 minutes more, or until the shrimp start to turn pink.
5. Remove the skillet from the heat and add the parsley. Stir to combine and serve warm.

Per Serving

calories: 619 | fat: 55.5g | protein: 24.1g | carbs: 3.7g | fiber: 0g | sodium: 735mg

Lemony Shrimp with Orzo Salad

Prep Time: 10 minutes | **Cooking Time:** 22 minutes | **Servings:** 4

Ingredients

1 cup orzo
1 hothouse cucumber, deseeded and chopped
½ cup finely diced red onion
2 tablespoons extra-virgin olive oil
2 pounds (907 g) shrimp, peeled and deveined
3 lemons, juiced
Salt and freshly ground black pepper, to taste
¾ cup crumbled feta cheese
2 tablespoons dried dill
1 cup chopped fresh flat-leaf parsley

Directions

1. Bring a large pot of water to a boil. Add the orzo and cook covered for 15 to 18 minutes, or until the orzo is tender. Transfer to a colander to drain and set aside to cool.
2. Mix the cucumber and red onion in a bowl. Set aside.
3. Heat the olive oil in a medium skillet over medium heat until it shimmers.
4. Reduce the heat, add the shrimp, and cook each side for 2 minutes until cooked through.
5. Add the cooked shrimp to the bowl of cucumber and red onion. Mix in the cooked orzo and lemon juice and toss to combine. Sprinkle with salt and pepper. Scatter the top with the feta cheese and dill. Garnish with the parsley and serve immediately.

Per Serving

calories: 565 | fat: 17.8g | protein: 63.3g | carbs: 43.9g | fiber: 4.1g | sodium: 2225mg

Spicy Grilled Shrimp with Lemon Wedges

Prep Time: 15 minutes | **Cooking Time:** 6 minutes | **Servings:** 6

Ingredients

1 large clove garlic, crushed
1 teaspoon coarse salt
1 teaspoon paprika
½ teaspoon cayenne pepper
2 teaspoons lemon juice
2tablespoons plus 1 teaspoon olive oil, divided
2 pounds (907 g) large shrimp, peeled and deveined
8 wedges lemon, for garnish

Directions

1. Preheat the grill to medium heat.
2. Stir together the garlic, salt, paprika, cayenne pepper, lemon juice, and 2 tablespoons of olive oil in a small bowl until a paste forms. Add the shrimp and toss until well coated.
3. Grease the grill grates lightly with remaining 1 teaspoon of olive oil.
4. Grill the shrimp for 4 to 6 minutes, flipping the shrimp halfway through, or until the shrimp is totally pink and opaque.
5. Garnish the shrimp with lemon wedges and serve hot.

Per Serving

calories: 163 | fat: 5.8g | protein: 25.2g | carbs: 2.8g | fiber: 0.4g | sodium: 585mg

Grilled Tilapia with Mango Salsa (Spanish)

Prep Time: 45 minutes **Cooking Time:** 10 minutes
Servings: 2

Ingredients

1/3 cup extra virgin olive oil	1 tablespoon chopped fresh parsley
1 tablespoon lemon juice	1 clove of garlic, minced
1 teaspoon dried basil	1 teaspoon ground black pepper
1/2 teaspoon salt	
2 tilapia fillets (1 oz. each)	1 large ripe mango, peeled, pitted and diced
1/2 red pepper, diced	
2 tablespoons chopped red onion	1 tablespoon chopped fresh coriander
1 jalapeño pepper, seeded and minced	2 tablespoons lime juice
1 tablespoon lemon juice	salt and pepper to taste

Directions

1. Mix extra virgin olive oil, 1 tablespoon lemon juice, parsley, garlic, basil, 1 teaspoon pepper, and 1/2 teaspoon salt in a bowl, then pour into a resealable plastic bag. Add the tilapia fillets, cover with the marinade, remove excess air, and close the bag. Marinate in the fridge for 1 hour.
2. Prepare the mango salsa by combining the mango, red pepper, red onion, coriander, and jalapeño pepper in a bowl. Add the lime juice and 1 tablespoon lemon juice and mix well. Season with salt and pepper and keep until serving. Preheat a grill over medium heat and lightly oil.
3. Remove the tilapia from the marinade and remove the excess. Discard the rest of the marinade. Grill the fillets until the fish is no longer translucent in the middle and flake easily with the fork for 3 to 4 minutes on each side, depending on the thickness of the fillets. Serve the tilapia topped with mango salsa.

Nutrition: 634 calories 40.2 grams of fat 33.4 g carbohydrates 36.3 g of protein 62 mg cholesterol 697 mg of sodium.

Asparagus Smoked Salmon (Spanish)

Prep Time: 15 minutes **Cooking Time:** 5 hours
Servings: 6

Ingredients

1 tablespoon extra-virgin olive oil	1 cup heavy (whipping) cream
	6 large eggs
2 teaspoons chopped fresh dill, plus additional for garnish	½ teaspoon kosher salt
¼ teaspoon freshly ground black pepper	1 1/2 cups shredded Havarti or Monterey Jack cheese
6 ounces smoked salmon, flaked	12 ounces asparagus, trimmed and sliced

Directions

1. Brush butter into a cooker Whisk in the heavy cream with eggs, dill, salt, and pepper. Stir in the cheese and asparagus. Gently fold in the salmon and then pour the mixture into the prepared insert. Cover and cook on low or 3 hours on high. Serve warm,

Nutrition: Calories 388 Fat 19 Carbs 1.0 Protein 21

One-Pot Seafood Chowder (Greek)

Prep Time: 10 minutes **Cooking Time:** 10 minutes
Servings: 3

Ingredients

3 cans coconut milk	1 tablespoon garlic, minced
3 cans clams, chopped	1 package fresh shrimps, shelled and deveined
2 cans shrimps, canned	
Salt and pepper to taste	1 can corn, drained
4 large potatoes, diced	2 carrots, peeled and chopped
	2 celery stalks, chopped

Directions

1. Place all in a pot and give a good stir to mix everything.
2. Close the lid and turn on the heat to medium.
3. Bring to a boil and allow to simmer for 10 minutes.
4. Place in individual containers.
5. Put a label and store in the fridge.
6. Allow to warm at room temperature before heating in the microwave oven.

Nutrition: Calories: 532; Carbs: 92.5g; Protein: 25.3g; Fat: 6.7g

Cedar Planked Salmon (Greek)

Prep Time: 15 minutes **Cooking Time:** 20 minutes
Servings: 6

Ingredients

2 untreated cedar boards	1/4 cup chopped green onions
1/3 cup of vegetable oil	
1/3 cup soy sauce	1 1/2 tablespoon rice vinegar
1 teaspoon finely chopped garlic	1 tbsp grated fresh ginger root
1 teaspoon sesame oil	2 skinless salmon fillets

Directions

1. Soak the cedar boards in hot water for at least 1 hour. Enjoy longer if you have time.
2. Combine vegetable oil, rice vinegar, sesame oil, soy sauce, green onions, ginger, and garlic in a shallow dish. Place the salmon fillets in the marinade and turn them over to coat them. Cover and marinate for a minimum of 15 minutes or a maximum of one hour.
3. Preheat an outside grill over medium heat. Place the shelves on the rack. The boards are ready when they start to smoke a little.
4. Place the salmon fillets on the shelves and discard the marinade — cover and grill for about 20 minutes. The fish is cooked if you can peel it with a fork.

Nutrition: 678 calories 45.8 g fat 1.7 g carbohydrates 61.3 g of protein 179 mg cholesterol 981 mg of sodium

Chapter 9
Fruits and Desserts

Roasted Orange Rice Pudding

Prep Time: 10 minutes | **Cooking Time:** 19 to 20 minutes | Servings: 6

Ingredients

2 medium oranges
2 teaspoons extra-virgin olive oil
⅛ teaspoon kosher salt
2 large eggs
2 cups unsweetened almond milk
1 cup orange juice
1 cup uncooked instant brown rice
¼ cup honey
½ tbsp ground cinnamon
1 teaspoon vanilla extract
Cooking spray

Directions

1. Preheat the oven to 450°F (235°C). Spritz a large, rimmed baking sheet with cooking spray. Set aside.
2. Slice the unpeeled oranges into ¼-inch rounds. Brush with the oil and sprinkle with salt. Place the slices on the baking sheet and roast for 4 minutes. Flip the slices and roast for 4 more minutes, or until they begin to brown. Remove from the oven and set aside.
3. Crack the eggs into a medium bowl. In a medium saucepan, whisk together the milk, orange juice, rice, honey and cinnamon. Bring to a boil over medium-high heat, stirring constantly. Reduce the heat to medium- low and simmer for 10 minutes, stirring occasionally.
4. Using a measuring cup, scoop out ½ cup of the hot rice mixture and whisk it into the eggs. While constantly stirring the mixture in the pan, slowly pour the egg mixture back into the saucepan.
5. Cook on low heat for 1 to 2 minutes, or until thickened, stirring constantly. Remove from the heat and stir in the vanilla. Let the pudding stand for a few minutes for the rice to soften. The rice will be cooked but slightly chewy. For softer rice, let stand for another half hour. Top with the roasted oranges. Serve warm or at room temperature.

Per Serving
calories: 204 | fat: 6.0g | protein: 5.0g | carbs: 34.0g | fiber: 1.0g | sodium: 148mg

Rice Pudding with Roasted Orange

Prep Time: 5 minutes | **Cooking Time:** 8 to 10 minutes | Servings: 14 to 16

Ingredients

1 cup hulled sesame seeds
1 cup sugar
8 tablespoons almond butter
2 large eggs
1¼ cups flour

Directions

1. Preheat the oven to 350°F (180°C).
2. Toast the sesame seeds on a baking sheet for 3 minutes. Set aside and let cool. Using a mixer, whisk together the sugar and butter. Add the eggs one at a time until well blended. Add the flour and toasted sesame seeds and mix until well blended. Drop spoonfuls of cookie dough onto a baking sheet and form them into round balls, about 1-inch in diameter, similar to a walnut.
3. Put in the oven and bake for 5 to 7 minutes, or until golden brown. Let the cookies cool for 5 minutes before serving.

Per Serving calories: 218 | fat: 12.0g | protein: 4.0g | carbs: 25.0g | fiber: 2.0g | sodium: 58mg

Watermelon and Blueberry Salad

Prep Time: 5 minutes | **Cooking Time:** 0 minutes | Servings: 6 to 8

Ingredients

1 medium watermelon
1 cup fresh blueberries
⅓ cup honey
2 tablespoons lemon juice
2 tablespoons finely chopped fresh mint leaves

Directions

1. Cut the watermelon into 1-inch cubes. Put them in a bowl.
2. Evenly distribute the blueberries over the watermelon.
3. In a separate bowl, whisk together the honey, lemon juice and mint. Drizzle the mint dressing over the watermelon and blueberries. Serve cold.

Per Serving calories: 238 | fat: 1.0g | protein: 4.0g | carbs: 61.0g | fiber: 3.0g | sodium: 11mg

Walnut and Date Balls

Prep Time: 5 minutes | **Cooking Time:** 8 to 10 minutes | **Servings:** 6 to 8

Ingredients

1 cup walnuts
1 cup unsweetened shredded coconut
14 medjool dates, pitted
8 tablespoons almond butter

Directions

1. Preheat the oven to 350°F (180°C).
2. Put the walnuts on a baking sheet and toast in the oven for 5 minutes.
3. Put the shredded coconut on a clean baking sheet. Toast for about 3 to 5 minutes, or until it turns golden brown. Once done, remove it from the oven and put it in a shallow bowl.
4. In a food processor, process the toasted walnuts until they have a medium chop. Transfer the chopped walnuts into a medium bowl.
5. Add the dates and butter to the food processor and blend until the dates become a thick paste. Pour the chopped walnuts into the food processor with the dates and pulse just until the mixture is combined, about 5 to 7 pulses.
6. Remove the mixture from the food processor and scrape it into a large bowl. To make the balls, spoon 1 to 2 tablespoons of the date mixture into the palm of your hand and roll around between your hands until you form a ball. Put the ball on a clean, lined baking sheet. Repeat until all the mixture is formed into balls.
7. Roll each ball in the toasted coconut until the outside of the ball is coated. Put the ball back on the baking sheet and repeat.
8. Put all the balls into the refrigerator for 20 minutes before serving. Store any leftovers in the refrigerator in an airtight container.

Per Serving

calories: 489 | fat: 35.0g | protein: 5.0g | carbs: 48.0g | fiber: 7.0g | sodium: 114mg

Coconut Blueberries with Brown Rice

Prep Time: 55 minutes | **Cooking Time:** 10 minutes | **Servings:** 4

Ingredients

1 cup fresh blueberries
2 cups unsweetened coconut milk
1 teaspoon ground ginger
¼ cup maple syrup
Sea salt, to taste
2 cups cooked brown rice

Directions

1. Put all the , except for the brown rice, in a pot. Stir to combine well.
2. Cook over medium-high heat for 7 minutes or until the blueberries are tender.
3. Pour in the brown rice and cook for 3 more minute or until the rice is soft. Stir constantly.
4. Serve immediately.

Per Serving

calories: 470 | fat: 24.8g | protein: 6.2g | carbs: 60.1g | fiber: 5.0g | sodium: 75mg

Bars with bananas, cranberries, and oats

Prep Time: 15 minutes | **Cooking Time:** 40 minutes | **Makes** 16 bars

Ingredients

2 tablespoon extra-virgin olive oil
2 medium ripe bananas, mashed
½ cup almond butter
½ cup maple syrup
⅓ cup dried cranberries
1½ cups old-fashioned rolled oats
¼ cup oat flour
¼ cup ground flaxseed
¼ teaspoon ground cloves
½ cup shredded coconut
½ teaspoon ground cinnamon
1 teaspoon vanilla extract

Directions

1. Preheat the oven to 400°F (205°C). Line a 8-inch square pan with parchment paper, then grease with olive oil.
2. Combine the mashed bananas, almond butter, and maple syrup in a bowl. Stir to mix well.
3. Mix in the remaining and stir to mix well until thick and sticky.
4. Spread the mixture evenly on the square pan with a spatula, then bake in the preheated oven for 40 minutes or until a toothpick inserted in the center comes out clean.
5. Remove them from the oven and slice into 16 bars to serve.

Per Serving calories: 145 | fat: 7.2g | protein: 3.1g | carbs: 18.9g | fiber: 2.0g | sodium: 3mg

Chocolate and Avocado Mousse

Prep Time: 40 minutes | **Cooking Time:** 5 minutes | **Servings:** 4 to 6

Ingredients

8 ounces (227 g) dark chocolate (60% cocoa or higher), chopped
¼ cup unsweetened coconut milk
2 tablespoons coconut oil
2 ripe avocados, deseeded
¼ cup raw honey
Sea salt, to taste

Directions

1. Put the chocolate in a saucepan. Pour in the coconut milk and add the coconut oil.
2. Cook for 3 minutes or until the chocolate and coconut oil melt. Stir constantly.
3. Put the avocado in a food processor, then drizzle with honey and melted chocolate. Pulse to combine until smooth.
4. Pour the mixture in a serving bowl, then sprinkle with salt. Refrigerate to chill for 30 minutes and serve.

Per Serving

calories: 654 | fat: 46.8g | protein: 7.2g | carbs: 55.9g | fiber: 9.0g | sodium: 112mg

Berry and Rhubarb Cobbler

Prep Time: 15 minutes | **Cooking Time:** 35 minutes | **Servings:** 8

Ingredients

Cobbler:
1 cup fresh raspberries
2 cups fresh blueberries
1 cup sliced (½-inch) rhubarb pieces
1 tablespoon arrowroot powder
¼ cup unsweetened apple juice
2 tablespoons melted coconut oil

Topping:
1 cup almond flour
1 tablespoon arrowroot powder
½ cup shredded coconut
¼ cup raw honey
½ cup coconut oil
¼ cup raw honey

Directions

Make the Cobbler

1. Preheat the oven to 350°F (180°C). Grease a baking dish with melted coconut oil.
2. Combine the for the cobbler in a large bowl. Stir to mix well.
3. Spread the mixture in the single layer on the baking dish. Set aside.

Make the Topping

4. Combine the almond flour, arrowroot powder, and coconut in a bowl. Stir to mix well.
5. Fold in the honey and coconut oil. Stir with a fork until the mixture crumbled.
6. Spread the topping over the cobbler, then bake in the preheated oven for 35 minutes or until frothy and golden brown.
7. Serve immediately.

Per Serving

calories: 305 | fat: 22.1g | protein: 3.2g | carbs: 29.8g | fiber: 4.0g | sodium: 3mg

Chocolate, Almond, and Cherry Clusters

Prep Time: 15 minutes | **Cooking Time:** 3 minutes | Makes 10 clusters

Ingredients

1 cup dark chocolate (60% cocoa or higher), chopped
1 tablespoon coconut oil
½ cup dried cherries
1 cup roasted salted almonds

Directions

1. Line a baking sheet with parchment paper.
2. Melt the chocolate and coconut oil in a saucepan for 3 minutes. Stir constantly.
3. Turn off the heat and mix in the cherries and almonds.
4. Drop the mixture on the baking sheet with a spoon. Place the sheet in the refrigerator and chill for at least 1 hour or until firm.
5. Serve chilled.

Per Serving

calories: 197 | fat: 13.2g | protein: 4.1g | carbs: 17.8g | fiber: 4.0g | sodium: 57mg

Citrus Cranberry and Quinoa Energy Bites

Prep Time: 25 minutes | **Cooking Time:** 0 minutes | Makes 12 bites

Ingredients

2 tablespoons almond butter
2 tablespoons maple syrup
¾ cup cooked quinoa
1 tablespoon dried cranberries
1 tablespoon chia seeds
¼ cup ground almonds
¼ cup sesame seeds, toasted
Zest of 1 orange
½ teaspoon vanilla extract

Directions

1. Line a baking sheet with parchment paper.
2. Combine the butter and maple syrup in a bowl. Stir to mix well.
3. Fold in the remaining and stir until the mixture holds together and smooth.
4. Divide the mixture into 12 equal parts, then shape each part into a ball.
5. Arrange the balls on the baking sheet, then refrigerate for at least 15 minutes.
6. Serve chilled.

Per Serving (1 bite)

calories: 110 | fat: 10.8g | protein: 3.1g | carbs: 4.9g | fiber: 3.0g | sodium: 211mg

Blueberry and Oat Crisp

Prep Time: 15 minutes | **Cooking Time:** 20 minutes | **Servings:** 4

Ingredients

2 tablespoons coconut oil, melted, plus more for greasing
4 cups fresh blueberries
Juice of ½ lemon
2 teaspoons lemon zest
¼ cup maple syrup
1 cup gluten-free rolled oats
½ cup chopped pecans
½ teaspoon ground cinnamon
Sea salt, to taste

Directions

1. Preheat the oven to 350°F (180°C). Grease a baking sheet with coconut oil.
2. Combine the blueberries, lemon juice and zest, and maple syrup in a bowl. Stir to mix well, then spread the mixture on the baking sheet.
3. Combine the remaining in a small bowl. Stir to mix well. Pour the mixture over the blueberries mixture.
4. Bake in the preheated oven for 20 minutes or until the oats are golden brown.
5. Serve immediately with spoons.

Per Serving

calories: 496 | fat: 32.9g | protein: 5.1g | carbs: 50.8g | fiber: 7.0g | sodium: 41mg

Honey Baked Cinnamon Apples

Prep Time: 5 minutes | **Cooking Time:** 20 minutes | **Servings:** 2

Ingredients

1 teaspoon extra-virgin olive oil
4 firm apples, peeled, cored, and sliced
½ teaspoon salt
1½ teaspoons ground cinnamon, divided
2 tablespoons unsweetened almond milk
2 tablespoons honey

Directions

1. Preheat the oven to 375°F (190°C). Coat a small casserole dish with the olive oil.
2. Toss the apple slices with the salt and ½ teaspoon of the cinnamon in a medium bowl. Spread the apples in the prepared casserole dish and bake in the preheated oven for 20 minutes. Meanwhile, in a small saucepan, heat the milk, honey, and remaining 1 teaspoon of cinnamon over medium heat, stirring frequently. When it reaches a simmer, remove the pan from the heat and cover to keep warm. Divide the apple slices between 2 plates and pour the sauce over the apples. Serve warm.

Per Serving

calories: 310 | fat: 3.4g | protein: 1.7g | carbs: 68.5g | fiber: 12.6g | sodium: 593mg

Strawberries with Balsamic Vinegar

Prep Time: 5 minutes | **Cooking Time:** 0 minutes | **Servings:** 2

Ingredients

2 cups strawberries, hulled and sliced
2 tablespoons sugar
2 tbsp balsamic vinegar

Directions

1. Place the sliced strawberries in a bowl, sprinkle with the sugar, and drizzle lightly with the balsamic vinegar.
2. Toss to combine well and allow to sit for about 10 minutes before serving.

Per Serving calories: 92 | fat: 0.4g | protein: 1.0g | carbs: 21.7g | fiber: 2.9g | sodium: 5mg

Frozen Mango Raspberry Delight

Prep Time: 5 minutes | **Cooking Time:** 0 minutes | **Servings:** 2

Ingredients

3 cups frozen raspberries
1 mango, peeled and pitted
1 peach, peeled and pitted
1 teaspoon honey

Directions

1. Place all the into a blender and purée, adding some water as needed.
2. Put in the freezer for 10 minutes to firm up if desired. Serve chilled or at room temperature.

Per Serving

calories: 276 | fat: 2.1g | protein: 4.5g | carbs: 60.3g | fiber: 17.5g | sodium: 4mg

Grilled Stone Fruit with Honey

Prep Time: 8 minutes | **Cooking Time:** 6 minutes | **Servings:** 2

Ingredients

3 apricots, halved and pitted
2 plums, halved and pitted
2 peaches, halved and pitted
½ cup low-fat ricotta cheese
2 tablespoons honey
Cooking spray

Directions

1. Preheat the grill to medium heat. Spray the grill grates with cooking spray.
2. Arrange the fruit, cut side down, on the grill, and cook for 2 to 3 minutes per side, or until lightly charred and softened.
3. Serve warm with a sprinkle of cheese and a drizzle of honey.

Per Serving

calories: 298 | fat: 7.8g | protein: 11.9g | carbs: 45.2g | fiber: 4.3g | sodium: 259mg

Mascarpone Baked Pears

Prep Time: 10 minutes | **Cooking Time:** 20 minutes | **Servings:** 2

Ingredients

2 ripe pears, peeled
1 tablespoon plus
2 teaspoons honey, divided
1 teaspoon vanilla, divided
¼ teaspoon ground coriander
¼ teaspoon ginger
¼ cup minced walnuts
¼ cup mascarpone cheese
Pinch salt
Cooking spray

Directions

1. Preheat the oven to 350°F (180°C). Spray a small baking dish with cooking spray.
2. Slice the pears in half lengthwise. Using a spoon, scoop out the core from each piece. Put the pears, cut side up, in the baking dish.
3. Whisk together 1 tablespoon of honey, ½ teaspoon of vanilla, ginger, and coriander in a small bowl. Pour this mixture evenly over the pear halves.
4. Scatter the walnuts over the pear halves.
5. Bake in the preheated oven for 20 minutes, or until the pears are golden and you're able to pierce them easily with a knife.
6. Meanwhile, combine the mascarpone cheese with the remaining 2 teaspoons of honey, ½ teaspoon of vanilla, and a pinch of salt. Stir to combine well.
7. Divide the mascarpone among the warm pear halves and serve.

Per Serving

calories: 308 | fat: 16.0g | protein: 4.1g | carbs: 42.7g | fiber: 6.0g | sodium: 88mg

Sweet Spiced Pumpkin Pudding

Prep Time: 2 hours 10 minutes | **Cooking Time:** 0 minutes | **Servings:** 6

Ingredients

1 cup pure pumpkin purée	½ teaspoon ground ginger
2 cups unsweetened coconut milk	Pinch cloves
1 teaspoon ground cinnamon	¼ cup pure maple syrup
¼ teaspoon ground nutmeg	2 tablespoons chopped pecans, for garnish

Directions

1. Combine all the , except for the chopped pecans, in a large bowl. Stir to mix well.
2. Wrap the bowl in plastic and refrigerate for at least 2 hours.
3. Remove the bowl from the refrigerator and discard the plastic. Spread the pudding with pecans and serve chilled.

Per Serving

calories: 249 | fat: 21.1g | protein: 2.8g | carbs: 17.2g | fiber: 3.0g | sodium: 46mg

Mango and Coconut Frozen Pie

Prep Time: 1 hour 10 minutes | **Cooking Time:** 0 minutes | **Servings:** 8

Ingredients

Crust:	**Filling:**
1 cup cashews	2 large mangoes, peeled and chopped
½ cup rolled oats	½ cup unsweetened shredded coconut
1 cup soft pitted dates	½ cup water
1 cup unsweetened coconut milk	

Directions

1. Combine the for the crust in a food processor. Pulse to combine well.
2. Pour the mixture in an 8-inch springform pan, then press to coat the bottom. Set aside.
3. Combine the for the filling in the food processor, then pulse to purée until smooth.
4. Pour the filling over the crust, then use a spatula to spread the filling evenly. Put the pan in the freeze for 30 minutes.
5. Remove the pan from the freezer and allow to sit for 15 minutes under room temperature before serving.

Per Serving (1 slice)

calories: 426 | fat: 28.2g | protein: 8.1g | carbs: 14.9g | fiber: 6.0g | sodium: 174mg

Mini Nuts and Fruits Crumble

Prep Time: 15 minutes | **Cooking Time:** 15 minutes | **Servings:** 6

Ingredients

Topping:	**Filling:**
¼ cup coarsely chopped hazelnuts	6 fresh figs, quartered
1 cup coarsely chopped walnuts	2 nectarines, pitted and sliced
1 teaspoon ground cinnamon	1 cup fresh blueberries
Sea salt, to taste	2 teaspoons lemon zest
1 tablespoon melted coconut oil	½ cup raw honey
	1 teaspoon vanilla extract

Directions

Make the Topping

1. Combine the for the topping in a bowl. Stir to mix well. Set aside until ready to use.

Make the Filling:

2. Preheat the oven to 375ºF (190ºC).
3. Combine the for the fillings in a bowl. Stir to mix well.
4. Divide the filling in six ramekins, then divide and top with nut topping. Bake in the preheated oven for 15 minutes or until the topping is lightly browned and the filling is frothy.
5. Serve immediately.

Per Serving

calories: 336 | fat: 18.8g | protein: 6.3g | carbs: 41.9g | fiber: 6.0g | sodium: 31mg

Cozy Superfood Hot Chocolate

Prep Time: 5 minutes | **Cooking Time:** 8 minutes | **Servings:** 2

Ingredients

2 cups unsweetened almond milk	1 teaspoon ground cinnamon
1 tablespoon avocado oil	1 teaspoon ground ginger
1 tablespoon collagen protein powder	1 teaspoon vanilla extract
2 teaspoons coconut sugar	½ teaspoon ground turmeric
2 tablespoons cocoa powder	Dash salt
	Dash cayenne pepper

Directions

1. In a small saucepan over medium heat, warm the almond milk and avocado oil for about 7 minutes, stirring frequently.
2. Fold in the protein powder, which will only properly dissolve in a heated liquid. Stir in the coconut sugar and cocoa powder until melted and dissolved.
3. Carefully transfer the warm liquid into a blender, along with the cinnamon, ginger, vanilla, turmeric, salt, and cayenne pepper (if desired). Blend for 15 seconds until frothy. Serve immediately.

Per Serving

calories: 217 | fat: 11.0g | protein: 11.2g | carbs: 14.8g | fiber: 6.0g | sodium: 202mg

Chapter 10
Sauces Recipes, Dips Recipes, & Dressings Recipes

Cucumber Cream Dip

Prep Time: 10 minutes | **Cooking Time:** 0 minutes | Servings: 6

Ingredients

1 medium cucumber, peeled and grated
¼ teaspoon salt
1 cup plain Greek yogurt
2 garlic cloves, minced
1 tablespoon extra-virgin olive oil
1 tablespoon freshly squeezed lemon juice
¼ teaspoon freshly ground black pepper

Directions

1. Place the grated cucumber in a colander set over a bowl and season with salt. Allow the cucumber to stand for 10 minutes. Using your hands, squeeze out as much liquid from the cucumber as possible. Transfer the grated cucumber to a medium bowl.
2. Add the yogurt, garlic, olive oil, lemon juice, and pepper to the bowl and stir until well blended.
3. Cover the bowl with plastic wrap and refrigerate for at least 2 hours to blend the flavors. Serve chilled.

Per Serving (¼ cup)

calories: 47 | fat: 2.8g | protein: 4.2g | carbs: 2.7g | fiber: 0g | sodium: 103mg

Italian Dressing

Prep Time: 5 minutes | **Cooking Time:** 0 minutes | Servings: 12

Ingredients

½ cup extra-virgin olive oil
¼ cup red wine vinegar
1 teaspoon dried Italian seasoning
1 teaspoon Dijon mustard
¼ teaspoon salt
¼ teaspoon freshly ground black pepper
1 garlic clove, minced

Directions

1. Place all the in a mason jar and cover. Shake vigorously for 1 minute until completely mixed.
2. Store in the refrigerator for up to 1 week.

Per Serving (1 tablespoon)

calories: 80 | fat: 8.6g | protein: 0g | carbs: 0g | fiber: 0g | sodium: 51mg

Cauliflower Dressing in Ranch Style

Prep Time: 10 minutes | **Cooking Time:** 0 minutes | Servings: 8

Ingredients

2 cups frozen cauliflower, thawed
½ cup unsweetened plain almond milk
2 tablespoons apple cider vinegar
2 tbsp extra-virgin olive oil
1 garlic clove, peeled
2 teaspoons finely chopped fresh parsley
2 teaspoons finely chopped scallions (both white and green parts)
1 teaspoon finely chopped fresh dill
½ teaspoon onion powder
½ teaspoon Dijon mustard
½ teaspoon salt
¼ teaspoon freshly ground black pepper

Directions

1. Place all the in a blender and pulse until creamy and smooth.
2. Serve immediately, or transfer to an airtight container to refrigerate for up to 3 days.

Per Serving (2 tablespoons)

calories: 41 | fat: 3.6g | protein: 1.0g | carbs: 1.9g | fiber: 1.1g | sodium: 148mg

Asian-Inspired Vinaigrette

Prep Time: 5 minutes | **Cooking Time:** 0 minutes | Servings: 2

Ingredients

¼ cup extra-virgin olive oil
3 tablespoons apple cider vinegar
1 garlic clove, minced
1 tablespoon peeled and grated fresh ginger
1 tablespoon chopped fresh cilantro
1 tablespoon freshly squeezed lime juice
½ teaspoon sriracha

Directions

1. Add all the in a small bowl and stir to mix well.
2. Serve immediately, or store covered in the refrigerator and shake before using.

Per Serving

calories: 251 | fat: 26.8g | protein: 0g | carbs: 1.8g | fiber: 0.7g | sodium: 3mg

Fruit Dessert Nachos (Italian)

Prep Time: 9 minutes **Cooking Time:** 13 minutes
Servings: 3

1tbsp. sugar	A pinch of ground cinnamon
1 ½ whole wheat tortillas	
¼ cup light cream cheese, softened	2½ tbsp. light dairy sour cream
½ tsp. orange peel, finely shredded	Cooking spray
1 tbsp. orange juice plus 30	1 cup assorted melon, chopped

Directions

1. Preheat the oven at 425°F.
2. Grease a large baking sheet with cooking spray.
3. Take a small bowl, combine the cinnamon and half of the sugar.
4. Take the tortillas and lightly coat them with cooking spray. Sprinkle each side with the sugar mix.
5. Cut the tortillas to make 8 wedges and place them on the baking sheet.
6. Bake the tortillas until they turn lightly browned, for 7–8 minutes. Turn once halfway.
7. Meanwhile, take a small-sized bowl and mix the sour cream, cream cheese, 30 g. orange juice, orange peel, and the remaining sugar. Once smooth, set it aside.
8. Take a medium bowl and combine melon and the remaining orange juice.
9. Serve by adding a spoon of melon mix on each tortilla wedge and 1 spoon of cream cheese mixture.

Nutrition: Calories: 121 Protein: 5.3 g. Fat: 5.2 g.

Ricotta Ramekins (Italian)

Prep Time: 10 minutes **Cooking Time:** 1 hour
Servings: 4

Ingredients

6 eggs, whisked	½ pounds ricotta cheese, soft
½ tsp. baking powder	
½ pound stevia	1 tsp. vanilla extract
Cooking spray	

Directions

1. In a bowl, mix the eggs with the ricotta and the other except the cooking spray and whisk well.
2. Grease 4 ramekins with the cooking spray, pour the ricotta cream in each and bake at 360F for 1 hour.
3. Serve cold.

Nutrition: Calories 180, Fat: 5.3g, Fiber: 5.4g, Carbs: 11.5g, Protein: 4g

Decadent Croissant Bread Pudding (Italian)

Prep Time: 5 minutes **Cooking Time:** 15 minutes
Servings: 6

Ingredients

1/2 cup double cream	1 teaspoon cinnamon
6 tablespoons honey	A pinch of salt
1/4 cup rum, divided	2 eggs, whisked
A pinch of grated nutmeg	8 croissants, torn into pieces
1 cup pistachios, toasted and chopped	1 teaspoon vanilla essence

Directions

1. Spritz a baking pan with cooking spray and set it aside.
2. In a mixing bowl, whisk the eggs, double cream, honey, rum, cinnamon, salt, nutmeg, and vanilla; whisk until everything is well incorporated.
3. Place the croissants in the prepared baking dish. Pour the custard over your croissants. Fold in the pistachios and press with a wide spatula.
4. Add 1 cup of water and metal rack to the inner pot of your Instant Pot. Lower the baking dish onto the rack.
5. Secure the lid. Choose the "Manual" mode and cook for 12 minutes at High pressure. Once cooking is complete, use a quick pressure release; carefully remove the lid.
6. Serve at room temperature or cold. Bon appétit!

Nutrition: 513 Calories; 27.9g Fat; 50.3g Carbohydrates; 12.5g Protein; 25.7g Sugars; 3.8g Fiber

Poached Apples with Greek Yogurt and Granola(Greek)

Prep Time: 5 minutes **Cooking Time:** 15 minutes
Servings: 4

Ingredients

4 medium-sized apples, peeled	1 vanilla bean
1 cinnamon stick	1/2 cup brown sugar
1/2 cup 2% Greek yogurt	1/2 cup cranberry juice
1/2 cup granola	1 cup water

Directions

1. Secure the lid. Choose the "Manual" mode and cook for 5 minutes at High pressure. Once cooking is complete, use a natural pressure release for 5 minutes; carefully remove the lid. Reserve poached apples.
2. Press the "Sauté" button and let the sauce simmer on "Less" mode until it has thickened.
3. Place the apples in serving bowls. Add the syrup and top each apple with granola and Greek yogurt. Enjoy!

Nutrition: 247 Calories; 3.1g Fat; 52.6g Carbohydrates; 3.5g Protein; 40g Sugars; 5.3g Fiber

Rhubarb Strawberry Crunch (Greek)

Prep Time: 15 minutes **Cooking Time:** 45 minutes
Servings: 18

Ingredients

1 cup of white sugar
3 cups fresh strawberries, sliced
1 cup butter
1 cup packed brown sugar
3 tbsps. all-purpose flour
1 ½ cup flour
3 cups rhubarb, cut into cubes
1 cup oatmeal

Directions

1. Preheat the oven to 190°C.
2. Combine the white sugar, 3 tbsps. of flour, strawberries, and rhubarb in a large bowl.
3. Place the mixture in a 9x13-inch baking dish.
4. Mix 1 ½ cups of flour, brown sugar, butter, and oats until a crumbly texture is obtained. You may want to use a blender for this.
5. Crumble the mixture of rhubarb and strawberry.
6. Bake for 45 minutes.

Nutrition: Calories: 253 Fat: 10.8 g. Protein: 2.3 g.

Vanilla Cream (Italian)

Prep Time: 2 hours **Cooking Time:** 10 minutes
Servings: 4

Ingredients

1 cup almond milk
2tbsps. cinnamon powder
1 tsp. vanilla extract
1cup coconut cream
2 cups coconut sugar

Directions

1. Heat a pan with the almond milk over medium heat, add the rest of the , whisk, and cook for 10 minutes more.
2. Divide the mix into bowls, cool down, and keep in the fridge for 2 hours before serving.

Nutrition: Calories: 254 Fat: 7.5 g. Protein: 9.5 g.

Cocoa Almond Pudding (Spanish)

Prep Time: 10 minutes **Cooking Time:** 10 minutes
Servings: 4

Ingredients

2 tbsps. coconut sugar
3 tbsps. coconut flour
½ tsp. vanilla extract
2eggs, whisked
2 tbsps. cocoa powder
2 cups almond milk

Directions

1. Fill the milk in a pan, add the cocoa and the other, whisk, simmer over medium heat for 10 minutes, pour into small cups, and serve cold.

Nutrition: Calories: 385 Fat: 31.7 g. Protein: 7.3 g.

Nutmeg Cream (Greek)

Prep Time: 10 minutes **Cooking Time:** 0 minutes
Servings: 6

Ingredients

2cups almond milk
2 tsps. vanilla extract
1cup walnuts, chopped
1 tsp. nutmeg, ground
4 tsps. coconut sugar

Directions

1. In a bowl, combine the milk with the nutmeg and the other, whisk well, divide into small cups and serve cold.

Nutrition: Calories: 243 Fat: 12.4 g. Protein: 9.7 g.

Vanilla Avocado Cream (Greek)

Prep Time: 70 minutes **Cooking Time:** 0 minutes
Servings: 4

Ingredients

1cups coconut cream
2 tbsps. coconut sugar
1tsp. vanilla extract
2 avocados, peeled, pitted, and mashed

Directions

1. Blend the cream with the avocados and the other , pulse well, divide into cups and keep in the fridge for 1 hour before serving.

Nutrition: Calories: 532 Fat: 48.2 g. Protein: 5.2 g.

Ice Cream Sandwich Dessert (Italian)

Prep Time: 20 minutes **Cooking Time:** 0 minute
Servings: 12

Ingredients

22 ice cream sandwiches
1 (12 oz.) jar caramel ice cream
1½ cups salted peanuts
16 oz. container frozen whipped topping, thawed

Directions

1. Cut a sandwich with ice in 2. Place a whole sandwich and a half sandwich on a short side of a 9x13-inch baking dish. Repeat this until the bottom is covered. Alternate the full sandwich, and the half sandwich.
2. Spread half of the whipped topping. Pour the caramel over it. Sprinkle with half the peanuts. Do layers with the rest of the ice cream sandwiches, whipped cream, and peanuts.
3. Cover and freeze for up to 2 months. Remove from the freezer 20 minutes before serving. Cut into squares.

Nutrition: Calories: 559 Fat: 28.8 g. Protein: 10 g.

Lemon-Tahini Sauce

Prep Time: 10 minutes | **Cooking Time:** 0 minutes | Makes 1 cup

Ingredients

½ cup tahini
1 garlic clove, minced
Juice and zest of 1 lemon
½ tbsp salt, plus more as needed
½ cup warm water, plus

Directions

1. Combine the tahini and garlic in a small bowl.
2. Add the lemon juice and zest and salt to the bowl and stir to mix well. Fold in the warm water and whisk until well combined and creamy. Feel free to add more warm water if you like a thinner consistency. Taste and add more salt as needed. Store the sauce in a sealed container in the refrigerator for up to 5 days.

Per Serving (¼ cup)

calories: 179 | fat: 15.5g | protein: 5.1g | carbs: 6.8g | fiber: 3.0g | sodium: 324mg

Peri-Peri Sauce

Prep Time: 10 minutes | **Cooking Time:** 5 minutes | **Servings:** 4

Ingredients

1 tomato, chopped
1 red onion, chopped
1 red bell pepper, deseeded and chopped
1 red chile, deseeded and chopped
4 garlic cloves, minced
2 tablespoons extra-virgin olive oil
Juice of 1 lemon
1 tablespoon dried oregano
1 tablespoon smoked paprika
1 teaspoon sea salt

Directions

1. Process all the in a food processor or a blender until smooth. Transfer the mixture to a small saucepan over medium-high heat and bring to a boil, stirring often.
2. Reduce the heat to medium and allow to simmer for 5 minutes until heated through. You can store the sauce in an airtight container in the refrigerator for up to 5 days.

Per Serving calories: 98 | fat: 6.5g | protein: 1.0g | carbs: 7.8g | fiber: 3.0g | sodium: 295mg

Garlic Lemon-Tahini Dressing

Prep Time: 5 minutes | **Cooking Time:** 0 minutes | **Servings:** 8 to 10

Ingredients

½ cup tahini
¼ cup extra-virgin olive oil
2 teaspoons salt
1 garlic clove, finely minced
¼ cup freshly squeezed lemon juice

Directions

1. In a glass mason jar with a lid, combine the tahini, olive oil, lemon juice, garlic, and salt. Cover and shake well until combined and creamy. Store in the refrigerator for up to 2 weeks.

Per Serving

calories: 121 | fat: 12.0g | protein: 2.0g | carbs: 3.0g | fiber: 1.0g | sodium: 479mg

Peanut Sauce with Honey

Prep Time: 5 minutes | **Cooking Time:** 0 minutes | **Servings:** 4

Ingredients

¼ cup peanut butter
1 tablespoon peeled and grated fresh ginger
1 tablespoon honey
1 tablespoon low-sodium soy sauce
1 garlic clove, minced
Juice of 1 lime
Pinch red pepper flakes

Directions

1. Whisk together all the in a small bowl until well incorporated. Transfer to an airtight container and refrigerate for up to 5 days.

Per Serving calories: 117 | fat: 7.6g | protein: 4.1g | carbs: 8.8g | fiber: 1.0g | sodium: 136mg

Cilantro-Tomato Salsa

Prep Time: 10 minutes | **Cooking Time:** 0 minutes | **Servings:** 6

Ingredients

2 or 3 medium, ripe tomatoes, diced
1 serrano pepper, seeded and minced
½ red onion, minced
¼ cup minced fresh cilantro
Juice of 1 lime
¼ teaspoon salt, plus more as needed

Directions

1. Place the tomatoes, serrano pepper, onion, cilantro, lime juice, and salt in a small bowl and mix well. Taste and add additional salt, if needed. Store in an airtight container in the refrigerator for up to 3 days.

Per Serving (¼ cup) calories: 17 | fat: 0g | protein: 1.0g | carbs: 3.9g | fiber: 1.0g | sodium: 83mg

Cheesy Pea Pesto

Prep Time: 5 minutes | **Cooking Time:** 0 minutes | **Servings:** 4

Ingredients

½ cup fresh green peas
½ cup grated Parmesan cheese
¼ cup extra-virgin olive oil
¼ cup pine nuts
¼ cup fresh basil leaves
2 garlic cloves, minced
¼ teaspoon sea salt

Directions

1. Add all the to a food processor or blender and pulse until the nuts are chopped finely.
2. Transfer to an airtight container and refrigerate for up to 2 days. You can also store it in ice cube trays in the freezer for up to 6 months.

Per Serving calories: 247 | fat: 22.8g | protein: 7.1g | carbs: 4.8g | fiber: 1.0g | sodium: 337mg

Matcha Chocolate Balls (Greek)

Prep Time: 10 minutes **Cooking Time:** 5 minutes
Servings: 15

Ingredients

1tbsp unsweetened cocoa powder
½ cup almonds
2tbsp matcha powder
½ cup pine nuts
3 tbsp oats, gluten-free
1cup dates, pitted

Directions

1. Add oats, pine nuts, almonds, and dates into a food processor and process until well combined.
2. Place matcha powder in a small dish.
3. Make small balls from mixture and coat with matcha powder.
4. Enjoy or store in refrigerator until ready to eat.

Nutrition: Calories 88, Fat 4.9g, Carbohydrates 11.3g, Sugar 7.8g, Protein 1.9g, Cholesterol 0mg

Blueberries Bowls (Greek)

Prep Time: 10 minutes **Cooking Time:** 0 minutes
Servings: 4

Ingredients

1 tsp. vanilla extract
2 cups blueberries
1 tsp. coconut sugar
8 oz. Greek yogurt

Directions

1. Mix strawberries with the vanilla and the other , toss and serve cold.

Nutrition: Calories: 343 Fat 13.4 g. Protein: 5.5 g.

Brownies (Greek)

Prep Time: 10 minutes **Cooking Time:** 25 minutes
Servings: 8

Ingredients

1 cup pecans, chopped
3 tbsps. coconut sugar
2 tsps. vanilla extract
½ tsp. baking powder
Cooking spray
cup avocado oil
2 tbsps. cocoa powder
3 eggs, whisked

Directions

1. In your food processor, combine the pecans with the coconut sugar and the other except for the cooking spray and pulse well.
2. Grease a square pan with the cooking spray, add the brownies mix, spread, introduce in the oven, bake at 350°F for 25 minutes, leave aside to cool down, slice, and serve.

Nutrition: Calories: 370 Fat: 14.3 g. Protein: 5.6 g.

Raspberries Cream Cheese Bowls (Italian)

Prep Time: 10 minutes **Cooking Time:** 25 minutes
Servings: 4

Ingredients

1tbsps. almond flour
1 cup coconut cream
3 cups raspberries
1 cup coconut sugar
8 oz. cream cheese

Directions

1. In a bowl, the flour with the cream and the other , whisk, transfer to a round pan, cook at 360°F for 25 minutes, divide into bowls and serve.

Nutrition: Calories: 429 Fat: 36.3 g. Protein: 7.8 g.

Minty Coconut Cream (Spanish)

Prep Time: 4 minutes **Cooking Time:** 0 minutes
Servings: 2

Ingredients

1banana, peeled
3 tablespoons mint
1and ½ cups coconut water
2 tablespoons stevia
2cups coconut flesh, shredded
½ avocado, pitted and peeled

Directions

1. In a blender, combine the coconut with the banana and the rest of the , pulse well, divide into cups and serve cold.

Nutrition: Calories 193; Fat 5.4 g; Fiber 3.4 g; Carbs 7.6 g; Protein 3 g

Almond Honey Ricotta Spread (Greek)

Prep Time: 7 minutes **Cooking Time:** 0 minutes
Servings: 3

Ingredients

½ cup whole milk Ricotta
¼ cup almonds, sliced
1/8 tsp. almond extract
1Peaches, sliced Hone to drizzle
¼ cup orange zest
½ tsp. honey
Bread of your choice

Directions

1. Take a medium bowl, and combine the almonds, almond extract, and Ricotta.
2. Once you have stirred it well, place it in a bowl to serve.
3. Sprinkle with the sliced almonds and drizzle some honey on the Ricotta.
4. Extent 1 tbsp. the spread to your choice of bread, top it with some honey and sliced peaches.

Nutrition: Calories: 199 Protein: 8.5 g. Fat: 12 g.

Creamy Yogurt Banana Bowls (Greek)

Prep Time: 10 minutes **Cooking Time:** 0 minutes
Servings: 4

Ingredients

2 bananas, sliced	½ tsp ground nutmeg
¼ cup creamy peanut butter	3 tbsp flaxseed meal
4 cups Greek yogurt	

Directions

1. Divide Greek yogurt between 4 serving bowls and top with sliced bananas.
2. Add peanut butter in microwave-safe bowl and microwave for 30 seconds.
3. Drizzle 1 tablespoon of melted peanut butter on each bowl on top of the sliced bananas.
4. Sprinkle cinnamon and flax meal on top and serve.

Nutrition: Calories 351, Fat 13.1g, Carbohydrates 35.6g, Sugar 26.1g, Protein 19.6g, Cholesterol 15mg

Watermelon Cream (Italian)

Prep Time: 15 minutes **Cooking Time:** 0 minutes
Servings: 2

Ingredients

1-pound watermelon, peeled and chopped	1 cup heavy cream
1 teaspoon vanilla extract	1 teaspoon lime juice
	2 tablespoons stevia

Directions

1. In a blender, combine the watermelon with the cream and the rest of the , pulse well, divide into cups and keep in the fridge for 15 minutes before serving.

Nutrition: Calories 122; Fat 5.7 g; Fiber 3.2 g; Carbs 5.3 g; Protein 0.4 g

Mango Bowls (Spanish)

Prep Time: 10 minutes **Cooking Time:** 0 minutes
Servings: 4

Ingredients

2cups mango, peeled & cubed	1 cup coconut cream
1 tsp. chia seeds	1 tsp. vanilla extract
	1 tbsp. mint, chopped

Directions

1. Mix the mango with the cream and the other , toss, divide into smaller bowls and keep in the fridge for 10 minutes before serving.

Nutrition: Calories: 238 Fat: 16.6 g. Protein: 3.3 g.

Mousse de chocolat (Greek)

Prep Time: 10 minutes **Cooking Time:** 6 minutes
Servings: 5

Ingredients

4 egg yolks	½ tsp vanilla
½ cup unsweetened almond milk	¼ cup cocoa powder
¼ cup water	1 cup whipping cream
	½ cup Swerve
	1/8 tsp salt

Directions

1. Add egg yolks to a large bowl and whisk until well beaten.
2. In a saucepan, add swerve, cocoa powder, and water and whisk until well combined.
3. Add almond milk and cream to the saucepan and whisk until well mix.
4. Once saucepan mixtures are heated up then turn off the heat.
5. Add vanilla and salt and stir well.
6. Add a tablespoon of chocolate mixture into the eggs and whisk until well combined.
7. Slowly pour remaining chocolate to the eggs and whisk until well combined.
8. Pour batter into the ramekins.
9. Pour 1 ½ cups of water into the instant pot then place a trivet in the pot.
10. Place ramekins on a trivet.
11. Seal pot with lid and select manual and set timer for 6 minutes.
12. Release pressure using quick release method than open the lid.
13. Carefully remove ramekins from the instant pot and let them cool completely.
14. Serve and enjoy.

Nutrition: Calories 128, Fat 11.9g, Carbohydrates 4g, Sugar 0.2g, Protein 3.6g, Cholesterol 194mg

Pistachio Balls (Italian)

Prep Time: 10 minutes **Cooking Time:** 5 minutes
Servings: 16

½ cup pistachios, unsalted	½ tsp ground fennel seeds
1 cup dates, pitted	
½ cup raisins Pinch of pepper	

Directions

1. Add all into the food processor and process until well combined.
2. Make small balls and place onto the baking tray.
3. Serve and enjoy.

Nutrition: Calories 55, Fat 0.9g, Carbohydrates 12.5g, Sugar 9.9g, Protein 0.8g, Cholesterol 0mg

Apricot Energy Bites (Greek)

Prep Time: 16 minutes **Cooking Time:** 0 minute
Servings: 10

Ingredients

1cup unsalted raw cashew nuts	¼ tsp. ground ginger
½ cup dried apricots	2 tbsps. dates, chopped
1 tsp. lemon zest	2¾ tbsp. unsweetened coconut, shredded
1 tsp. orange zest	¼ tsp. cinnamon Salt to taste

Directions

1. Grind the apricots, coconut, dates, and cashew nuts in a food processor.
2. Pulse until a crumbly mixture has formed.
3. Add the spices, salt, and citrus zest to the mixture.
4. Pulse it again to mix well.
5. Process the batter on HIGH till it sticks together.
6. Take a dish or a tray and line it with parchment paper.
7. Shape the balls in your palm, make around 20 balls.
8. Keep in the refrigerator. Serve as needed.

Nutrition: Calories: 102 Protein: 2 g. Fat: 6 g.

Cranberry Orange Cookies (Italian)

Prep Time: 20 minutes **Cooking Time:** 16 minutes
Servings: 24

Ingredients

1 cup soft butter	½ cup brown sugar
1tsp. orange peel, grated	2½ cups flour
2 tbsps. orange juice	1 cup white sugar
½ tsp. baking powder	½ tsp. salt
2 cups cranberries, chopped	½ cup walnuts, chopped
1 egg	(optional) For the icing:
½ tsp. orange peel, grated	1½ cup confectioner's sugar
3 tbsps. orange juice	

Directions

1. Preheat the oven to 190°C.
2. Blend the butter, white sugar, and brown sugar. Beat the egg until everything is well mixed. Mix 1 tsp. orange zest and 2 tbsps. of orange juice. Mix the flour, baking powder, and salt; stir in the orange mixture.
3. Mix the cranberries and, if used, the nuts until well distributed. Place the dough with a spoon on ungreased baking trays.
4. Bake in the preheated oven for 12–14 minutes. Cool on racks.
5. In a small bowl, mix icing . Spread over cooled cookies.

Nutrition: Calories: 110 Fat: 4.8 g. Protein: 1.1 g.

Rhubarb Cream (Greek)

Prep Time: 10 minutes **Cooking Time:** 14 minutes
Servings: 4

Ingredients

1/3 cup cream cheese	½ cup coconut cream
1lbs. rhubarb, roughly chopped	3 tbsps. coconut sugar

Directions

1. Blend the cream cheese with the cream and the other well.
2. Divide into small cups, introduce in the oven, and bake at 350°F for 14 minutes.
3. Serve cold.

Nutrition: Calories: 360 Fat: 14.3 g. Protein: 5.2 g.

Dipped Sprouts (Italian)

Prep Time: 12 minutes **Cooking Time:** 10 minutes
Servings: 2

Ingredients

16 oz. Brussels sprouts	6 tbsps. raisins and nuts, crushed
4 tbsps. honey	

Directions

1. Boil water in a pot
2. Add the sprouts, and cook for 10 minutes until soft.
3. Glaze the sprouts in the honey and coat well. Add the nuts and raisins.

Nutrition: Calories: 221 Fat: 15.1 g. Protein: 5.3 g.

Healthy & Quick Energy Bites (Italian)

Prep Time: 10 minutes **Cooking Time:** 0 minutes
Servings: 20

Ingredients

2 cups cashew nuts	¼ tsp cinnamon
4 tbsp dates, chopped	1/3 cup unsweetened shredded coconut
1 tsp lemon zest	
¾ cup dried apricots	

Directions

1. Line baking tray with parchment paper and set aside.
2. Add all in a food processor and process until the mixture is crumbly and well combined.
3. Make small balls from mixture and place on a prepared baking tray.
4. Serve and enjoy.

Nutrition: Calories 100, Fat 7.5g, Carbohydrates 7.2g, Sugar 2.8g, Protein 2.4g, Cholesterol 0mg

CHAPTER 11
Dinner Recipes

Skewers for Salad (Greek)

Prep Time: 10 minutes **Cooking Time:** 0 minutes
Servings: 1

Ingredients

1wooden skewers, soaked in water for 30 minutes before use.
1 yellow pepper, cut into eight squares.
3.5-oz. (about 10cm) cucumber, cut into four slices and halved.
For the dressing:
Juice of ½ lemon.
A right amount of salt and freshly ground black pepper..

8 cherry tomatoes.
8 large black olives.
oz. feta, cut into 8 cubes
½ red onion, chopped in half and separated into eight pieces.
1 tsp. balsamic vinegar
Leaves oregano, chopped
1 tbsp. extra-virgin olive oil.
Few leaves basil, finely chopped (or ½ tsp dried mixed herbs to replace basil and oregano).
½ clove garlic, peeled and crushed.

Directions

1. Thread each skewer in the order with salad olive, tomato, yellow pepper, red onion, cucumber, feta, basil, olive, yellow pepper, red ointment, cucumber, feta.
2. Put all the ingredients of the dressing in a small bowl and blend well together. Pour over the spoils.

Nutrition: Calories: 315 g. Fat: 30 g. Protein: 56 g. Carbs: 45 g. Cholesterol: 230 mg. Sugar: 0 g.

Artichoke Petals Bites (Spanish)

Prep Time: 10 minutes **Cooking Time:** 10 minutes
Servings: 8

Ingredients

8 oz. artichoke petals, boiled, drained, without salt.
4 oz. Parmesan, grated.

½ cup almond flour.
2 tbsps. almond butter, melted.

Directions

1. In the mixing bowl, mix up together almond flour and grated Parmesan.
2. Preheat the oven to 355° F.
3. Dip the artichoke petals in the almond butter and then coat in the almond flour mixture.
4. Place them in the tray.
5. Transfer the tray to the preheated oven and cook the petals for 10 minutes.
6. Chill the cooked petal bites a little before serving.

Nutrition: Calories: 140 g. Fat: 6.4 g. Fiber: 7.6 g. Carbs: 14.6 g. Protein: 10 g.

Salad Kebab Skewers (Greek)

Prep Time: 20 minutes **Cooking Time:** 50 minutes
Servings: 1

Ingredients

3 oz. turkey.
1 pepper Bird's Eye.
1 tsp. fresh ginger.
1 clove of garlic.
oz. dried tomatoes.
0.3-oz. parsley.
¼ fresh lemon juice.

1-oz. cauliflower.
2 oz. red onion.
3 tbsps. extra virgin olive oil.
2 tsps. turmeric.
Dried sage to taste.
1 tbsp. capers.

Directions

1. Blend the raw cauliflower tops and cook them in a tsp. of extra virgin olive oil, garlic, red onion, chili pepper, ginger, and a tsp. of turmeric.
2. Leave to flavor on the fire for a minute, then add the chopped sun-dried tomatoes and 5 g of parsley. Season the turkey slice with a tsp. of extra virgin olive oil, the dried sage, and cook it in another tsp. of extra virgin olive oil. Once ready, season with a tbsp. of capers, ¼ of lemon juice, 5 g of parsley, a tbsp. of water and add the cauliflower.

Nutrition: Calories: 120 g. Fat: 10 g. Protein: 56 g. Carbs: 45 g. Cholesterol: 230 mg. Sugar: 0 g.

Italian Style Ground Beef (Italian)

Prep Time: 10 minutes **Cooking Time:** 20 minutes
Servings: 4

Ingredients

2 lbs. ground beef
Salt
3tbsp olive oil
1/2 tsp dried sage
2tsp thyme

2eggs, lightly beaten
1/4 tsp dried basil
11/2 tsp dried parsley
1 tsp oregano
1 tsp rosemary Pepper

Directions

1. Pour 1 1/2 cups of water into the instant pot then place the trivet in the pool.
2. Spray loaf pan with cooking spray.
3. Add all ingredients into the mixing bowl and mix until well combined.
4. Transfer meat mixture into the prepared loaf pan and place loaf pan on top of the trivet in the pot.
5. Seal pot with lid and cook on high for 35 minutes.
6. Once done, allow to release pressure naturally for 10 minutes then release remaining using quick release. Remove lid.
7. Serve and enjoy.

Nutrition: Calories 365 Fat 18 g Carbohydrates 0.7 g Sugar 0.1 g Protein 47.8 g Cholesterol 190 mg

Prawn Arrabbiata (Greek)

Prep Time: 10 minutes **Cooking Time:** 40 minutes
Servings: 1

Ingredients

Raw or cooked prawns (Ideally king prawns). .
Red onion, finely chopped.
1.2-oz. celery, finely chopped
1 Bird's eye chili, finely chopped.
1 tsp. dried mixed herbs.
1 tbsp. chopped parsley.

1 tbsp. extra-virgin olive oil.
For the arrabbiata sauce:
1 garlic clove, finely chopped.
oz. buckwheat pasta
1tsp. extra-virgin olive oil.
2tbsps. white wine (optional).
14-oz. tinned chopped tomatoes.

Directions

1. Firstly, fry the onion, garlic, celery, and chili over medium-low heat and dry herbs in the oil for 1–2 minutes. Switch the flame to medium, then add the wine and cook for 1 minute. Add the tomatoes and leave the sauce to cook for 20–30 minutes over medium-low heat until it has a nice rich consistency. If you feel the sauce becomes too thick, add some water.
2. While the sauce is cooking, boil a pan of water, and cook the pasta as directed by the packet. Drain, toss with the olive oil when cooked to your liking, and keep in the pan until needed.
3. Add the raw prawns to the sauce and cook for another 3–4 minutes until they have turned pink and opaque, then attach the parsley and serve. If you use cooked prawns add the parsley, bring the sauce to a boil and eat.
4. Add the cooked pasta to the sauce, blend well, and then serve gently.

Nutrition: Calories: 185 g. Fat: 30 g. Protein: 56 g. Carbs: 45 g. Cholesterol: 230 mg. Sugar: 0 g.

Coated Cauliflower Head (Spanish)

Prep Time: 10 minutes **Cooking Time:** 40 minutes
Servings: 6

Ingredients

2-lb. cauliflower head.
3 tbsps. olive oil.
1 egg, whisked.
1 tsp. salt.

1 tbsp. butter softened.
1 tsp. ground coriander.
1 tsp. dried cilantro.
1 tsp. dried oregano.
1 tsp. Tahini paste.

Directions

1. Trim cauliflower head if needed. Preheat oven to 350° F.
2. In the mixing bowl, mix up together olive oil, softened butter, ground coriander, salt, whisked egg, dried cilantro, dried oregano, and tahini paste.
3. Then brush the cauliflower head with this mixture generously and transfer it to the tray.
4. Bake the cauliflower head for 40 minutes.
5. Brush it with the remaining oil mixture every 10 minutes.

Nutrition: Calories: 131 g. Fat: 10.3 g. Fiber: 4 g. Carbs: 8.4 g. Protein: 4.1 g.

Chicken Shawarma with Spicy Sauce (Greek)

Prep Time: 15 minutes **Cooking Time:** 6 minutes
Servings: 4

Ingredients

1 lb. chicken breast
½ cup plum tomato, chopped
¼ cup red onion, chopped
2 tbsps. lemon juice, divided
2 tbsps. parsley, finely chopped
½ tsp. salt
¼ tsp. ground cumin
1/8 tsp. ground coriander

4(6-inch) halved pitas
½ cup cucumber, chopped
5tbsps. plain low-fat Greek-style yogurt, divided
1tbsp. tahini
2 tbsps. extra-virgin olive oil
½ tsp. crushed red pepper
¼ tsp. ground ginger

Directions

1. Combine the parsley, salt, red pepper, ginger, cumin, coriander, 1 tbsp. yogurt, 1 tbsp. juice, and 2 cloves of garlic. Add the chicken, stir to coat. Preheat the oil in a nonstick pan over medium-high heat. Add the chicken mixture to the pan and cook for 6 minutes.
2. In the meantime, combine the remaining 1 tbsp. lemon juice, the remaining ¼ cup of yogurt, the remaining 1 clove of garlic, and the tahini, mixing well. Put 1 ½ tsp. the tahini mixture inside each half of the pita, divide the chicken between the pita halves. Fill each half of the pita with 1 tbsp. cucumber, 1 tbsp. tomato, and 1 ½ tsp. onion.

Nutrition: Calories: 440 Protein: 37 g. Fat: 19 g.

Chicken Sausage and Peppers (Spanish)

Prep Time: 10 minutes **Cooking Time:** 20 minutes
Servings: 6

Ingredients

1tbsps. extra-virgin olive oil
6 Italian chicken sausage links
1 green bell pepper
½ cup dry white wine
pepper Pinch red pepper flakes

1 red bell pepper
1 onion
¼ tsp. freshly ground black
3 garlic cloves, minced
½ tsp. sea salt

Directions

1. Heat the olive oil in a skillet at medium-high heat.
2. Add the sausages and cook for 5–7 minutes, turning occasionally, until browned, and they reach an internal temperature of 165°F. With tongs, remove the sausage from the pan and set it aside on a platter, tented with aluminum foil to keep warm.
3. Put the skillet back to heat and add the onion, red bell pepper, and green bell pepper. Cook them for 5–7 minutes.
4. Cook the garlic for 30 seconds, stirring constantly.
5. Stir in the wine, sea salt, pepper, and red pepper flakes. Scrape and fold in any browned bits from the bottom. Simmer for 4 minutes more. Spoon the peppers over the sausages and serve.

Nutrition: Calories: 173 Protein: 22 g. Fat: 5 g.

Chicken Merlot with Mushrooms (Spanish)

Prep Time: 10 minutes **Cooking Time:** 40 minutes
Servings: 2

Ingredients

6 boneless, skinless chicken breasts, cubed.	1 large red onion, chopped.
¾ cup chicken broth.	2 cloves garlic, minced.
¼ cup Merlot.	1 (6 oz.) can tomato paste.
2 tbsps. basil, chopped finely.	3 tbsps. chia seeds.
1 (10 oz.) package buckwheat ramen noodles, cooked.	Salt and pepper to taste.
	3 cups mushrooms, sliced.
	2 tbsps. Parmesan, shaved.
	2 tsps. sugar.

Directions

1. Rinse chicken; set aside.
2. Add mushrooms, onion, and garlic to the crockpot and mix.
3. Place chicken cubes on top of the vegetables and do not mix.
4. In a large bowl, combine broth, tomato paste, wine, chia seeds, basil, sugar, salt, and pepper. Pour over the chicken.
5. Cover and cook on low for 7–8 hours or on high for 3 ½–4 hours.
6. To serve, spoon chicken, mushroom mixture, and sauce over hot cooked buckwheat ramen noodles. Top with shaved Parmesan.

Nutrition: Calories: 213 g. Fat: 10 g. Protein: 56 g. Carbs: 45 g. Cholesterol: 230 mg. Sugar: 0 g.

Stuffed Beef Loin in Sticky Sauce (Italian)

Prep Time: 15 minutes **Cooking Time:** 6 minutes
Servings: 4

Ingredients

1 tbsp. Erythritol.	1 tbsp. lemon juice.
½ tsp. tomato sauce.	¼ tsp. dried rosemary.
½ cup of water.	9 oz. beef loin.
3 oz. celery root, grated.	1 tbsp. walnuts, chopped.
3 oz. bacon, sliced.	2 tsps. butter.
¾ tsps. garlic, diced.	1tbsp. olive oil.
	1 tsp. salt.

Directions

1. Cut the beef loin into the layer and spread it with the dried rosemary, butter, and salt.
2. Then place over the beef loin: grated celery root, sliced bacon, walnuts, and diced garlic.
3. Roll the beef loin and brush it with olive oil.
4. Secure the meat with the help of the toothpicks.
5. Place it in the tray and add a ½ cup of water.
6. Cook the meat in the preheated to 365º F oven for 40 minutes.
7. Meanwhile, make the sticky sauce: mix up together Erythritol, lemon juice, 4 tbsps. of water, and butter.
8. Preheat the mixture until it starts to boil.
9. Then add tomato sauce and whisk it well.
10. Bring the sauce to boil and remove from the heat.
11. When the beef loin is cooked, remove it from the oven and brush it with the cooked sticky sauce very generously.
12. Slice the beef roll and sprinkle with the remaining sauce.

Nutrition: Calories: 248 g. Fat: 17.5 g. Fiber: 0.5 g. Carbs: 2.2 g. Protein:20.7 g.

Olive Feta Beef (Greek)

Prep Time: 10 minutes **Cooking Time:** 6 hours
Servings: 8

Ingredients

1lbs. beef stew meat, cut into half-inch pieces.	30 oz. can tomato, diced.
½ tsp. salt.	1 cup olives, pitted, and cut in half.
½ cup feta cheese, crumbled.	¼ tsp. pepper.

Directions

1. Add all ingredients into the crockpot and stir well.
2. Cover and cook on high for 6 hours.
3. Season with pepper and salt.
4. Stir well and serve.

Nutrition: Calories: 370 g. Fat: 12 g. Fiber: 1 g. Carbs: 10 g. Protein: 50 g.

Excellent Beef Meal (Spanish)

Prep Time: 15 minutes **Cooking Time:** 7 hours 4 minutes
Servings: 6

Ingredients

1 tbsp. vegetable oil	4 garlic cloves
2 lb. beef stew meat	1 can diced tomatoes with juice 1/2 C.
1 can artichoke hearts	Kalamata olives, pitted
1 container beef broth	1 tsp. dried oregano
1 can tomato sauce	1 tsp. dried parsley
1 tsp. dried basil	1 bay leaf, crumbled
1 onion	
1/2 tsp. ground cumin	

Directions

1. In a skillet, heat the oil over medium-high heat and cook the beef for about 2 minutes per side.
2. Transfer the beef into a slow cooker and top with artichoke hearts, followed by the onion and garlic.
3. Place the remaining ingredients on top.
4. Set the slow cooker on "Low" and cook, covered for about 7 hours.

Nutrition: Calories: 410; Carbohydrates: 0.9g; Protein: 53.1g; Fat: 14.2g; Sugar: 6.7g; Sodium: 1116mg; Fiber: 6.4g

Chicken and Tzatziki Pitas (Greek)

Prep Time: 10 minutes **Cooking Time:** 0 minutes
Servings: 8

Ingredients

2pita breads	10 oz chicken fillet, grilled
8 teaspoons tzatziki sauce	1 cup lettuce, chopped

Directions

1. Cut every pita bread on the halves to get 8 pita pockets.
2. Then fill every pita pocket with chopped lettuce and sprinkle greens with tzatziki sauce.
3. Chop chicken fillet and add it in the pita pockets too.

Nutrition: calories 106, fat 3.8, fiber 0.2, carbs 6.1, protein 11

Lamb with String Beans (Spanish)

Prep Time: 10 minutes
Cooking Time: 1 hour
Servings: 6

Ingredients

¼ cup extra-virgin olive oil	1 tsp. sea salt
½ tsp. black pepper	1lb. green beans
2 tbsps. tomato paste	1 onion
1 ½ cups hot water	6 lamb chops
2 tomatoes	

Directions

1. In a skillet at medium-high heat, pour 2 tbsps. of olive oil.
2. Season the lamb chops with ½ tsp. sea salt and 1/8 tsp. pepper. Cook the lamb in the hot oil for 4 minutes. Transfer the meat to a platter and set it aside.
3. Put back to the heat then put the 2 tbsps. of olive oil. Heat until it shimmers.
4. Blend the tomato paste and the hot water. Mix to the hot skillet along with the green beans, onion, tomatoes, and the remaining ½ tsp. sea salt and ¼ tsp. pepper. Bring to a simmer.
5. Return the lamb chops to the pan. Bring to boil and reduce the heat to medium-low. Simmer for 45 minutes until the beans are soft, adding additional water as needed to adjust the thickness of the sauce.

Nutrition: Calories: 439 Protein: 50 g. Fat: 22 g.

Chicken Piccata (Italian)

Prep Time: 10 minutes **Cooking Time:** 10 minutes
Servings: 6

Ingredients

½ cup whole-wheat flour	½ tsp. sea salt
1/8 tsp. freshly ground black pepper 1 ½ lb. boneless	3 tbsps. extra-virgin olive oil
½ cup dry white wine 1 lemon juice	1 cup unsalted chicken broth
	1 lemon zest
¼ cup capers, drained and rinsed	¼ cup fresh parsley leaves, chopped

Directions

1. In a shallow dish, whisk the flour, sea salt, and pepper. Dredge the chicken in the flour and tap off any excess.
2. Heat the olive oil in a pan over medium-high heat.
3. Add the chicken and cook for 4 minutes. Remove the chicken from the pan and set aside, tented with aluminum foil to keep warm.
4. Return to the heat and mix the broth, wine, lemon juice, and lemon zest, and capers. Simmer for 3–4 minutes, stirring. Remove the skillet from the heat and return the chicken to the pan. Turn to coat. Stir in the parsley and serve.

Nutrition: Calories: 153 Protein: 8 g. Fat: 9 g.

One-Pan Tuscan Chicken (Italian)

Prep Time: 10 minutes **Cooking Time:** 25 minutes
Servings: 6

Ingredients

¼ cup extra-virgin olive oil, divided	1 onion
	1 lb. boneless chicken
1 red bell pepper 3 garlic cloves	½ cup dry white wine 2 (14 oz.) can tomatoes
1 (14 oz.) can white beans	1 tbsp. dried Italian seasoning
½ tsp. sea salt	1/8 tsp. freshly ground black pepper
1/8 tsp. red pepper flakes	
¼ cup fresh basil leaves, chopped	

Directions

1. In a huge skillet over medium-high heat, preheat 2 tbsps. of olive oil.
2. Add the chicken and cook for 6 minutes, stirring. Take out the chicken and set it aside on a platter, tented with aluminum foil to keep warm.
3. Return the skillet to heat and heat the remaining 2 tbsps. of olive oil.
4. Add the onion and red bell pepper. Cook for 5 minutes.
5. Cook the garlic for 30 seconds.
6. Stir in the wine. Cook for 1 minute, stirring.
7. Add the crushed and chopped tomatoes, white beans, Italian seasoning, sea salt, pepper, and red pepper flakes. Bring to a simmer and reduce the heat to medium. Cook for 5 minutes, stirring occasionally.
8. Take the chicken and any juices that have collected back to the skillet. Cook for 1–2 minutes. Pull out from the heat and stir in the basil before serving.

Nutrition: Calories: 271 Protein: 14 g. Fat: 0.1 g.

Mediterranean Rice and Sausage (Italian)

Prep Time: 15 minutes **Cooking Time:** 8 hours
Servings: 6

Ingredients

1½ lb. Italian sausage, crumbled	2 tbsps. steak sauce
	1 medium onion, chopped
2 cups long-grain rice, uncooked	1 (14 oz.) can diced tomatoes with juice
½ cup water	1 medium green pepper, diced Olive oil or nonstick cooking spray

Directions

1. Spray your slow cooker with olive oil or nonstick cooking spray.
2. Add the sausage, onion, and steak sauce to the slow cooker.
3. Cook on low for 8–10 hours.
4. After 8 hours, add the rice, tomatoes, water, and green pepper. Stir to combine thoroughly.
5. Cook for 20–25 minutes.

Nutrition: Calories: 650 Fat: 36 g. Protein: 22 g.

Sunday Dinner Brisket (Spanish)

Prep Time: 10 minutes **Cooking Time:** 8 hours 10 minutes
Servings: 6

Ingredients

2 1/2 lb. beef brisket, trimmed	Salt and freshly ground black pepper, to taste
2 medium onions, chopped	1 (15-oz.) can diced tomatoes, drained
2 large garlic cloves, sliced	2 tsp. Dijon mustard
1 tbsp. Herbs de Provence	2 tsp. olive oil
1 C. dry red wine	

Directions

1. Season the brisket with salt and black pepper evenly.
2. In a non-stick skillet, heat the oil over medium heat and cook the brisket for about 4-5 minutes per side.
3. Transfer the brisket into a slow cooker.
4. Add the remaining ingredients and stir to combine.
5. Set the slow cooker on "Low" and cook, covered for about 8 hours.
6. Uncover the slow cooker and with a slotted spoon, transfer the brisket onto a platter.
7. Cut the brisket into desired sized slices and serve with the topping of pan sauce.

Nutrition: Calories: 427; Carbohydrates: 7.7g; Protein: 58.5g; Fat: 193.6g; Sugar: 3.7g; Sodium: 178mg; Fiber: 1.7g

Leg of Lamb with Rosemary and Garlic (Greek)

Prep Time: 15 minutes **Cooking Time:** 8 hours
Servings: 4–6

Ingredients

3–4-lb. leg of lamb	4 garlic cloves, sliced thin
5–8 sprigs of fresh rosemary, more if desired	1 lemon, halved
2 tbsps. olive oil	
¼ cup flour	

Directions

1. Put a skillet over high heat and pour the olive oil.
2. When the olive oil is hot, add the leg of lamb and sear on both sides until brown.
3. Spray the slow cooker with olive oil and then transfer the lamb to the slow cooker.
4. Squeeze the lemon over the meat and then place it in the pot next to the lamb.
5. Take a sharp knife, make small incisions in the meat, and then stuff the holes you created with rosemary and garlic.
6. Place any remaining rosemary and garlic on top of the roast.
7. Cook on low for 8 hours.

Nutrition: Calories: 557 Fat: 39 g. Protein: 46 g.

Lemon Honey Lamb Shoulder (Spanish)

Prep Time: 10 minutes **Cooking Time:** 8 hours
Servings: 4

Ingredients

3 garlic cloves, thinly sliced	1 tbsp. fresh rosemary, chopped
1 tsp. lemon zest, grated	4–5-lb. boneless lamb shoulder roast
½ tsp. each salt and pepper	6 shallots, quartered
3 tbsps. lemon juice	2 tsps. Olive oil
1 tbsp. honey	
2 tsps. cornstarch	

Directions

1. Stir the garlic, rosemary, lemon zest, salt, and pepper.
2. Rub the spice mixture into the lamb shoulder. Make sure to coat the whole roast.
3. Spray the slow cooker with olive oil and add the lamb.
4. Mix the honey and lemon juice and then pour over the meat.
5. Arrange the shallots beside the meat in the slow cooker.
6. Cook on low for 8 hours.
7. Serve. You can make a gravy by transferring the juice from the slow cooker to a medium saucepan. Thoroughly mix the cornstarch into a bit of water until smooth. Then mix into the juice and bring to a simmer. Simmer until mixture thickens.

Nutrition: Calories: 240 Fat: 11 g. Protein: 31 g.

Lemony Trout with Caramelized Shallots (Greek)

Prep Time: 10 minutes **Cooking Time:** 20 minutes
Servings: 2

Ingredients

For the shallots:	1tsp. almond butter
2shallots, thinly sliced Dash	For the trout:
1tbsp. almond butter	2(4 oz./113 g.) trout fillets
3tbsps. capers	¼ cup freshly squeezed lemon juice
salt	Dash freshly grounds black pepper
¼ tsp. salt	1 lemon, thinly sliced

Directions

1. For the shallots:
1. Place a skillet over medium heat, cook the butter, shallots, and salt for 20 minutes, stirring every 5 minutes.
2. For the trout:
3. Meanwhile, in another large skillet over medium heat, heat 1 tsp. almond butter.
4. Add the trout fillets and cook each side for 3 minutes, or until flaky. Transfer to a plate and set aside.
5. In the skillet used for the trout, stir in the capers, lemon juice, salt, and pepper, then bring to a simmer. Whisk in the remaining 1 tbsp. almond butter. Spoon the sauce over the fish.
6. Garnish the fish with lemon slices and caramelized shallots before serving.

Nutrition: Calories: 344 Fat: 18 g. Protein: 21 g.

Skillet Braised Cod with Asparagus and Potatoes(Spanish)

Prep Time: 20 minutes **Cooking Time:** 20 minutes
Servings: 4

Ingredients

4 skinless cod fillets	12 oz. halved small purple
1 lb. asparagus	potatoes
½ lemon zest, finely grated	½ lemon juice
½ cup white wine	¼ cup torn fresh basil
1 ½ tbsp. olive oil	leaves
1 tbsp. capers	3 garlic cloves, sliced
½ tsp. salt	¼ tsp. pepper

Directions

1. Take a large and tall pan on the sides and heat the oil over medium- high.
2. Season the cod abundantly with salt and pepper and put in the pan, with the hot oil, for 1 minute. Carefully flip for 1 more minute and after transferring the cod to a plate. Set aside. Add the lemon zest, capers, and garlic to the pan and mix to coat with the remaining oil in the pan, and cook for 1 minute. Add the wine and deglaze the pan. Add the lemon juice, potatoes, ½ tsp. salt, ¼ tsp. pepper and 2 cups of water and bring to a boil, reduce the heat, and simmer until potatoes are tender, for 10–12 minutes.
3. Mix the asparagus and cook for 2 minutes. Bring back the cod filets and any juices accumulated in the pan. Cook until the asparagus are tender, for 3 minutes.
4. Divide the cod fillets into shallow bowls and add the potatoes and asparagus. Mix the basil in the broth left in the pan and pour over the cod.

Nutrition: Calories: 461 Protein: 40 g. Fat: 16 g.

Savory Vegetable Pancakes (Greek)

Prep Time: 10 minutes **Cooking Time:** 40 minutes
Servings: 7

Ingredients

8 peeled carrots	2 garlic cloves
1 zucchini	1 bunch green onions
½ bunch parsley	1 recipe pancake batter
Salt to taste	3 tbsps. of olive oil

Directions

1. Grate chop the zucchini and carrots using the grater. Finely chop the onions, mince the garlic and roughly chop the parsley. Prepare the pancakes with your favorite recipe or buy them in the store, but use ¼ cup of liquid less than required, zucchini will add a large amount of liquid to the mix. Fold the vegetables in the prepared pancake batter.
2. Heat a pan over medium-high heat and brush it gently with the olive oil. Use a 1/3 measuring cup to scoop the batter on the heated pan. Cook for 3–4 minutes, until the outer edge has set, then turn over. Cook for another 2 minutes and remove from the heat.
3. Season the pancakes with plenty of salt. Serve with butter, sour cream, or even a salted jam.

Nutrition: Calories: 291 Protein: 24 g. Fat: 10 g.

Niçoise-inspired Salad with Sardines (Spanish)

Prep Time: 9 minutes **Cooking Time:** 16 minutes
Servings: 4

Ingredients

4 eggs	12 ounces baby red
6 ounces green beans,	potatoes (about 12
halved	potatoes)
4 cups baby spinach leaves	1 bunch radishes, quartered
or mixed greens	(about 1 1/3 cups)
20 Kalamata or Niçoise	3 (3.75-ounce) cans skinless,
olives (about 1/3 cup)	boneless sardines packed in
1 cup cherry tomatoes	olive oil, drained
8 tablespoons Dijon Red	
Wine Vinaigrette	

Directions

1. Situate the eggs in a saucepan and cover with water. Bring the water to a boil. Once the water starts to boil, close then turn the heat off. Set a timer for minutes.
2. Once the timer goes off, strain the hot water and run cold water over the eggs to cool. Peel the eggs when cool and cut in half.
3. Poke each potato a few times using fork. Place them on a microwave- safe plate and microwave on high for 4 to 5 minutes, until the potatoes are tender. Let cool and cut in half. Place green beans on a microwave-safe plate and microwave on high for 1½ to 2 minutes, until the beans are crisp-tender. Cool.
4. Place 1 egg, ½ cup of green beans, 6 potato halves, 1 cup of spinach, 1/3 cup of radishes, ¼ cup of tomatoes, olives, and 3 sardines in each of 4 containers. Pour 2 tablespoons of vinaigrette into each of 4 sauce containers.

Nutrition: Calories: 450 Fat: 32g Protein: 21g

Tuscan Beef Stew (Spanish)

Prep Time: 10 minutes **Cooking Time:** 4 hours
Servings: 8

Ingredients

1lbs. beef stew meat	2 (14 ½ oz.) cans tomatoes
1 medium onion	1 package McCormick®
1 tsp. rosemary leaves	Slow Cookers Hearty Beef
8 slices Italian bread	Stew Seasoning
½ cup water	½ cup dry red wine
4 carrots	

Directions

1. Place the cubed beef in the slow cooker along with the carrots, diced tomatoes, and onion wedges.
2. Mix the seasoning package in ½ cup of water and stir well, making sure no lumps are remaining.
3. Add the red wine to the water and stir slightly. Add the rosemary leaves to the water-and-wine mixture and then pour over the meat, stirring to ensure the meat is completely covered.
4. Turn the slow cooker to LOW and cook for 8 hours, or cook for 4 hours on HIGH.
5. Serve with toasted Italian bread.

Nutrition: Calories: 329 Fat: 15 g. Protein: 25.6 g.

Fragrant Asian Hotpot (Spanish)

Prep Time: 15 minutes **Cooking Time:** 45 minutes
Servings: 2

Ingredients

1 tsp. tomato purée.
Small handful parsley, stalks finely chopped.
Small handful coriander, stalks finely chopped.
Broccoli, cut into small florets.
1 tbsp. good-quality miso paste. oz. raw tiger prawns.
oz. firm tofu, chopped.
500 ml chicken stock, fresh or made with one cube.

1-star anise, crushed (or ¼ tsp. ground anise).
Juice of ½ lime.
½ carrot, peeled and cut.
Beansprouts.
oz. rice noodles that are cooked according to packet instructions. Cooked water chestnuts, drained.
Little Sushi ginger, chopped.

Directions

1. In a large saucepan, put the tomato purée, star anise, parsley stalks, coriander stalks, lime juice, and chicken stock and bring to boil for 10 minutes.
2. Stir in the carrot, broccoli, prawns, tofu, noodles, and water chestnuts, and cook gently until the prawns are cooked. Take it from heat and stir in the ginger sushi and the paste miso.
3. Serve sprinkled with peregrine leaves and coriander.

Nutrition: Calories: 185 g. Fat: 30 g. Protein: 56 g. Carbs: 45 g. Cholesterol: 230 mg. Sugar: 0 g.

Turkey Burgers with Mango Salsa (Greek)

Prep Time: 15 minutes **Cooking Time:** 10 minutes
Servings: 6

Ingredients

1½ lb. ground turkey breast
1 tsp. sea salt, divided
2mangos, peeled, pitted, and cubed
1garlic clove, minced
2 tbsps. extra-virgin olive oil
1 lime juice

¼ tsp. freshly ground black pepper
½ red onion, finely chopped
½ jalapeño pepper, seeded and finely minced
2 tbsps. fresh cilantro leaves, chopped

Directions

1. Form the turkey breast into 4 patties and season with ½ tsp. sea salt and pepper.
2. In a nonstick skillet over medium-high heat, heat the olive oil until it shimmers.
3. Add the turkey patties and cook for 5 minutes per side until browned.
4. While the patties cook, mix the mango, red onion, lime juice, garlic, jalapeño, cilantro, and remaining ½ tsp. sea salt in a small bowl. Spoon the salsa over the turkey patties and serve.

Nutrition: Calories: 384 Protein: 3 g. Fat: 16 g.

Asian King Prawn Stir Fry with Buck wheat Noodles (Italian)

Prep Time: 10 minutes **Cooking Time:** 20 minutes
Servings: 1

Ingredients

oz. shelled raw king prawns, deveined.
2 tsps. tamaris.
1 garlic clove, finely chopped.
oz. celery, trimmed and sliced.
Red onions, sliced. Green beans, chopped.

oz. soba (buckwheat noodles).
2 tsps. extra virgin olive oil.
1 bird's eye chili, finely chopped.
1 tsp. finely chopped fresh ginger.
oz. kale, roughly chopped.
Little lovage or celery leaves. Chicken stock.

Directions

1. Heat a frying pan over a high flame, then cook the prawns for 2–3 minutes in 1 tsp. tamari and 1 tsp. oil. Place the prawns onto a tray. Wipe the pan out with paper from the kitchen, as you will be using it again.
2. Cook the noodles for 5–8 minutes in boiling water, or as directed on the packet. Drain and put away.
3. Meanwhile, over medium-high heat, fry the garlic, chili, and ginger, red onion, celery, beans, and kale in the remaining oil for 2–3 minutes. Add the stock and boil, then cook for 2–3 minutes until the vegetables are cooked but crunchy.
4. Add the prawns, noodles, and leaves of lovage/celery to the pan, bring back to the boil, then remove and eat.

Nutrition: Calories: 185 g. Fat: 30 g. Protein: 56 g. Carbs: 20 g. Cholesterol: 230 mg. Sugar: 0 g.

Herb-Roasted Turkey Breast (Greek)

Prep Time: 15 minutes **Cooking Time:** 90 minutes
Servings: 6

Ingredients

1tbsps. extra-virgin olive oil
1 tbsp. fresh thyme leaves
2tbsps. fresh Italian parsley leaves
¼ tsp. black pepper
1 cup dry white wine

1 lemon zest
1tbsp. fresh rosemary leaves
1 tsp. sea salt
4 garlic cloves, minced
1 (6 lbs.) bone-in, skin-on turkey breast
1 tsp. ground mustard

Directions

1. Preheat the oven to 325°F.
2. Scourge the olive oil, garlic, lemon zest, thyme, rosemary, parsley, mustard, sea salt, and pepper. Layout the herb mixture evenly over the surface of the turkey breast, and loosen the skin, and rub underneath as well. Place the turkey breast in a roasting pan on a rack, skin-side up.
3. Pour the wine into the pan. Roast for 1–1 ½ hour. Take out from the oven and rest for 20 minutes, tented with aluminum foil to keep it warm, before carving.

Nutrition: Calories: 392 Protein: 84 g. Fat: 6 g.

Risotto with Butternut Squash (Italian)

Prep Time: 10 minutes **Cooking Time:** 15 minutes
Servings: 4

Ingredients

3 tbsps. butter.
¼ tsp. black pepper, ground.
½ cup dry sherry.
½ cup butternut squash, cooked and mashed.
½ cup mascarpone cheese.
1/8 tsp. grated nutmeg.
2 tbsps. minced sage.
1 tsp. salt.
1 tsp. minced rosemary.
4 cups riced cauliflower.
½ cup parmesan cheese, grated.
1tsp. minced garlic.

Directions

1. Melt your butter inside of a large frying pan turned to a medium level of heat.
2. Add your rosemary, your sage, and the garlic. Cook this for about 1 minute or until this mixture begins to become fragrant.
3. Add in the cauliflower rice, pepper and salt, and the mashed squash. Cook this for 3 minutes. You will know it is ready for the next step when cauliflower is starting to soften up for you.
4. Add in your sherry and cook this for an additional 6 minutes, or until the majority of the liquid is absorbed into the rice, or when the cauliflower is much softer.
5. Stir in the mascarpone cheese, the parmesan cheese, as well as the nutmeg (grated).
6. Cook all of this on a medium heat level, being sure to stir it occasionally and do this until the cheese has melted and the risotto has gotten creamy. This will take around 4–5 minutes.
7. Taste the risotto and add more pepper and salt to season if you wish.
8. Remove your pan from the burner and garnish your risotto with more of the herbs as well as some grated parmesan.
9. Serve and enjoy

Nutrition: Calories: 337 g. Fats: 25 g. Carbs: 9 g. Protein: 8 g.

Healthy Chickpea Burger (Spanish)

Prep Time: 15 minutes **Cooking Time:** 10 minutes
Servings: 2

Ingredients

1 cup chickpeas, boiled.
A pinch of paprika.
1 tbsp. tomato puree.
Salt to taste.
½ cup bell pepper, sliced.
1 tsp. olive oil.
1tsp. soy sauce.
A pinch of white pepper.
1 onion, diced.
2lettuce leaves.
1avocado, sliced.
2burger buns to serve.

Directions

1. Mash the chickpeas and combine with bell pepper, salt, pepper, paprika, soy sauce, and tomato puree.
2. Use your hands to make patties.
3. Fry the patties golden brown with oil.
4. Assemble the burgers with lettuce, onion, avocado, and enjoy.

Nutrition: Calories: 254 g. Fat: 12 g. Protein: 9 g. Carbs: 7.8 g.

Fall-Apart Tender Beef (Spanish)

Prep Time: 10 minutes **Cooking Time:** 11 hours
Servings: 12

Ingredients

4 lb. boneless beef chuck roast, trimmed
2 large onions, sliced into thin strips
1C. BBQ sauce
2tbsp. prepared yellow mustard
4 celery stalks, sliced 4 garlic cloves, minced
1 1/2 C. catsup
1/4 C. molasses
1/4 C. apple cider vinegar
Fresh ground black pepper, to taste
1/4 tsp. red chili powder

Directions

1. In a slow cooker, place all the ingredients and stir to combine.
2. Set the slow cooker on "Low" and cook, covered for about 8-10 hours.
3. Uncover the slow cooker and with 2 forks, shred the meat.
4. Stir the meat with pan sauce.
5. Set the slow cooker on "Low" and cook, covered for about 1 hour.
6. Serve hot.

Nutrition: Calories: 454; Carbohydrates: 43.4g; Protein: 48.3g; Fat: 10g; Sugar: 35.5g; Sodium: 1000mg; Fiber: 1.2g

Cheesy Broccoli Soup (Greek)

Prep Time: 5 minutes **Cooking Time:** 30 minutes
Servings: 6

Ingredients

1lbs. broccoli, chopped. Salt to taste.
¼ cup shredded cheddar cheese..
2 garlic cloves, mince.
Pepper to taste.
5 cups vegetable broth.
1 tbsp. olive oil
¼ cup lemon juice.
1 white onion, chopped.

Directions

1. Heat the olive oil in a pan with medium heat.
2. Fry the onion for 1 minute and then add the garlic. Fry until the garlic becomes golden in color.
3. Toss in the broccoli and stir for 3 minutes.
4. Pour in the vegetable broth.
5. Add salt, pepper and mix well.
6. Cook for 20 minutes or until your broccoli is perfectly cooked through.
7. Take off the heat and let it cool down a bit.
8. Add to a blender, and blend it until your soup is perfectly smooth.
9. Transfer the soup into the pot again and heat it over medium heat.
10. Add lemon juice, cheddar cheese, and check if it needs more seasoning.
11. Serve hot with more cheese on top.

Nutrition: Calories: 97 g. Fats: 3.6 g. Carbs: 13.4 g. Proteins: 5 g.

Pasta with Garlic and Shrimp (Italian)

Prep Time: 4 minutes **Cooking Time:** 16 minutes
Servings: 4

Ingredients

6 ounces whole wheat spaghetti	12 ounces raw shrimp, peeled and deveined, cut into 1-inch pieces
1 bunch asparagus, trimmed	3 garlic cloves, chopped
1 large bell pepper, thinly sliced	1 cup fresh peas
1 and ¼ teaspoons kosher salt	½ and ½ cups non-fat plain yogurt
1 tablespoon extra-virgin olive oil	½ teaspoon fresh ground black pepper
¼ cup pine nuts, toasted	3 tablespoon lemon juice

Directions

1. Take a large sized pot and bring water to a boil
2. Add your spaghetti and cook them for about minutes less than the directed package instruction
3. Add shrimp, bell pepper, asparagus and cook for about 2-4 minutes until the shrimp are tender
4. Drain the pasta and the contents well
5. Take a large bowl and mash garlic until a paste form
6. Whisk in yogurt, parsley, oil, pepper and lemon juice into the garlic paste
7. Add pasta mix and toss well
8. Serve by sprinkling some pine nuts!

Nutrition: Calories: 406 Fat: 22g Protein: 26g

Rosemary Baked Chicken Drumsticks (Spanish)

Prep Time: 5 minutes **Cooking Time:** 1 hour
Servings: 6

Ingredients

1tbsps. fresh rosemary leaves, chopped	½ tsp. sea salt
1/8 tsp. freshly ground black pepper	1 tsp. garlic powder
	12 chicken drumsticks
	1 lemon zest

Directions

1. Preheat the oven to 350°F.
2. Blend the rosemary, garlic powder, sea salt, pepper, and lemon zest.
3. Place the drumsticks in a 9-by-13-inch baking dish and sprinkle with the rosemary mixture. Bake for 1 hour.

Nutrition: Calories: 163 Protein: 26 g. Fat: 6 g.

Mediterranean Avocado Salmon Salad (Greek)

Prep Time: 6 minutes **Cooking Time:** 10 minutes
Servings: 4

Ingredients

1 lb. skinless salmon fillets	3 tbsp. olive oil
Marinade/Dressing:	1 tbsp. red wine vinegar
2 tbsp. lemon juice fresh, squeezed	2 tsp garlic minced
1 tbsp. fresh chopped parsley	1 tsp dried oregano
Cracked pepper, to taste	1 tsp salt
Salad:	1 large cucumber
2 Roma tomatoes	4 cups Romaine (or Cos) lettuce leaves
1avocado	1 red onion
1/3 cup pitted Kalamata olives	1/2 cup feta cheese

Directions

1. Scourge the olive oil, lemon juice, red wine vinegar, chopped parsley, garlic minced, oregano, salt and pepper
2. Fill out half of the marinade into a large, shallow dish, refrigerate the remaining marinade to use as the dressing
3. Coat the salmon in the rest of the marinade
4. Place a skillet pan or grill over medium-high, add 1 tbsp oil and sear salmon on both sides until crispy and cooked through
5. Allow the salmon to cool Distribute the salmon among the containers, store in the fridge for 2-3 days
6. To Serve: Prep the salad by putting the romaine lettuce, cucumber, Roma tomatoes, red onion, avocado, feta cheese, and olives in a bowl. Reheat the salmon in the microwave for 30seconds to 1 minute or until heated through.
7. Slice the salmon and arrange over salad. Drizzle the salad with the remaining untouched dressing, serve with lemon wedges.

Nutrition: Calories:411 Fat: 27g Protein: 28g

Chicken with Onions, Potatoes, Figs, and Carrots(Greek)

Prep Time: 5 minutes **Cooking Time:** 45 minutes
Servings: 4

Ingredients

2 cups fingerling potatoes, halved	2 carrots, julienned
2 tbsps. extra-virgin olive oil	4 fresh figs, quartered
1 tsp. sea salt, divided	¼ tsp. freshly ground black pepper
2 tbsps. fresh parsley leaves, chopped	4 chicken leg-thigh quarters

Directions

1. Preheat the oven to 425°F.
2. In a small bowl, toss the potatoes, figs, and carrots with the olive oil, ½ tsp. sea salt, and pepper. Spread in a 9-by-13-inch baking dish. Rub the chicken with the remaining ½ tsp. sea salt. Place it on top of the vegetables.
3. Bake for 35–45 minutes.
4. Sprinkle with the parsley and serve.

Nutrition: Calories: 429 Protein: 52 g. Fat: 12 g

Steak with Red Wine–Mushroom Sauce (Italian)

Prep Time: 10 minutes **Cooking Time:** 20 minutes
Servings: 4

Ingredients

For the marinade and steak
2 tbsps. extra-virgin olive oil
1 tbsp. low-sodium soy sauce
2tbsps. extra-virgin olive oil
2 tbsps. extra-virgin olive oil
1 lb. cremini mushrooms
1tsp. dried thyme
1/8 tsp. black pepper

3 garlic cloves, minced
1tsp. Dijon mustard
1 cup dry red wine
1 tbsp. dried thyme
For the mushroom sauce
½ tsp. sea salt
1 ½ lb. skirt steak
2garlic cloves, minced
1 cup dry red wine

Directions

For the marinade and steak:

1. In a small bowl, whisk the wine, garlic, olive oil, soy sauce, thyme, and mustard. Pour into a resealable bag and add the steak. Refrigerate the steak to marinate for 4–8 hours. Remove the steak from the marinade and pat it dry with paper towels.
2. In a big skillet over medium-high heat, warm up olive oil.
3. Cook the steak for 4 minutes per side. Pull out steak from the skillet and put it on a plate tented with aluminum foil to keep warm, while you prepare the mushroom sauce.
4. When the mushroom sauce is ready, slice the steak against the grain into½-inch-thick slices.

For the mushroom sauce:

1. Preheat the skillet over medium-high heat, heat the olive oil.
2. Add the mushrooms, sea salt, thyme, and pepper. Cook for 6 minutes.
3. Cook the garlic for 30 seconds.
4. Stir in the wine, and use the side of a wooden spoon to scrape and fold in any browned bits from the bottom of the skillet. Cook for 4 minutes. Serve the mushrooms spooned over the steak.

Nutrition: Calories: 405 Protein: 33 g. Fat: 22 g.

Dijon Fish Fillets (Greek)

Prep Time: 15 minutes **Cooking Time:** 3 minutes
Servings: 2

Ingredients

2 white fish fillets
Salt

1 tbsp Dijon mustard 1 cup of water Pepper

Directions

1. Pour water into the instant pot and place trivet in the pot.
2. Brush fish fillets with mustard and season with pepper and salt and place on top of the trivet.
3. Seal pot with lid and cook on high for 3 minutes.
4. Once done, release pressure using quick release. Remove lid.
5. Serve and enjoy.

Nutrition: Calories 270 Fat 11.9 g Carbohydrates 0.5 g Sugar 0.1 g Protein 38 g Cholesterol 119 mg

Quinoa Protein Bars (Spanish)

Prep Time: 15 minutes **Cooking Time:** 40 minutes
Servings: 16

Ingredients

½ cup almonds, chopped.
½ cup coconut oil, melted.
½ cup honey.
1cup quinoa, dry.

½ cup chocolate chips.
½ cup flaxseed, ground.
½ tsp. salt.
2¼ cups quick oats.
3 large egg whites.

Directions

1. Preheat oven to 325° F
2. On the bottom of a clean, dry baking sheet evenly spread oats, quinoa, and almonds.
3. Bake for about 15 minutes or until lightly brown. You may want to stir the items in the cookie sheet every few minutes to ensure nothing burns.
4. Remove grains and nuts from the oven and allow to cool completely, but don't turn off the oven.
5. Whisk the egg whites in a bowl and beat the coconut oil and honey into them.
6. Combine flaxseed, chocolate chips, and salt into the cooled grains and nuts, and then pour that mixture into the mixing bowl, coating everything completely.
7. Line your baking sheet with parchment paper and spread the mixture evenly onto it, pressing it into one even layer. You may want to shape the sides of the mass, depending on whether or not it reaches the edges of your baking sheet without thinning out too much.
8. Bake for 30 minutes, then remove from the oven.
9. Let cool for one hour before slicing into evenly-shaped bars, then cool completely.
10. Enjoy!

Nutrition: Calories: 269 g. Carbs: 30 g. Fats: 15 g. Protein: 6 g.

Paprika Butter Shrimps (Spanish)

Prep Time: 6 minutes **Cooking Time:** 31 minutes
Servings: 2

Ingredients

¼ tablespoon smoked paprika
1/8 cup sour cream
Salt and black pepper, to taste

½ pound tiger shrimps
1/8 cup butter

Directions

1. Prep the oven to 390F and grease a baking dish.
2. Mix all the ingredients in a large bowl and transfer into the baking dish.
3. Situate in the oven and bake for about 15 minutes.
4. Place paprika shrimp in a dish and set aside to cool for meal prepping. Divide it in 2 containers and cover the lid. Refrigerate for 1-2 days and reheat in microwave before serving.

Nutrition: Calories: 330 Protein: 32.6g Fat: 21.5g

CHAPTER 12
Snack Recipes & Appetizer Recipes

Artichokes with Garlic and Parmesan (Greek)
Prep Time: 9 minutes **Cooking Time:** 10 minutes
Servings: 4

Ingredients
4 artichokes, wash, trim, and cut top
¼ cup Parmesan cheese, grated
½ cup vegetable broth
1 tbsp. olive oil
2 tsps. garlic, minced Salt

Directions
1. Pour the broth into the electric pressure cooker, then place the steamer rack in the pot.
2. Place the artichoke steam side down on the steamer rack into the pot.
3. Sprinkle the garlic and grated cheese on top of artichokes and season with salt. Drizzle the oil over artichokes.
4. Seal pot with the lid and cook on high for 10 minutes.
5. Once done, release pressure using quick release. Remove the lid.
6. Serve and enjoy.

Nutrition: Calories: 132 Fat: 5.2 g. Protein: 7.9 g.

Manchego Crackers (Spanish)
Prep Time: 55 minutes **Cooking Time:** 15 minutes
Servings: 4

Ingredients
4 tbsps. butter, at room temperature
1 cup Manchego cheese
1 large egg
1 cup almond flour
1 tsp. salt, divided
¼ tsp. black pepper

Directions
1. Scourge butter and shredded cheese using an electric mixer.
2. Mix the almond flour with ½ tsp. salt and pepper. Mix the almond flour mixture to the cheese, constantly mixing to form a ball.
3. Put it onto plastic wrap and roll into a cylinder log about 1 ½-inch thick. Wrap tightly and refrigerate for at least 1 hour.
4. Preheat the oven to 350°F. Prepare 2 baking sheets with parchment paper.
5. For egg wash, blend egg and remaining ½ tsp. salt.
6. Slice the refrigerated dough into small rounds, about ¼-inch thick, and place on the lined baking sheets.
7. Top the crackers with egg wash and bake for 15 minutes. Pull out from the oven and situate in a wire rack.
8. Serve.

Nutrition: Calories: 243 Fat: 23 g. Protein: 8 g.

Deviled Eggs in Greek Style (Greek)
Prep Time: 45 minutes **Cooking Time:** 15 minutes
Servings: 4

Ingredients
4 large hardboiled eggs
½ cup Feta cheese
2 tbsps. sun-dried tomatoes, chopped
¼ tsp. black pepper
2 tbsps. roasted garlic aioli
8 pitted Kalamata olives
½ tsp. dried dill
1 tbsp. red onion, minced

Directions
1. Slice the hardboiled eggs in half lengthwise, remove the yolks, and place the yolks in a medium bowl.
2. Reserve the egg white halves and set them aside.
3. Smash the yolks well with a fork.
4. Add the aioli, Feta cheese, olives, sun-dried tomatoes, onion, dill, and pepper and stir to combine until smooth and creamy.
5. Spoon the filling into each egg white half and chill for 30 minutes, or up to 24 hours, covered.

Nutrition: Calories: 147 Fat: 11 g. Protein: 9 g.

Burrata Caprese Stack (Greek)
Prep Time: 5 minutes **Cooking Time:** 0 minutes
Servings: 4

Ingredients
1 large organic tomato
¼ tsp. black pepper
8 fresh basil leaves
2 tbsps. extra-virgin olive oil
1 tbsp. red wine
½ tsp. salt
1 (4 oz.) ball of Burrata cheese

Directions
1. Slice the tomato into 4 thick slices, removing any tough center core, and sprinkle with salt and pepper. Place the tomatoes, seasoned-side up, on a plate.
2. On a separate rimmed plate, slice the Burrata cheese into 4 thick slices and place 1 slice on top of each tomato slice. Top each with 2 basil leaves and pour any reserved Burrata cream from the rimmed plate over the top.
3. Drizzle with olive oil and vinegar and serve with a fork and knife.

Nutrition: Calories: 153 Fat: 13 g. Protein: 7 g.

Cod Cakes (Greek)

Prep Time: 25 minutes **Cooking Time:** 30 minutes
Servings: 12

Ingredients

Cod (12 oz, cooked)
Turnip's puree (12 oz.)
Whole eggs (2 ½ oz, beaten)
Whole wheat flour Egg wash Breadcrumbs
Tomatoes sauce

White pepper (to taste)
Ground ginger (pinch)
Standard Breading
Procedure:
Egg yolk (1 yolk, beaten)
Salt (to taste)

Directions

1. Shred the fish.
2. Combine with the turnips, egg, and egg yolk.
3. Season with salt, pepper, and ground ginger.
4. Divide the mixture into 2 ½ oz portions. Shape the mixture into a ball and then slightly flatten the mixture cakes.
5. Place the mixture through the Standard Breading Procedure.
6. Deep-fry at 350 F until golden brown.
7. Serve 2 cakes per portion. Accompany with tomato sauce.

Nutrition: 280 Calories 6g Fat 23g Protein

Avocado Gazpacho (Spanish)

Prep Time: 15 minutes **Cooking Time:** 0 minute
Servings: 4

Ingredients

1cups chopped tomatoes
2 large ripe avocados
1 medium bell pepper

¼ cup extra-virgin olive oil

¼ cup scallions, chopped 2 tbsps. red wine vinegar 2 limes or 1 lemon juice
¼ tsp. black pepper

1 large cucumber

1cup plain whole-milk Greek yogurt
¼ cup fresh cilantro, chopped
½–1 tsp. salt

Directions

1. If using an immersion blender in a blender or a large bowl, combine the tomatoes, avocados, cucumber, bell pepper, yogurt, olive oil, cilantro, scallions, vinegar, and lime juice. Blend until smooth. If using a stand blender, you may need to blend in 2–3 batches.
2. Season with salt and pepper and blend to combine the flavors.
3. Chill for 2 hours before serving. Serve cold.

Nutrition: Calories: 392 Fat: 32 g. Protein: 6 g.

Pitted Olives and Anchovies (Greek)

Prep Time: 1 hour and 10 minutes **Cooking Time:** 0 minute
Servings: 2

Ingredients

1cups pitted Kalamata olives or other black olives
2 anchovy fillets, chopped
1 teaspoon Dijon mustard
Seedy Crackers, Versatile Sandwich Round, or vegetables, for serving (optional)

2 teaspoons chopped capers
1 garlic clove, finely minced
1 cooked egg yolk
¼ cup extra-virgin olive oil

Directions

1. Wash the olives in cold water and strain well. In a food processor, blender, or a large jar (if using an immersion blender) place the drained olives, anchovies, capers, garlic, egg yolk, and Dijon. Process until it forms a thick paste. While running, gradually stream in the olive oil.
2. Handover to a small bowl, cover, and refrigerate at least 1 hour to let the flavors develop. Serve with Seedy Crackers, atop a Versatile Sandwich Round, or with your favorite crunchy vegetables.

Nutrition 179 Calories 19g Fat 2g Carbohydrates 2g Protein

Cheese Crackers (Italian)

Prep Time: 1 hour and 15 minutes
Cooking Time: 15 minutes
Servings: 20

Ingredients

4 tablespoons butter, at room temperature
1 cup finely shredded Manchego cheese
1 large egg

1 teaspoon salt, divided
¼ teaspoon freshly ground black pepper
1 cup almond flour

Directions

1. Using an electric mixer, scourge together the butter and shredded cheese until well combined and smooth. Incorporate the almond flour with ½ teaspoon salt and pepper. Gradually put the almond flour mixture to the cheese, mixing constantly until the dough just comes together to form a ball.
2. Situate a piece of parchment or plastic wrap and roll into a cylinder log about 1½ inches thick. Seal tightly then freezes for at least 1 hour. Preheat the oven to 350°F. Put parchment paper or silicone baking mats into 2 baking sheets.
3. To make the egg wash, scourge together the egg and remaining ½ teaspoon salt. Slice the refrigerated dough into small rounds, about ¼ inch thick, and place on the lined baking sheets. Egg washes the tops of the crackers and bake until the crackers are golden and crispy. Situate on a wire rack to cool.
4. Serve warm or, once fully cooled, store in an airtight container in the refrigerator for up to 1 week.

Nutrition 243 Calories 23g Fat 1g Carbohydrates 8g Protein

Vegetable Fritters (Italian)

Prep Time: 15 minutes **Cooking Time:** 6 minutes
Servings: 5

Ingredients

Egg (3, beaten)	Whole wheat flour (8 oz)
Milk (8 Fl oz)	Baking powder (1 tbsp)
Maple syrup (1/2 oz)	Carrot (12 oz,)
Vegetables:	Salt (½ tsp)
Baby lima beans (12 oz)	Celery (12 oz)
Turnip (12 oz)	Eggplant (12 oz)
Cauliflower (12 oz)	Zucchini (12 oz)
Parsnips (12 oz)	Asparagus (12 oz)

Directions

1. Combine the eggs and milk.
2. Mix the flour, baking powder, salt, and maple syrup. Stir in to the milk and eggs and mix until smooth.
3. Set aside the batter for several hours in a refrigerator.
4. Stir the cold, cooked vegetable into the batter.
5. Drop with a No. 24 scoop into deep fat at 350 F. Toss the content from the scoop carefully in the hot oil. Fry until golden brown.
6. Drain well and serve.

Nutrition: 140 Calories 6g Fat 4g Protein

Avocado and Turkey Mix Panini (Italian)

Prep Time: 5 minutes **Cooking Time:** 8 minutes
Servings: 2

Ingredients

2 red peppers, roasted and sliced into strips	¼ lb. thinly sliced mesquite smoked turkey breast
2 slices provolone cheese	¼ cup mayonnaise
1 tbsp olive oil, divided	1 cup whole fresh spinach leaves, divided
2 ciabatta rolls	
½ ripe avocado	

Directions

1. In a bowl, mash thoroughly together mayonnaise and avocado. Then preheat Panini press.
2. Chop the bread rolls in half and spread olive oil on the insides of the bread. Then fill it with filling, layering them as you go: provolone, turkey breast, roasted red pepper, spinach leaves and spread avocado mixture and cover with the other bread slice.
3. Place sandwich in the Panini press and grill for 5 to 8 minutes until cheese has melted and bread is crisped and ridged.

Nutrition 546 Calories 34.8g Fat 31.9g Carbohydrates 27.8g Protein

Cucumber, Chicken and Mango Wrap (Greek)

Prep Time: 5 minutes **Cooking Time:** 20 minutes
Servings: 1

Ingredients

½ of a medium cucumber cut lengthwise	½ of ripe mango
1tbsp salad dressing of choice	1 whole wheat tortilla wrap
2 tbsp oil for frying	1-inch-thick slice of chicken breast around 6-inch in length
2tbsp whole wheat flour	Salt and pepper to taste
2 to 4 lettuce leaves	

Directions

1. Slice a chicken breast into 1-inch strips and just cook a total of 6-inch strips. That would be like two strips of chicken. Store remaining chicken for future use.
2. Season chicken with pepper and salt. Dredge in whole wheat flour. On medium fire, place a small and nonstick fry pan and heat oil. Once oil is hot, add chicken strips and fry until golden brown around 5 minutes per side.
3. While chicken is cooking, place tortilla wraps in oven and cook for 3 to 5 minutes. Then set aside and transfer in a plate.
4. Slice cucumber lengthwise, use only ½ of it and store remaining cucumber. Peel cucumber cut into quarter and remove pith. Place the two slices of cucumber on the tortilla wrap, 1-inch away from the edge.
5. Slice mango and store the other half with seed. Peel the mango without seed, slice into strips and place on top of the cucumber on the tortilla wrap. Once chicken is cooked, place chicken beside the cucumber in a line.
6. Add cucumber leaf, drizzle with salad dressing of choice.
7. Roll the tortilla wrap, serve and enjoy.

Nutrition 434 Calories 10g Fat 65g Carbohydrates 21g Protein

Raisin Rice Pilaf (Italian)

Prep Time: 13 minutes **Cooking Time:** 8 minutes
Servings: 5

Ingredients

1 tbsp. olive oil 1 tsp. cumin	1cup onion, chopped
½ cup carrot, shredded	½ tsp. cinnamon
2cups instant brown rice 1	1 cup golden raisins
¾ cup orange juice	
¼ cup water	½ cup pistachios, shelled
Fresh chives, chopped for garnish	

Directions

1. Place a medium saucepan over medium-high heat before adding in the oil. Add in the onion, and stir often, so it doesn't burn. Cook for 5 minutes, and then add in the cumin, cinnamon, and carrot. Cook for another minute.
2. Add in the orange juice, water, and rice. Boil before covering the saucepan. Turn the heat down to medium-low and then allow it to simmer for 6–7 minutes.
3. Stir in the pistachios, chives, and raisins. Serve warm.

Nutrition: Calories: 320 Protein: 6 g. Fat: 7 g.

Tuna Tartare (Spanish)

Prep Time: 15 minutes **Cooking Time:** 0 minute
Servings: 8

Ingredients

Sashimi quality tuna (26.5 g, well-trimmed)	Parsley (2 tbsp, chopped)
Fresh tarragon (2 tbsp, chopped)	Shallots (1 oz, minced)
Lime juice (2 tbsp)	Dijon-style mustard (1 Fl oz)
	Olive oil (2 Fl oz)

Directions

1. Use a knife to mince the tuna.
2. Mixed the rest of the ingredients with the chopped tuna.
3. Use a ring mold to make a beautifully presented tuna tartare.
4. Season to taste with pepper and salt.

Nutrition 200 Calories 12g Fat 21g Protein

Goat Cheese–Mackerel Pâté (Italian)

Prep Time: 10 minutes **Cooking Time:** 0 minute
Servings: 4

Ingredients

4 oz. olive oil-packed wild-caught mackerel	1 lemon zest and juice
2 tbsps. fresh parsley, chopped	2 oz. goat cheese
1 tbsp. extra-virgin olive oil	2 tsps. capers, chopped
2 tsps. fresh horseradish (optional)	2 tbsps. fresh arugula, chopped

Directions

1. In a food processor, blender, or large bowl with an immersion blender, combine the mackerel, goat cheese, lemon zest and juice, parsley, arugula, olive oil, capers, and horseradish (if using). Process or blend until smooth and creamy. Serve with crackers, cucumber rounds, endive spears, or celery.

Nutrition: Calories: 118 Fat: 8 g. Protein: 9 g.

Taste of the Mediterranean Fat Bombs (Greek)

Prep Time: 15 minutes + 4 hours **Cooking Time:** 0 minute
Servings: 6

Ingredients

1 cup goat cheese, crumbled	12 pitted Kalamata olives
4 tbsps. jarred pesto	1 tbsp. fresh rosemary, chopped
½ cup walnuts, finely chopped	

Directions

1. Mix the goat cheese, pesto, and olives. Cool for 4 hours to harden.
2. Make 6 balls from the mixture, about ¾-inch diameter. The mixture will be sticky.
3. Place the walnuts and rosemary in a small bowl and roll the goat cheese balls in the nut mixture to coat.

Nutrition: Calories: 166 Fat: 15 g. Protein: 5 g.

Cream of Cauliflower Gazpacho (Spanish)

Prep Time: 15 minutes **Cooking Time:** 25 minutes
Servings: 6

Ingredients

1 cup raw almonds	½ tsp. salt
½ cup, plus 1 tbsp. extra-virgin olive oil	1 small head cauliflower
2 cups chicken stock	2 garlic cloves
¼ tsp. freshly ground black pepper	1 tbsp. red wine vinegar
	1 small white onion

Directions

1. Boil the almonds in the water for 1 minute. Drain in a colander and run under cold water. Pat dry. Discard the skins. In a food processor or blender, blend the almonds and salt. With the processor running, drizzle in ½ cup extra-virgin olive oil, scraping down the sides as needed. Set the almond paste aside.
2. In a stockpot, cook the remaining 1 tbsp. olive oil over medium-high heat. Sauté onion for 4 minutes. Add the cauliflower florets and sauté for another 3–4 minutes. Cook the garlic for 1 minute more.
3. Add 2 cups of stock and bring to a boil. Cover, reduce the heat to medium-low and simmer the vegetables until tender, 8–10 minutes. Pull out from the heat and allow to cool slightly.
4. Blend the vinegar and pepper with an immersion blender. With the blender running, add the almond paste and blend until smooth, adding extra stock if the soup is too thick. Serve warm, or chill in the refrigerator for at least 4–6 hours to serve a cold gazpacho.

Nutrition: Calories: 505 Fat: 45 g. Protein: 10 g.

Red Pepper Hummus (Greek)

Prep Time: 7 minutes **Cooking Time:** 34 minutes
Servings: 4

Ingredients

1 cup dried chickpeas	1 tbsp., plus ¼ cup extra-virgin olive oil, divided
4 cups water	
½ cup roasted red pepper, chopped, divided	1 tsp. ground cumin
½ tsp. ground black pepper	3/4 tsp. salt
1/3 cup tahini	¼ tsp. smoked paprika
½ tsp. garlic, minced	1/3 cup lemon juice

Directions

1. Put chickpeas, water, and 1 tbsp. oil in the electric pressure cooker. Seal put steam release to sealing, select the manual button, and time to 30 minutes.
2. When the timer rings, quick-release the pressure. Click the cancel button and open it. Drain and next set aside the cooking liquid.
3. Process the chickpeas, 1/3 cup roasted red pepper, the remaining ¼ cup of oil, tahini, cumin, salt, black pepper, paprika, lemon juice, and garlic using a food processor. Serve, garnished with reserved roasted red pepper on top.

Nutrition: Calories: 96 Fat: 8 g. Protein: 2 g.

Citrus-Marinated Olives (Greek)

Prep Time: 10 minutes + 4 hours **Cooking Time:** 0 minute
Servings: 4

Ingredients

2 cups mixed green olives with pits	¼ cup red wine vinegar
¼ cup extra-virgin olive oil	1 orange zest and juice
2 bay leaves	4 garlic cloves, finely minced
1tsp. red pepper flakes	½ tsp. ground cumin
½ tsp. ground allspice	

Directions

1. In a jar, mix the olives, vinegar, oil, garlic, orange zest and juice, red pepper flakes, bay leaves, cumin, and allspice.
2. Cover and chill for 4 hours, tossing again before serving.

Nutrition: Calories: 133 Fat: 14 g. Protein: 1 g.

Zucchini-Ricotta Fritters with Lemon-GarlicAioli (Italian)

Prep Time: 30 minutes **Cooking Time:** 25 minutes
Servings: 4

Ingredients

1 large zucchini	1 tsp. salt, divided
½ cup whole-milk	1large egg
2garlic cloves	2 tbsps. fresh mint (optional)
Ricotta cheese 2 scallions	2 tsps. grated lemon zest
8 tbsps. roasted garlic aioli	½ cup almond flour
¼ tsp. freshly ground black pepper	1 tsp. baking powder
8 tbsps. extra-virgin olive oil	

Directions

1. Place the shredded zucchini in a colander or on several layers of paper towels. Sprinkle with ½ tsp. salt and let sit for 10 minutes. Using another layer of paper towel, press down on the zucchini to release any excess moisture and pat dry.
2. In a large bowl, combine the drained zucchini, Ricotta, scallions, egg, garlic, mint (if using), lemon zest, the remaining ½ tsp. salt, and pepper and stir well.
3. Blend the almond flour and baking powder. Mix in flour mixture into the zucchini mixture and let rest for 10 minutes.
4. In a large skillet, working in 4 batches, fry the fritters. For each batch of 4, heat 2 tbsps. of olive oil over medium-high heat. Add 1 heaping tbsp. zucchini batter per fritter, pressing down with the back of a spoon to form 2–3-inch fritters. Cover and let fry 2 minutes before flipping. Fry another 2–3 minutes, covered.
5. Repeat for the remaining 3 batches, using 2 tbsps. of olive oil for each batch.
6. Serve with aioli.

Nutrition: Calories: 448 Fat: 42 g. Protein: 8 g.

Zucchini Feta Roulades (Italian)

Prep Time: 10 minutes **Cooking Time:** 10 minutes
Servings: 6

Ingredients

½ cup feta	1garlic clove, minced
2tablespoons fresh basil, minced	1/8 teaspoon salt
1/8 teaspoon red pepper flakes	1 tbsp capers, minced
	2 medium zucchinis
12 toothpicks	1 tablespoon lemon juice

Directions

1. Preheat the air fryer to 360°F. (If using a grill attachment, make sure it is inside the air fryer during preheating.) In a small bowl, mix the feta, garlic, basil, capers, salt, red pepper flakes, and lemon juice.
2. Slice the zucchini into 1/8-inch strips lengthwise. (Each zucchini should yield around 6 strips.) Spread 1 tablespoon of the cheese filling onto each slice of zucchini, then roll it up and locked it with a toothpick through the middle.
3. Place the zucchini roulades into the air fryer basket in a one layer, individually. Bake or grill in the air fryer for 10 minutes. Remove the zucchini roulades from the air fryer and gently remove the toothpicks before serving.

Nutrition 46 Calories 3g Fat 6g Carbohydrates 3g Protein

Garlic-Roasted Tomatoes and Olives (Greek)

Prep Time: 5 minutes **Cooking Time:** 20 minutes
Servings: 6

Ingredients

2 cups cherry tomatoes	4 garlic cloves, roughly chopped
1 cup black olives	
½ red onion, roughly chopped	1 cup green olives
1 tablespoon fresh basil, minced	2 tablespoons olive oil
	1 tablespoon fresh oregano, minced
¼ to ½ teaspoon salt	

Directions

1. Preheat the air fryer to 380°F. In a large bowl, incorporate all of the ingredients and toss together so that the tomatoes and olives are coated well with the olive oil and herbs.
2. Pour the mixture into the air fryer basket, and roast for 10 minutes. Stir the mixture well, then continue roasting for an additional 10 minutes. Remove from the air fryer, transfer to a serving bowl, and enjoy.

Nutrition 109 Calories 10g Fat 5g Carbohydrates 1g Protein

Baked Vegetables that are Simple and Healthy (Italian)

Prep Time: 9 minutes **Cooking Time:** 75 minutes
Servings: 6

Ingredients

2 lbs. Brussels sprouts, trimmed

3 lbs. butternut squash

1 lb. pork breakfast sausage

1 tbsp. fat from fried sausage

Directions

1. Grease a 9-inch baking pan and preheat the oven to 350°F.
2. With medium-high heat, put a nonstick saucepan and cook sausage. Break up the sausages and cook until browned.
3. In a greased pan, mix browned sausage, squash, sprouts, sea salt, and fat. Toss to mix well. Pop into the oven and cook for 1 hour.
4. Remove from oven and serve warm.

Nutrition: Calories: 364 Protein: 19 g. Fat: 17 g.

Morning Tostadas (Spanish)

Prep Time: 15 minutes **Cooking Time:** 6 minutes
Servings: 6

Ingredients

½ white onion, diced

1 tablespoon fresh cilantro, chopped

1 tomato, chopped

6 corn tortillas

2oz Cheddar cheese, shredded

½ teaspoon butter

6 eggs

1 cucumber, chopped

½ jalapeno pepper, chopped

1 tablespoon lime juice

1tablespoon canola oil

½ cup white beans, canned, drained

½ teaspoon Sea salt

Directions

1. Make Pico de Galo: in the salad bowl combine together diced white onion, tomato, cucumber, fresh cilantro, and jalapeno pepper. Then add lime juice and a ½ tablespoon of canola oil. Mix up the mixture well. Pico de Galo is cooked.
2. After this, preheat the oven to 390F. Line the tray with baking paper. Arrange the corn tortillas on the baking paper and brush with remaining canola oil from both sides. Bake the tortillas until they start to be crunchy. Chill the cooked crunchy tortillas well. Meanwhile, toss the butter in the skillet.
3. Crack the eggs in the melted butter and sprinkle them with sea salt. Fry the eggs until the egg whites become white (cooked). Approximately for 3-5 minutes over the medium heat. After this, mash the beans until you get puree texture. Spread the bean puree on the corn tortillas.
4. Add fried eggs. Then top the eggs with Pico de Galo and shredded Cheddar cheese.

Nutrition 246 Calories 11g Fat 4.7g Carbohydrates 13.7g Protein

Cheese Omelet (Italian)

Prep Time: 5 minutes **Cooking Time:** 10 minutes
Servings: 2

Ingredients

1 tablespoon cream cheese

½ teaspoon dried oregano

2 eggs, beaten

¼ teaspoon paprika

¼ teaspoon dried dill

1 oz Parmesan, grated

1 teaspoon coconut oil

Directions

1. Mix up together cream cheese with eggs, dried oregano, and dill. Pour coconut oil in the skillet and heat it up until it will coat all the skillet.
2. Then fill the skillet with the egg mixture and flatten it. Add grated Parmesan and close the lid. Cook omelet for 10 minutes over the low heat. Then transfer the cooked omelet in the serving plate and sprinkle with paprika.

Nutrition 148 Calories 11.5g Fat 0.3g Carbohydrates 10.6g Protein

Fruity Pizza (Italian)

Prep Time: 10 minutes **Cooking Time:** 0 minute
Servings: 2

Ingredients

1 tbsp fresh cilantro chopped

1 tbsp Pomegranate sauce

9 oz watermelon slice

2 oz Feta cheese, crumbled

Directions

1. Place the watermelon slice in the plate and sprinkle with crumbled Feta cheese. Add fresh cilantro. After this, sprinkle the pizza with Pomegranate juice generously. Cut the pizza into the Servings

Nutrition 143 Calories 6.2g Fat 0.6g Carbohydrates 5.1g Protein

Herb and Ham Muffins (Greek)

Prep Time: 10 minutes **Cooking Time:** 15 minutes
Servings: 4

Ingredients

3 oz ham, chopped

½ teaspoon dried oregano

4 eggs, beaten

2 tablespoons coconut flour

¼ teaspoon dried cilantro

Cooking spray

Directions

1. Spray the muffin's molds with cooking spray from inside. In the bowl mix up together beaten eggs, coconut flour, dried oregano, cilantro, and ham. When the liquid is homogenous, pour it in the prepared muffin molds.
2. Bake the muffins for 15 minutes at 360F. Chill the cooked meal well and only after this remove from the molds.

Nutrition 128 Calories 7.2g Fat 2.9g Carbohydrates 10.1g Protein

Appendix 3   Index

Leave a Review

As an independent author with a small marketing budget, reviews are my livelihood on this platform. If you enjoyed this book, I'd appreciate it if you could leave your honest feedback. I read EVERY single review because I love the feedback from MY readers!

Thank you for staying with me.

Manufactured by Amazon.ca
Bolton, ON

32230588R00061